The Road Ahead

Transition to Adult Life for Persons with Disabilities

Edited by
Keith Storey
Paul Bates
Dawn Hunter

Training Resource Network, Inc. ■ St. Augustine, Florida

First Edition

This publication is sold with the understanding that the publisher is not engaged in rendering legal, financial, medical, or other such services. If legal advice or other such expert assistance is required, a competent professional in the appropriate field should be sought. All brand and product names are trademarks or registered trademarks of their respective companies.

Printed in the United States of America on acid-free paper.

Published by Training Resource Network, Inc., PO Box 439, St. Augustine, FL 32085-0439. You may order direct from the publisher for $32.95 plus $4.00 shipping by calling toll-free at 866-823-9800 or visiting our web-site at www.trninc.com.

Library of Congress Cataloging-in-Publication Data
The road ahead : transition to adult life for persons with disabilities / edited by Keith Storey, Paul Bates, Dawn Hunter
    p. cm.
  Includes bibliographical references and index.
  ISBN 1-883302-46-3
  1. Youth with disabilities--Vocational guidance--United States. 2. Youth with disabilities--Education--United States. 3. Youth with disabilities--Employment--United States. I. Storey, Keith, date. II. Bates, Paul, date. III. Hunter, Dawn, date.

    HV1569.3.Y68 R66 2002
    362.4'0484--dc21

                                2002019169

Table of Contents

Dedication

For my parents for their love and support through all these years.

I would also like to thank the following people for their positive influence during various stages of my professional career: Paul Bates, Mary Berman, Doug Blandy, Hazel Bond, Nick Certo, Janis Chadsey, Emma Doerr, Norm Douglass, Brigid Flannery, Joyce Forte, Damon Foster, Robert Gaylord-Ross, Harry Hanson, Curt Hendricks, Vicki House, Rob Horner, Dawn Hunter, Dawn Inafuku, Betsy Lance, Linda Lengyel, Dave Mank, Eva Moore, Lanny Morreau, Ernie Pancsofar, Michal Post, Larry Rhodes, Jean Rowland, Dennis Sandow, Irene Wilde, and Xiaoyan Yan.

I also would like to acknowledge my intellectual debt to Ian Hunter, Robert Ingersoll, Aron Nimzovich, Winston O'Boogie, Tom Rover, and B. F. Skinner.

Keith Storey

I would like to thank my parents, Ted and Ellen Bates, for providing me with both the foundation and optimism needed to build a life centered around family, home, and community. In the midst of their challenges with aging and Alzheimer's disease, they continue to inspire me to new depths of understanding regarding human dignity and generosity.

To all of my university students, individuals with disabilities, and family members that I've been privileged to know, thank you for sharing your time, energy, occasional frustrations, and moments of joy. By valuing one another, we are forever changed for the better. I am also indebted to Paul Wehman and Adelle Renzaglia, valued colleagues who were my mentors and inspiration.

Finally, Barbara, Megan, Dylan, Laurel, Julia, Jackson, and Aaron, thank-you for making yesterday worth remembering, today worth living, and tomorrow a day I eagerly anticipate.

Paul Bates

To my parents Dorothy and George Hunter, Pam and Jim Vasseur, Jim and Karen Hunter, and Mel Murakami for their love, laughter, and for always being there for me.

I also would like to express my deep appreciation to the following people for their unconditional and caring support, wise guidance, healing energy, endless patience, and for keeping me both grounded and maintaining a sense of humor during the creation of this book: Michael Brady, Sharla Brown, Don Cardinal, Angela Carlson, Jane Fischer, Carrie Hayward, Maura McEveety and the girls, Sybil Jacobson, Jan Mower, David Murakami, Lisa O'Brien, Rick Olson, the School of Education faculty and staff at Chapman University, Meryl and Murray Schrantz, Keith Storey, Eckhart Tolle, Nicholas, Brooke, and Dan Vasseur, and, of course, to my graduate and undergraduate students who continue to teach me about teaching and inspire me daily to live up to their expectations.

Dawn Hunter

Contributors

Keith Storey, Ph.D. (Editor)
School of Education
Chapman University
2600 Stanwell Dr.
Concord, CA 94520
925-246-6128
storey@chapman.edu

Paul Bates, Ph.D. (Editor)
Professor
Department of Special Education
Southern Illinois University
Carbondale, IL 62901
618-453-2311
Fax: 618-453-1646
pbates@siu.edu

Dawn Hunter, Ph.D. (Editor)
Associate Professor
School of Education
Chapman University
One University Dr.
Orange, CA 92866
714-744-7674
dhunter@chapman.edu

Michael P. Brady, Ph.D.
Florida Atlantic University
Department of Exceptional Student
   Education
777 Glades Rd.
PO Box 3091
Boca Raton, FL 33431-0991
561-297-3280

Janis G. Chadsey, Ph.D.
Professor
University of Illinois
Department of Special Education
1310 S. 6th St.
Champaign, IL 61820
217-333-0260
chadsey@uiuc.edu

Penny Church-Pupke
University of Florida
Department of Special Education
G-315 Norman Hall
PO Box 117050
Gainesville, FL 32611-7050

Susan R. Copeland, Ph.D.
Assistant Professor of Special Education
Department of Educational Specialties
University of New Mexico
College of Education
Albuquerque, NM 87131-1231

Paula Davis, Ph.D.
Professor
Rehabilitation Institute
Southern Illinois University
Carbondale, IL 62901-4609
618-536-7704
pdavis@siu.edu

Stephanie E. Fowler, Ph.D.
Vanderbilt University
Peabody College
Box 328
Nashville, TN 37203

Teresa Grossi, Ph.D.
Indiana Institute on Disability and
   Community
The University Affiliated Program
   of Indiana
Indiana University
2853 E. Tenth St.
Bloomington, IN 47408-2601
812-855-6508
Fax: 812-855-9630
tgrossi@indiana.edu

Carolyn Hughes, Ph.D.
Department of Special Education
Box 328, Peabody College
Vanderbilt University
Nashville, TN 37203
615-322-8186
Fax: 615-343-1570
carolyn.hughes@vanderbilt.edu

Margaret P. Hutchins, Ph.D.
Illinois State University
Department of Special Education
Campus Box 5910
Normal, IL 61790
309-438-7067
mphutch@ilstu.edu

Dave Mank, Ph.D.
Director
Indiana Institute on Disability and
    Community
Indiana University
2853 E. Tenth St.
Bloomington, IN 47408-2601
812-855-6508
Fax: 812-855-9630
dmank@isdd.isdd.indiana.edu

Craig Miner, Ph.D.
California State University, Fresno
Department of Counseling and Special
    Education
5005 N. Maple Ave. M/S ED3
Fresno, CA 93740-8025
559-278-0326
cminer@csufresno.edu

Lisa O'Brien, M.A., M.A.E.
Carl Harvey School,
Santa Ana Unified School District
1635 S. Center
Santa Ana, CA 92704
714-430-6200

Adelle Renzaglia, Ph.D.
Professor and Head
Department of Special Education
University of Illinois
288 Education Building
1310 S. Sixth
Champaign, IL 61820

Howard Rosenberg, Ed.D
Florida International University
College of Education
Miami, FL 33199
305-348-2552

Larry Schaaf, M.S.
Center on Community Living and Careers
Indiana Institute on Disability and
    Community
The University Affiliated Program of
    Indiana
Indiana University
2853 E. Tenth St.
Bloomington, IN 47408-2601

Debra Shelden, M.S., C.R.C.
Research Associate
Transition Research Institute
University of Illinois at Urbana-Champaign
117 CRC, 51 Gerty Dr.
Champaign, IL 61820
217-333-2325
dshelden@uiuc.edu

Marcia Steigerwald, B.S.
Center on Community Living and Careers
Indiana Institute on Disability and
    Community
The University Affiliated Program of
    Indiana
Indiana University
2853 East Tenth St.
Bloomington, IN 47408-2601

Introduction
Curriculum Design and Programmatic Issues Involving Youth in Transition

Keith Storey

Chapman University

Transition from school to adult life has been difficult for people with disabilities, especially in the area of employment. If, and where, people with disabilities should work, has been an issue that people with disabilities and their families, school systems, adult service systems, and governments have struggled with (Wehman, 1988; 1998). Questions concerning whether or not people with disabilities were capable of working, whether they need to get "ready" to work, whether they should work in sheltered or integrated environments, and the type of supports that are appropriate for workers with disabilities are confronting the field and have not been resolved clearly (Mank, 1994; Wehman & Kregel, 1995; Wehman & Moon, 1988).

The vast majority of people with disabilities are either unemployed or underemployed with low wages and no benefits. Though there has been some improvement with the service delivery system over the past few years, unemployment is still a way of life for most people with disabilities. Many governments are struggling with how to provide benefits to people with disabilities without creating disincentives to work (Biggs, Humphries, & Flett, 1998; Floyd, 1995; Moallem & Moallem, 1998). These changes are important because, of those people with a disability who were not employed, the vast majority say that they want to work but that the many disincentives make it difficult.

This introduction will provide an overview of why transition and employment in integrated settings is important for people with disabilities. It examines why it is important for people to work, as this has not always been articulated clearly or agreed upon by professionals in the field or by the general public or policy makers.

Importance of Work in Integrated Settings
Philosophical/Ethical Judgment

A philosophical and ethical judgment must be made whether integration and work are important for all people and all types of cultures (i.e., minorities, women), including people with disabilities. This judgment obviously will have long lasting

I

effects. For instance, if a secondary teacher of students with disabilities does not believe that it is important for her students to have a job while in school and after graduation, then she is less likely to teach relevant employment skills. This will thus diminish the chances of her students being employed after graduation.

Civil Rights

In many countries it is the law that separate is not equal regarding educational and other opportunities (Brown v. Board of Education, 1954). It is interesting to note that one of the legal arguments against Brown was that it would apply to students with disabilities. Integration for persons with disabilities has been an extension of the civil rights movement (Bogdan & Biklen, 1977; Russell, 1994; Shapiro, 1993), and the importance of integration applies for adults as well as for students with disabilities.

Normalization

Normalization broadly refers to what is "typical" behavior of peers (Wolfensberger, 1972). It is generally expected that as an adult, one becomes employed in some capacity. Thus, denying people with disabilities employment contributes to making them different from people without disabilities.

Community Participation

It is important that people with disabilities be part of their communities, whether it be where they live, shop, recreate, or work. Through work, people with disabilities are more likely to be involved in their community. They will be more likely to have money to rent or own a place of their own, be able to buy things, go on vacations, join clubs or service organizations, or work out at a health club. In other words, they will be able to do the things that other people in the community do.

Influencing Society

Work and integration can be very powerful factors in changing attitudes and expectations towards people with disabilities. If employers, co-workers, customers, and others see people with disabilities performing competently in real jobs, then people with disabilities are more likely to be seen as competent in their abilities. This makes them more likely to be accepted as equals. This is especially true if people are working in jobs that are seen as "nontraditional" roles for people with disabilities.

People with disabilities are often viewed with pity. Stereotypes of people with disabilities as unable to work, needing charity, and being lesser beings are reinforced through vehicles such as telethons and poster children (Finger, 1994; Shapiro, 1993). A 1991 Louis Harris poll in the US concerning "Public Attitudes toward People with Disabilities" indicated that though 98% of the respondents believed that everyone, including people with disabilities, should have equal opportunity to participate in American society. Still, 77% felt pity toward people with disabilities.

Valued

Work is commonly valued (Turkel, 1972). When you meet someone new, one of the first questions you ask is "What do you do for a living?" An individual's status or worth often is based upon his or her employment and economic status. If Steve says that he is a teacher or researcher, then he is more likely to be looked upon favorably than if he said, "I sort nuts and bolts at the sheltered workshop."

Helps Individuals Through Stress and Difficulties

When people are having a difficult time they often turn to co-workers (Gallo, 1982; House, 1974; 1981). Though there has not been research that specifically targets people with disabilities, it appears logical that if a worker with a disability does not have an adequate social support network (which often involves co-workers who are capable of providing such support), then the stress and difficulty that he or she is going through may be increased.

Economic Independence

With good wages and good benefits, people with disabilities can avoid the poverty and dependency in which the vast majority of people with disabilities live. The unemployment rate for people with disabilities is much higher than any other group. This has led to dependency upon welfare, Supplemental Security Income, Medicare, Medicaid, and other government assistance programs. Along with economic independence comes political participation, which is how people with disabilities ultimately will influence and control the service delivery system (Longmore, 1995).

Professionals Cannot Meet All Needs of Persons with Disabilities

Though professionals may be important, professionals come and go in the lives of people with disabilities. Friends, co-workers, and family members are more likely to be stable in their lives and more likely to provide reciprocity and social networks (Kennedy, Horner, & Newton, 1989; Newton, Olson, Horner, & Ard, 1996). With employment in integrated settings, people with disabilities are more likely to have friends and significant others to meet their needs.

Life-Long Learning

Lifelong learning is important for all adults in terms of factors such as intellectual stimulation and learning new skills that could be important in future work environments. Denying work to adults with disabilities inhibits their ability to use the skills that they have learned and to continue to learn new skills.

Transition and Employment

The emphasis in transition has been increasingly placed on lifestyle outcomes such as wages and benefits, integration, friendships and social networks, community involvement, etc. (Horner, 1991; Rusch, 1990; Schalock, 1990; Wehman & Kregel, 1995). Rather than getting people ready to work, the emphasis is on placing people and then training them ("place and train") and providing supports. This is in contrast to the "train and place" model of sheltered workshops.

The supported employment movement is a dramatic shift from previous vocational services for people with disabilities. This traditional approach relied upon segregated services in day training programs, sheltered workshops or institutions, and stressed prevocational or readiness skills (Bellamy, Rhodes, Bourbeau, & Mank, 1986; Bellamy, Rhodes, Mank, & Albin, 1988; Wehman & Moon, 1988). Supported employment has been promoted as more desirable than sheltered service delivery systems because it is more capable of delivering outcomes of wages, integration, and support (Wehman & Kregel, 1988; Will, 1984).

The current educational and adult service systems have done an inadequate job of preparing and employing people with disabilities. Poor quality of life outcomes and almost total unemployment remains among adults with disabilities. This book provides strategies and ideas for improving the lives of the people that you serve. Any situation needs to be judged by the ability to deliver quality of life outcomes to people with disabilities and to meet the criterion of ultimate functioning (Brown, Nietupski, & Hamre-Nietupski, 1976). To paraphrase Helen Keller, "People with disabilities not only need to be given lives, they need to be given lives worth living."

References

Bellamy, G. T., Rhodes, L. E., Bourbeau, P. E., & Mank, D. M. (1986). Mental retardation services in sheltered workshops and day activity programs: Consumer benefits and policy alternatives. In F. R. Rusch (Ed.), *Competitive employment issues and strategies* (257-271). Baltimore: Paul H. Brookes.

Bellamy, G. T., Rhodes, L. E., Mank, D. M., & Albin, J. M. (1988). *Supported employment: A community implementation guide.* Baltimore, MD: Paul H. Brookes.

Biggs, H. C., Humphries, S. A., & Flett, R. A. (1998). Perspectives on vocational rehabilitation: A New Zealand analysis. *Journal of Vocational Rehabilitation, 11,* 13-20.

Bogdan, R., & Biklen, D. (1977). Handicapism. *Social Policy, 7,* 59-63.

Brown V. Board of Education of Topeka, 347 US 483, 493 (1954).

Brown, L., Nietupski, J., & Hamre-Nietupski, S. (1976). Criterion of ultimate functioning. In M. A. Thomas (Ed.), *Hey, don't forget about me!* (2-15). Reston, VA: Council for Exceptional Children.

Finger, A. (1994). ...and the greatest of these is charity. In B. Shaw (Ed.), *The ragged edge: The disability experience from the pages of the first fifteen years of the Disability Rag* (115-119). Louisville, KY: The Advocado Press.

Floyd, M. (1995). Self-employment and disabled people in the United Kingdom. *International Journal of Practical Approaches to Disability, 19,* 9-14.

Gallo, F. (1982). The effects of social support networks on the health of the elderly. *Social Work in Health Care, 8,* 65-74.

Horner, R. H. (1991). The future of applied behavior analysis for people with severe disabilities: Commentary I. In L. H. Meyer, C. A. Peck, & L. Brown, (Eds.), *Critical issues in the lives of people with severe disabilities* (607-611). Baltimore, MD: Paul H. Brookes.

House, J. S. (1974). Occupational stress and physical health. In J. O'Toole (Ed.), *Work and the quality of life: Resource papers for work in America* (145-170). Cambridge, MA: The Massachusetts Institute of Technology Press.

House, J. S. (1981). *Work, stress, and social support.* Reading, MA: Addison-Wesley.

Kennedy, C. H., Horner, R. H., & Newton, J. S. (1989). Social contacts of adults with severe disabilities living in the community: A descriptive analysis of relationship patterns. *Journal of The Association for Persons with Severe Handicaps, 14,* 190-196.

Longmore, P. K. (1995). The second phase: From disability rights to disability culture. *The Disability Rag & ReSource, 16*(5), 4-11.

Mank, D. M. (1994). The underachievement of supported employment: A call for reinvestment. *Journal of Disability Policy Studies, 5,* 1-24.

Moallem, A., & Moallem, M. (1998). Systematic change in vocational training institutions in France. *International Journal of Disability, Development and Education, 45,* 17-33.

Newton, J. S., Olson, D., Horner, R. H., & Ard, W. R. (1996). Social skills and the stability of social relationships between individuals with intellectual disabilities and other community members. *Research in Developmental Disabilities, 17,* 15-26.

Rusch, F. R. (1990). *Supported employment issues and strategies.* Sycamore, IL: Sycamore Press.

Russell, M. (1994). Malcom teaches us, too. In B. Shaw (Ed.), *The ragged edge: The disability experience from the pages of the first fifteen years of the Disability Rag* (11-14). Louisville, KY: The Advocado Press.

Schalock, R. L. (1990). *Quality of life: Perspectives and issues.* Washington, DC: American Association on Mental Retardation.

Shapiro, J. P. (1993). *No pity: People with disabilities forging a new civil rights movement.* New York: Times Books.

Storey, K., Stern, R., & Parker, R. (1990). A comparison of attitudes towards typical recreational activities versus the Special Olympics. *Education and Training in Mental Retardation, 25,* 94-99.

Turkel, S. (1972). *Working.* New York: Pantheon Press.

Wehman, P. (1988). Supported employment: Toward equal employment opportunity for persons with severe disabilities. *Mental Retardation, 26,* 357-361.

Wehman, P. (1998). Work, unemployment and disability: Meeting the challenges. *Journal of Vocational Rehabilitation, 11,* 1-3.

Wehman, P., & Kregel, J. (1988). Adult employment programs. In R. Gaylord-Ross (Ed.), *Vocational education for persons with handicaps* (205-233). Mountain View, CA: Mayfield.

Wehman, P., & Kregel, J. (1995). At the crossroads: Supported employment a decade later. *Journal of the Association for Persons with Severe Handicaps, 20,* 286-299.

Wehman, P., & Moon, M. S. (1988). *Vocational rehabilitation and supported employment.* Baltimore: Paul H. Brookes.

Will, M. (1984). *Supported employment for adults with severe disabilities: An OSERS program initiative.* Washington, DC: Office of Special Education and Rehabilitative Services.

Wolfensberger, W. (1972). *The principle of normalization in human services.* Downsview, Toronto, Canada: National Institute on Mental Retardation.

Chapter 1
Person-Centered Transition Planning:
Creating Lifestyles of Community Inclusion and Autonomy

Craig Miner
California State University, Fresno
Paul Bates
Southern Illinois University

Key Questions
1. Why does transition planning need to be person-centered?
2. What is person-centered planning?
3. How often does person-centered planning occur?
4. Who should be involved in person-centered planning teams?
5. Who can facilitate a person-centered planning meeting?
6. How can someone facilitate person-centered planning?
7. How can person-centered planning information be incorporated into the IEP/transition plan?

Key Question #1: Why does transition planning need to be person-centered?

The importance of preparing students for adult life after leaving school has been increasingly recognized as a vital component to secondary special education. The IEP process specifically requires planning for the transition from school to adulthood. For secondary-age students, the focus of transition planning should be centered on the goals that students and their families set for themselves rather than on the priorities of teachers and other professionals (Wehman, 1992).

Person-centered planning provides a format for the development of a rich description of post-school goals and promotes creative problem solving for the realization of these goals. Language within both the Rehabilitation Act Amendments of 1992 and the Individuals with Disabilities Education Act (PL 101-476, 1990) support an empowered role for persons with disabilities in the transition planning process. In both of these legislative acts, transition services are defined identically and include the statement that "the coordinated set of (transition) activities shall be based upon the individual student's needs, taking into account the student's preferences and interests…" The Rehabilitation Act Amendments go further and require a statement from the consumer regarding how he or she was involved in developing his or her individual program plan.

When students and families are more actively involved in their own planning, they are empowered in many ways. In an empirical investigation of person-centered planning activities, Miner and Bates (1997) found parent participation in IEP meetings to increase following person-centered planning activities. Miner and Bates (1997) also found that participation in person-centered planning increased parental perceptions regarding the quantity and quality of their child's input into his or her IEP meetings.

Key Question #2: What is person-centered planning?

Person-centered planning is a general term that has been used to describe a variety of approaches for empowering students and families to assume a more assertive position in their own program planning. These approaches include "group action planning" (Turnbull & Turnbull, 1997), "lifestyle planning" (Wilcox & Bellamy, 1987), "personal futures planning" (Mount & Zwernick, 1988), the "McGill action planning system" (MAPS) (Vandercook, York, & Forest, 1989), "outcome-based planning" (Steere, Wood, Pancsofar, & Butterworth, 1990), and "essential lifestyle planning" (Smull & Harrison, 1992). Although there are unique characteristics associated with each of these approaches, all share a common focus on encouraging the individual's expression of his or her vision for the future and developing needed supports for realizing this vision.

Key Question #3: How often does person-centered planning occur?

The person-centered planning process varies from student to student and from family to family. The critical outcome is that students and their families create a vision of the future and take action toward realizing that vision. This outcome requires a different approach for each individual student and family. Some students and families may choose to meet with a few key individuals at school prior to the annual IEP/transition planning meeting for the purpose of promoting a more person-centered approach. Others may choose to meet frequently with a broader circle of support as part of an ongoing transition planning process. At a minimum, teachers should interview their students to obtain a more complete understanding of their desired futures. Regardless of the number of meetings or the specific activities that are utilized, person-centered transition planning is an outcome-based process involving students and important others working collaboratively to achieve personally identified adult living goals.

Many of the models for person-centered planning describe a process that involves ongoing meetings and follow-along support to assist individuals in attaining their transition goals, to promote community building around an individual's desired future, and to creatively solve the variety of unique problems or challenges that may be interfering with the individual's community adjustment beyond high school. Undoubtedly, such efforts are effective for students and families that have the skills, time commitment, and energy to participate in such an exhaustive effort. Not every student and family will be able to make such a commitment. For this reason and others it may be unwise to mandate person-centered planning for all students and families (Turnbull & Turnbull, 1997). However, the spirit of person-centered planning needs to be present within the already mandated IEP/transition planning process.

Key Question #4: Who should be involved in person-centered planning teams?

The nature of parents' involvement in their children's education is different for each family (Turnbull & Turnbull, 1997). Similarly, the makeup of the person-centered planning team is highly individualized and unique to family character-istics, personal preferences and interests, and transition goals. In some cases, extended family members, family friends, and others may be involved in the planning process. Other person-centered planning teams may include only the student and parent(s)/guardian(s). The members of the team will not be the same for every student. It is often beneficial to broaden the active members of the team in order to develop necessary supports for attaining desired futures. These individuals may be identified through activities conducted as part of the person-centered planning process itself. For example, the creation of an indi-vidualized circle of support map (Pearpoint, Forest, & Snow, 1992) is an activity that often results in the identification of a small group of committed individuals who can make a tremendous difference in a person's success.

The major difference between person-centered planning and more traditional planning models is the role of the student. Too many times students have been excluded from the IEP process based on the belief that they cannot contribute or understand the issues discussed. Person-centered planning places the student as the focus person in the process, with an active role in every interaction. Ideally, students assume greater and greater responsibility for their own planning and eventually assume the role of director/coordinator in their own IEP meeting.

Key Question #5: Who can facilitate a person-centered planning meeting?

The facilitator role within a person-centered planning meeting can be as-sumed by virtually anyone who is committed to the process, such as a school psychologist, teacher, social worker, family member, or, preferably, the student. Turnbull and Turnbull (1997) recommend that the person-centered planning pro-cess be conducted outside of school with educator participation. Although this recommendation has merit, it may be problematic to find an agreeable location or someone outside of the school system who is willing to devote time and energy in assisting the student and family in the development of a person-cen-tered plan. If it is necessary to initiate the process within the education system, the facilitator needs to be sensitive to his or her professional bias that might interfere with seeing things from the student's perspective.

A system centered approach may try to fit a student's transition goals into an existing program. For example, a discussion of post-school goals may take place at the very end of an IEP/transition planning meeting after annual goals and objectives are written. A challenging vision of the future should not be limited to options that are currently available in the school program. Ideally, person-cen-tered planning works best when a student-centered orientation reigns and there is no systems-centered bias that limits the discussion of possibilities.

Key Question #6: How can someone facilitate person-centered planning?

The person-centered planning approach described in this chapter for involv-ing students and their families more actively in the transition planning process should be conducted prior to the annually scheduled IEP meetings. Person-cen-tered planning is most appropriately initiated by contacting students and parents to assess their interest in participating in planning activities that may assist them in understanding more about how they can be more actively involved in their upcoming IEP meetings. For those families who express interest, meetings are scheduled at convenient times for each family in the comfort of their own home or other settings of their choice. These meetings consist of activities designed to develop a personal profile, select future lifestyle goals, determine action steps and responsible parties, and identify necessary changes in the service system.

A flipchart and colored markers are used to graphically record the discussion regarding each component of the person-centered transition planning process. A description of each component activity of person-centered transition planning is provided below. Case study examples are presented to illuminate these activities.

Personal Profile Development

Each meeting begins with the facilitator assisting the student, family members, and other important stakeholders to construct a personal profile of the student. The personal profile is similar to a resume in that it describes the individual in terms of unique capabilities and capacities. Specific components of a personal profile include a circle of support map, community presence chart, preferences list, and a gifts and capacities description.

Mapping a Circle of Support

The importance of relationships is evident in the lives of most people. However, the importance of meaningful relationships is often under-appreciated for individuals with disabilities. A circle of support map illustrates the interpersonal relationships in an individual's life. This map identifies the persons that have a stake in the future of the individual with a disability. These persons are a rich resource of interpersonal support. If there are few meaningful relationships in the individual's life, the obvious need to enhance personal relationships is evident.

One approach that has proven useful in explaining the importance of an individualized circle of support map is to present contrasting examples. The first of these (Figure 1) describes an individual with many close family/peer relationships and relatively few paid service providers. The other (Figure 2) depicts an individual with few family/peer relationships and extensive involvement with paid service providers such as doctors, therapists, and social workers. The contrast between the two circles of support maps illustrates the need for natural supports to play a more prominent role in transition planning.

Following a brief discussion of the contrasting examples and elaboration on the importance of broad-based interpersonal support in transition planning, the facilitator asks the planning team members to name the people that are important in the focus person's life. The names of these individuals are then written on the flipchart within the relevant circle of the concentric diagram. In the innermost circle of the diagram, the focus person's name is written. Next, the people most important to the individual are written around the inner circle, followed by additional names of important interpersonal resources in the next outward concentric. Situational relationships such as classmates, co-workers, fellow church members, etc. are entered in the next circle. Finally, paid providers in the person's life such as teachers, therapists, bus drivers, doctors, nurses, etc., are written around the outer circle. These paid providers may be quite important to the individual,

Figure 1
Circle of Support Map for a Young Adult without Disabilities

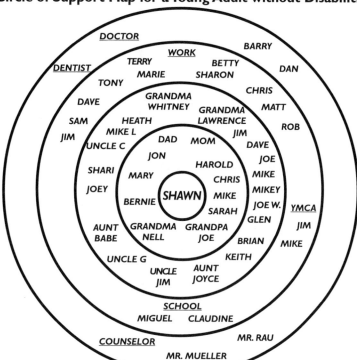

Figure 2
**Circle of Support Map for a Young Adult with Severe Disabilities
Living in a Group Home and Attending a Day Training Program**

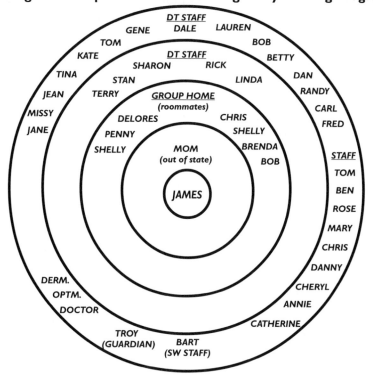

but are unlikely to be a part of the person's life when they are not being paid to do so. A completed circle of support map is a valuable component of the personal profile.

The people included on these maps may provide needed assistance in finding jobs, providing and/or developing natural supports, and facilitating other community connections. Many families underestimate the willingness and potential value of involving circle of support members in the creative problem solving process associated with transition planning. A simple invitation to become involved is often sufficient to secure valuable interpersonal resource assistance. When very few people are identified within the two inner circles, this signals an important need to focus on the development of closer interpersonal relationships as part of the person's transition plan. If the people involved in the focus person's life are primarily paid providers, it is imperative that they be encouraged to approach support from a person-centered perspective.

Illustrating Community Presence

The number and variety of places that an individual uses within his or her community can be an indicator of current lifestyle status. The community presence map provides a graphic display of places utilized within one's home community. Following the "circles of support" activity, the concept of community presence is introduced by the facilitator's presentation of contrasting examples, one of which reflects high presence (Figure 3) and one which exemplifies low presence (Figure 4).

These examples reinforce the desirability of high community presence and the relative inadequacy of low community involvement. At this point in the process, the facilitator asks the individual and planning team members to list the community settings used by the focus person on a daily, weekly, or occasional basis. Once this diagram is complete and placed on the flip chart for all to see, the facilitator reviews the individual's community presence entries and engages the planning team in a discussion regarding ways in which the focus person might increase his or her choices, involvement, or competence in community participation. The number of places, variety, and frequency of community presence are all considerations to address as part of this review. The single most important consideration when evaluating the quality of the focus person's community participation is his or her individual preferences and the opportunities available for that individual to express choice of community activities.

Developing a Preferences List

Preferences can be communicated in many ways. People with disabilities, who may not communicate in traditional ways, say a great deal about their preferences through their behavior. People who know the individual well are needed to identify preferences based on their experience with that individual in many situations. If individuals try to escape or avoid specific activities or people, this may indicate that they would rather be doing something else or be with someone else. On the other hand, if individuals actively seek out activities or individuals this indicates a desirable preference. An individualized preferences list should be used in conjunction with the previously developed community presence diagram to evaluate the individual's current and future lifestyle. Specifically, when our

Figure 3
Community Presence Map For A Young Adult Without Disabilities

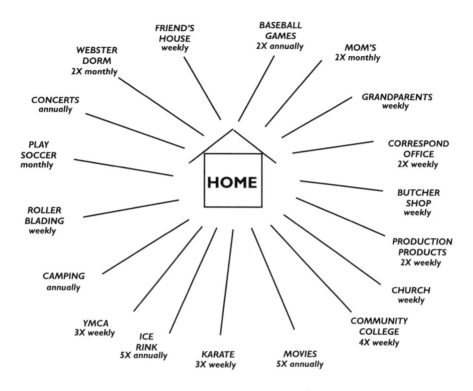

Figure 4
Community Presence Map for a Young Adult with Severe Disabilities Living in a Group Home and Attending a Day Training Program

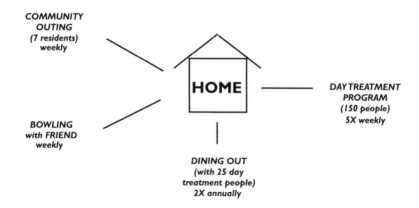

lives are lived in accordance with our preferences and minimize those things that we don't like, we are typically happier and healthier.

A helpful way to address a person's preferences is to delineate things that "work" and "don't work" for an individual (Mount & Zwernick, 1988). For example, Figure 5 provides a sample preference list for an individual with severe disabilities. This preference list establishes a much-needed context for making decisions regarding a person's desired future and his or her transition plan. In completing the preferences list activity within the personal profile, the facilitator emphasizes the difference between a system-centered planning approach to service delivery as opposed to a person-centered planning approach that values individual preferences. Once a listing of things that work and things that don't work is placed on the flip chart for all to review, the facilitator summarizes these preferences and emphasizes the importance of these preferences being reflected in all future discussions of desired lifestyle and needed supports.

For students who do not communicate in traditional ways, it is important to recognize that the preferences list may reflect the perceptions of other team members rather than the actual preferences of the individual. In these cases it is critical to utilize the basic principles of nondiscriminatory evaluation. Multiple team members should be able to agree on the preferences listed. Preferences

Figure 5
Preference List

THINGS THAT "WORK" FOR SAM	THINGS THAT "DON'T WORK" FOR SAM
• Fishing	• Brushing his teeth
• Watching TV late	• Putting rubber bands on his braces
• Listening to headphones	• Working the window at the cafeteria
• Nintendo™	• Cleaning the house or his room
• Stereo	• Indoors
• Scanner	• People with bad attitudes
• Shopping	• Bullies
• Riding his bike	
• Playing basketball	
• Four-wheeling	
• Outdoors	
• Action movies	
• Work/Money	
• Loading the dishwasher at work	
• Freezer work	

should be validated by direct observation whenever possible. For example, on-the-job assessments should be conducted to validate employment preferences. Finally, it always should be emphasized that the preferences list is a joint communication between the student and other team members.

The preferences list can be used as a basis for creating and evaluating a desirable lifestyle. The things that work in a person's life should be a major part of everyday life. When choosing a job, a place to live, or a recreation activity, compare what occurs in the environment to the preferences list. Similarly, the things that don't work should be avoided whenever possible. For example, if large crowds are identified as something the individual prefers to avoid, then going to concerts may not be a desirable leisure activity.

All preferences do not carry the same weight. Smull and Harrison (1992) refer to "non-negotiables" in a person's life as being those experiences or conditions that absolutely must be present or absent in one's life. For example, a person who uses a wheelchair for mobility must live and work in a place that is accessible. Similarly, someone who becomes extremely agitated in noisy situations must work in an environment that is free from loud, distracting stimuli. When creating these individualized preference lists, the student and other team members should note any particular preferences that are "nonnegotiable" to the student's quality of life. Some preferences are not as critical as others. Specific food preferences may not be as crucial as a preference for living near parents and family members. However, non-negotiables must be honored as essential considerations in a person's plan for a meaningful adult lifestyle.

The importance of including preferred activities in a typical daily schedule cannot be overemphasized. Most people make career choices, develop significant relationships, and decide upon weekend activities based on their personal preferences. By identifying these preferences within a student's personal profile, there is a much higher likelihood that these considerations will be reflected in the person's transition plan.

Expressing Gifts and Capacities

When parents tell others about their children, they tend not to dwell on their faults and shortcomings. In school, however, individuals with disabilities have extensive records pertaining to their deficits and weaknesses. The strengths listed on a typical IEP may not promote the awareness of an individual's unique capabilities. For example, the statement that the student "Knows his activities of daily living skills" does not provide a sufficiently complete description of positive qualities and may not lead to high expectations on the part of those who are in a position to support that individual.

The facilitator can best identify gifts and capacities by asking general questions such as: "What do people who like the individual say about her or him?" This question often stimulates responses similar to the things parents would say about their child when they brag to their friends. The facilitator's role in this process is to prompt contributions by encouraging the identification of unique skills and emphasizing the importance of valued community roles (e.g., club member). Figure 6 provides a gifts and capacities list for John, a student with severe disabilities. John's list is indicative of the kinds of qualities that are identified by people that know a student well, despite his significant disability.

A completed personal profile establishes an extremely important context for discussions regarding the student's desired future lifestyle. Each individual family situation is unique, possessing resources, preferences, interests, and skills that form a foundation for building an "enviable" life of community inclusion. Too often an individual's talents are overshadowed by deficits. The gifts and capacities activity is an excellent lead-in to the other person-centered planning activities described below. With this positive perspective expectations of a meaningful lifestyle are raised.

Figure 6
Gifts and Capacities List

JOHN IS:

- **A good worker**
- **Consistent**
- **Friendly**
- **Helpful**
- **Honest**

- **Caring**
- **Always on time**
- **Very responsible**
- **Neat/Clean**
- **Fun**

Future Lifestyle Planning

Creating a challenging vision of the future

With the personal profile fresh in the minds of participants, describe a challenging vision of the future. Dreams of the future should reflect an "enviable life" (Turnbull & Turnbull, 1998), one worth working to achieve. A collectively shared vision of a desirable future lifestyle is necessary for the level of commitment required if participants are going to take action on behalf of the individual with a disability.

After the personal profile is completed, the facilitator asks the focus person and other participants to describe a desirable future by answering the following questions:

1. Where will she or he live in this desired future (own home, with family, supported apartment, etc.)?
2. What will he or she do during the day and where will she or he do it (work, volunteer, etc.)?
3. What will he or she do for fun and recreation and with whom will she or he participate in these activities?

In completing this activity, the facilitator's role is to encourage the creation of a challenging vision based the focus person's desired future (including systems change if needed) rather than on the limits of an individual's disability or the opinions of others. A student may have a desire to work in construction, but the school may not provide community work experience in construction or there may be barriers due to local unions. The student's desired future should be developed and needed changes in school job development practices or exceptions to union rules should be identified. One strategy for evaluating this desired future is for the facilitator to ask each group member to consider whether or not an individual without an identified disability would find the proposed lifestyle goals desirable.

These three questions regarding community living, productive activity, and social-recreation appear somewhat simple at first glance, but can lead quickly to very complex discussions involving values, hopes, and dreams. (See Figure 7.) Responses to these questions should be reflected in the desired outcomes that are identified as part of the individual's transition plan within the IEP. As students and families are contemplating their responses, the facilitator may find it useful to use personal profile information to stimulate discussion and reflection. When one's future lifestyle goals truly reflect personal preferences and interests, there is a much greater likelihood that the person will make the commitment needed to realize positive transition outcomes.

Figure 7
Future Lifestyle Description for a Student with Severe Disabilities

Where will Jarrel live?
Jarrel plans on living with his parents after graduation. In the long term he would like to live in a suburban area. He would like to live in a house rather than an apartment. He would also like to have a roommate, rather than living alone. Public transportation would need to be available.

What will Jarrel do during the day and where will he do it?
Jarrel would like to have a job working as a janitor, maybe in a school. He would prefer working evenings. The ideal job would be working with others, indoors, and able to wear headphones.

What will Jarrel do for fun and recreation?
Jarrel expects to continue fishing often. He would like to participate in archery and other sports, such as basketball, in the future. He wants to go to hockey games and baseball games occasionally. He also wants to continue collecting baseball cards.
Jarrel would like to do some of these activities with friends from school and new friends he might meet, possibly at work. He wants to make new friends at the archery center.

There is a common concern that the student's description of a desired future lifestyle might be unrealistic. Teenagers often have dreams that are seen as unrealistic by others. Many high school students have had dreams of becoming professional athletes, entertainers, or some other high profile professional. Students with disabilities will undoubtedly describe future lifestyles that appear to be improbable. This is, in part, the reason that transition planning must be a dynamic, ongoing process. A challenging vision of the future often changes over time. The way in which individuals learn what is or is not realistic is through experience.

Person-centered planning teams should identify steps to gain experience related to a future lifestyle rather than discount the student's dream as unrealistic. The negotiation of the desired future lifestyle is critical to the process. When a student's desires and his or her family expectation's conflict, the discussion needs to focus on the student's capacities and action steps for that student to have experiences needed to make an informed decision. What is or is not realistic does not need to be imposed; it will be self-discovered through one's experiences. With such an experientially based orientation to determining "realistic" lifestyle goals, arbitrary obstacles are removed and creative strategies for realizing the "impossible" are often found.

Action Steps and Responsible Parties

No personal profile or vision of the future is worthwhile without action towards making the vision come true. When a few short-term tasks are accomplished successfully, increasingly more challenging steps toward an individual's desired lifestyle can be taken. Completion of action steps is one of the very best ways to ignite a support circle's efforts on behalf of a person's future lifestyle planning and transition goals.

With the individual's desired future as a focal point, the facilitator coordinates the process of negotiating action steps and assigning responsible parties for attaining these future goals. In this process, the facilitator often takes the lead by asking the participants to identify three to five activities that should be undertaken to provide immediate movement toward the focus person's desired lifestyle. The facilitator records responses to this question on the flip chart under the "activities" column. Those individuals responsible for performing the activity or overseeing its performance are identified and listed under the "who" column.

Voluntary commitment is important. Whenever possible the focus person should be encouraged to take responsibility or co-responsibility for seeing that an activity is completed. No one should be coerced into accepting responsibility for an action step. Figure 8 illustrates an example in which the student, Jamie, has responsibility for three of the four action steps. The action steps and responsible party component of the person-centered planning process fits nicely with the transition planning requirements of the IEP. One or more of these action steps should be translated into an IEP transition goal and proposed as such in the student's IEP meeting.

When identifying supports to be developed through action steps, the team should place an emphasis on natural supports (Nisbet, 1992). Too often, identified supports and services are limited to the paid resources available to individuals with disabilities. Experiences and activities outside of the school system are critical to the attainment of desired outcomes. The team initially should consider unpaid, natural supports, utilizing them whenever appropriate. If no appropriate natural support is available, generic services should be considered. If natural supports or generic services cannot be accessed, then formal supports/services should be considered.

It is highly recommended that the action steps include some activities of immediate benefit to the individual. These initial successes are important for student "buy-in" and commitment to their own transition planning. From these initial accomplishments, people are more inclined to dream of what might be instead of settling for what is available.

Needed Service System Changes

If students with disabilities are going to realize their desired future, the ways in which school and post-school services have traditionally been provided will have to change. Improving, rather than abolishing, the current service system is the goal. As school and post-school services become more accountable to persons with disabilities and their families, needed system change is likely to occur through the reallocation of resources to more effective practices. The facilitator

Figure 8
Action Steps and Responsible Parties

ACTIVITIES	WHO
1. Attend IEP/Transition Planning Meeting	Jamie, Mom Dad
2. Take consumer education class	Mr. Mayes
3. Invite ORS representative to IEP meeting	Jamie, Ms. Swartz
4. Obtain employment as receptionist	Jamie, Ms. Powell

solicits system change suggestions by asking participants to identify those aspects of the current system that would have to change for the individual to realize a desired future.

System changes in employment, housing, post-secondary education opportunities, and transportation are likely to be stimulated by this type of problem-solving discussion. Here is an example of necessary systems changes identified by one high school student and his family:

1. Families should be given better explanation of available services (the earlier, the better).
2. Affordable health care.

The necessary system changes identified during these meetings should be shared with appropriate administrators of local services and supports and others such as teachers, ministers, politicians, and business owners. To every extent possible, the individual with a disability should be actively involved in relating this information to service providers and other community members. This active involvement promotes self-advocacy leadership skills on the part of the individual and listening skills on the part of others.

Figure 9 provides a checklist to facilitate the person-centered planning activities described in this chapter. While teams and meetings may vary, these steps have proven effective in promoting a challenging vision of the future and identifying the steps needed to achieve it.

Families that have participated in these person-centered planning activities have been very pleased with the experience. Many have expressed that person-centered planning has empowered them as consumers to assume a more active role in the IEP/transition planning process. Relatively, the total time requirement for these planning activities is low and the perceived benefit by students, their parents, and professionals is quite high.

Key Question #7: How can person-centered planning information be incorporated into the IEP/transition plan?

One of the best strategies for promoting use of person-centered planning information is to provide copies of all materials to the students and families and encourage their use as part of the student's IEP meeting. The facilitator plays a pivotal role in this process. He or she prepares a summary of the information gathered in the person-centered planning meeting and organizes the materials for presentation to the IEP team. The facilitator's presence at the IEP meeting is also highly desired since he or she may need to play a strong advocacy role to ensure that the student's and family's voices are heard.

As described previously, the person-centered planning information fits nicely with the transition requirements of the IEP. Specifically, desired outcomes from the person-centered planning process have direct implications for the student's IEP. For example, Joe's person-centered planning team concluded, "Joe plans to live with his parents immediately after graduation. His long term plans are to live independently with a possible need for time-limited support." Joe also "…expects to be competitively employed with no need for formal support and to attend community college in the evenings." In the area of recreation and leisure, Joe's plans are to "…participate in recreation activities such as tandem bike riding with ongoing support." These desired outcomes have direct implications for Joe's

Figure 9
Suggested Steps for Person-Centered Transition Planning

Personal Profile Development
- Provide the student and family with the "Introduction to Person-Centered Planning Activities" handout
- Review process described in the handout.
- Present sample circle of support map for non-handicapped high school graduate.
- Describe the relationship of individuals in each circle.
- Present sample of circle of support map for the person with severe disabilities.
- Develop a circle of support map for the individual.
- Suggest that the student's map should more closely resemble the first sample than the second sample.
- Present community presence map samples.
- Develop the student's community presence map.
- Present a sample preferences list for an individual with severe disabilities.
- Develop a preferences list of things that "work" and "don't work" for the student.
- Present sample of gifts and capacities list for individual with severe disabilities.
- Develop gifts and capacities list for student.
- Review the personal profile and solicit necessary changes.

Future Lifestyle Planning
- Suggest that participants base their vision of the future on the student's desires and needed systems change, not on the student's disability.
- Ask participants to describe where the student will live immediately after school exit.
- Ask participants to describe where the student will live five years after school exit.
- Ask participants what the student will do during the day and where she or he will do it.
- Ask participants to describe what the student will do for fun and recreation.
- Ask participants to list the individuals with whom the student will participate in recreation and leisure activities.

Action Steps and Responsible Parties
- Write the words "activities" and "who" on the flip chart.
- To begin process, list "attend transition planning meeting" as first activity and student and parents as responsible individuals.
- Ask the participants to identify activities and responsible individuals that will begin to move toward the realization of the vision of the future.
- Mark out "attend transition planning meeting" and student and/or family as responsible individuals if participants do not agree.
- Suggest that the group identify two to five additional activities.

Systems Change
- Ask the participants to make any statements of necessary changes in service system to achieve future lifestyle for student and list them on flip chart.

Person-centered planning materials should be developed from information on the flipcharts and provided to all participants as soon as possible. Suggest that these materials be utilized during subsequent IEP/transition planning meetings to promote a person-centered approach.

IEP. For these outcomes to be attained, Joe's transition goals should reflect these plans, his secondary curriculum experiences should prepare him in these areas, and the needed interagency connections should be made to promote a smoother transition from school to post-school life.

Person-centered transition planning is a wonderful way to lay the groundwork for a productive IEP meeting. The personal profile information gives a holistic appreciation of the individual's interpersonal connectedness, community involvement, preferences and interests, and gifts and capacities. One of the very best ways to incorporate some of this information into the formal IEP interaction is to begin the meeting by giving a strength-based introduction of the individual. Such an introduction is in sharp contrast to past practices in which student deficit information dominated the context in which annual planning occurred. In many cases, the strength-based student introduction is followed by a self-directed IEP, a practice that further places emphasis on the student's capabilities rather than disabilities.

Transition planning is a required aspect of the IEP process for high-school-age students with disabilities. However, until students and their families assume a more empowered role in this process, the potential benefits of transition planning will not be realized. Person-centered planning activities are needed to invigorate the process and fulfill the promise of transition planning and the desirable post-school lifestyles of community inclusion that we all seek.

Window to the World
Steve: Negotiating and Realizing a Desirable Future

Steve was finishing his junior year in high school. He had always been a quiet, well-mannered student and the teachers at the high school liked him. When Steve's person-centered planning meeting began, he didn't say much, but just seemed to agree with most of the things that were said by his parents.

When discussing where he would live in the future, his mom suggested that it would have to be near public transportation as Steve didn't drive. Later, when the action steps were being identified, Steve stated that he wanted to take driver's education during his senior year. His mom objected, saying that it would be dangerous for Steve to drive. What if he was too slow to react and had a wreck?

Steve reminded his mom that one of his gifts was his persistence. It was agreed that he could talk to Mr. McCoy, the special education teacher, about taking the classroom portion of the driver's education course. During his senior year, Steve completed driver's education, got his license, and later bought a red pickup truck. Dreaming of a future for Steve was much different when planning from a capacities perspective rather than focusing on his deficits.

Window to the World
Carl: Accessing Generic and Natural Supports

Carl had been in a secondary program for students with moderate to severe mental retardation for three years. He was twenty years old and still had two years of school eligibility. His parents were very concerned about

what would happen after leaving high school. They knew other families that were unhappy with the day training program and residential options and felt that the future was bleak. When participating in person-centered planning activities, Carl and his parents described a future in which Carl would live with a friend in an apartment with ongoing support.

Brainstorming about future work yielded possible vocations in the service field, nursing home care, horticulture, or the care of animals. Carl's community work experience was limited to working as a dishwasher in the school cafeteria. Identifying action steps resulted in recognition that there were limited opportunities to gain work experience in horticulture or animal care. Carl's parents suggested that he take a class in horticulture at the local community college. This action step had the advantage of utilizing a setting where Carl would have the opportunity to meet other people his own age and learn more about the kind of work he was interested in.

In discussions about working with animals, Carl's mom mentioned that the family had recently adopted a Labrador retriever puppy. The puppy needed to attend obedience school and someone was required to be its "trainer." She suggested, and Carl quickly agreed, that he be the trainer for the puppy and learn more about training and caring for animals. Carl would gain experience and serve a valued role in the family.

If the family had confined action steps to only those formal educational services available for student with disabilities, Carl's opportunities would have been greatly limited. Considering services and supports that were available to people without disabilities and those available to anyone in Carl's family led to meaningful experiences for Carl.

Future Research Issues

1. What is the impact of person-centered planning meetings on the content of discussion in the school transition planning/IEP meetings?

2. What are the effects of person-centered planning on the post-school outcomes experienced by special education exiters?

3. What are the identified and validated enabling behaviors of professionals in person-centered transition planning/IEP meetings?

Best Practice Recommendations

1. Practitioners should focus on facilitating quality plans rather than achieve a goal of facilitating a plan for every student.
2. An emphasis on ensuring implementation and follow-up of action steps is essential to the ethical practice of person-centered planning. Facilitators should begin by developing their own person-centered plan.
3. Whenever possible, the facilitator should be someone other than a service provider involved with the student.
4. Teachers facilitating person-centered planning for their students should remain neutral during the planning activities.
5. Initiate person-centered planning with a student who has had difficulty developing a challenging vision of the future.

6. When developing action steps and responsible parties promote greater reliance on natural supports.
7. Develop person-centered planning materials from information on the flipcharts and provide them to all participants as soon as possible.
8. Suggest that these materials be utilized during subsequent IEP/transition planning meetings to promote a person-centered approach.
9. Incorporate the spirit of person-centered planning into transition planning activities for all students.

Discussion Questions

1. How can teachers control personal bias in regards to student preferences, future expectations, action steps, and necessary systems change when facilitating a person-centered plan?
2. How can teachers find the time needed to facilitate person-centered transition planning?
3. How can teachers secure broad-based input and interagency responsibility as part of a person-centered planning process?

Community-Based Activities

After reading this chapter, practitioners should:

1. Develop their own person-centered plan. This experience can provide insight into the personal nature of the process and examples to stimulate discussion when facilitating subsequent person-centered plans.
2. Facilitate a person-centered plan with a young man or woman without disabilities who graduated from high school within the last three to five years. This experience should provide a perspective of typical outcomes for youth in the years immediately after completing high school.
3. After completion of the previous suggested activities, facilitate a person-centered plan for a student volunteer along with volunteer participants such as family members, friends, and interested professionals with student approval.

After the reader has completed the Community-Based Activity Suggestions, initiate person-centered planning with a student who has had difficulty developing a challenging vision of the future. The spirit of person-centered planning can be incorporated into transition planning activities for all students.

References

Miner, C. A., & Bates, P. E. (1997). The effect of person-centered planning activities on the IEP/ transition planning process. *Education and Training in Mental Retardation and Developmental Disabilities, 32,* 105-112.

Mount, B., & Zwernick, K. (1988). *It's never too early. It's never too late. A booklet about personal futures planning for persons with developmental disabilities, their families and friends, case managers, service providers and advocates.* St. Paul, MN: Metropolitan Council.

Nisbet, J. (Ed.). (1992). *Natural supports in school, at work, and in the community for people with severe disabilities.* Baltimore: Paul H. Brookes.

Pearpoint, J., Forest, M., & Snow. (1992). *The inclusion papers: Strategies to make inclusion work.* Toronto: Inclusion Press.

Smull, M. W., & Harrison, S. (September, 1992). *Supporting people with severe reputations in the community.* (Available from National Association of State Mental Retardation Program Directors, Inc., 113 Oronoco St., Alexandria, Virginia 22314).

Steere, D., Wood, R., Pancsofar, E. L., & Butterworth, J. (1990). Outcome-based school to work transition planning for students with severe disabilities. *Career Development for Exceptional Individuals, 13,* 57-69.

Turnbull, H. R., & Turnbull, A. P. (1998, Winter). Getting an enviable life. *MRDD Express, 9,* 1.

Turnbull, A. P., & Turnbull, H. R. (1997). *Families, professionals, and exceptionality: A special partnership.* Upper Saddle River, NJ: Merrill.

Vandercook, T., York, J., & Forest, M. (1989). The McGill Action Planning System (MAPS): A strategy for building the vision. *Journal of The Association for Persons with Severe Handicaps, 14,* 205-215.

Wehman, P. (1992). Transition for young people with disabilities: Challenges for the 1990s. *Education and Training in Mental Retardation and Developmental Disabilities, 27,* 112-118.

Wilcox, B., & Bellamy, G. T. (1987). *A comprehensive guide to The Activities Catalog: An alternative curriculum for youth and adults with severe disabilities.* Baltimore: Paul H. Brookes.

Chapter 2
Instructional Assessment

Paul E. Bates
Southern Illinois University

Key Questions
1. What is the difference between norm-referenced instructional assessment and criterion-referenced instructional assessment?
2. What are socially significant instructional objectives?
3. What is an ecological inventory and how might it contribute to the selection of socially significant instructional objectives?
4. What is social validation assessment and how does it contribute to determinations regarding social significance?
5. What are the characteristics of a "quality" instructional objective?
6. What are some of the issues involved in selecting an appropriate direct observation assessment methodology for an instructional objective of interest?
7. What is task analytic assessment and when should this methodology be chosen?
8. What is frequency assessment and when should this methodology be chosen?
9. What is duration/latency assessment and when should this assessment methodology be chosen?
10. What are the different interval assessment procedures and under what conditions might you choose each of these methodologies?
11. What is inter-observer reliability?
12. What is procedural reliability?
13. What is the purpose of data-based decision-making?

Instructional assessment is a multifaceted process consisting of curriculum development activities and direct behavioral observation. The purpose of instructional assessment is to assist educators in making better decisions regarding what to teach and how to most efficiently teach valued school and community behaviors. In this chapter an instructional assessment model is described. This model emphasizes the importance of assessment in the process of determining personally and socially significant target behaviors. After these socially significant target behaviors are determined for individual students, they need to be incorporated into instructional objectives and relevant direct observation procedures selected for measuring the behavioral dimensions of interest. Direct observational data must be collected in such a manner that valid and reliable performance information is produced and reviewed as part of an ongoing data-based decision-making process. Each of these components is described in this chapter with case study examples to illustrate their application with students who experience disabilities.

Key Question #1: What is the difference between norm-referenced instructional assessment and criterion-referenced instructional assessment?

It is important to recognize that there are a variety of practices that fit under the broad umbrella of instructional assessment. Instructional assessment includes both norm-referenced assessment and criterion-referenced assessment. Typically, norm-referenced assessment refers to the administration of a standardized aptitude or achievement test to an individual and the comparison of that student's score with the average performance of a norm group, a comparison group of other students in the country who are of the same age or grade level (Overton, 2000). For example, a standardized reading achievement test administered to high school students may indicate that a particular student is functioning at the tenth percentile. Interpretation of this result means that the individual performed as well as or better than ten out of one hundred of the students included in the norm group. This type of assessment and score tells us very little about specific areas of performance and gives us relatively little instructionally relevant information.

Criterion referenced assessment, on the other hand, is distinguished from norm-referenced assessment in that the student's performance is compared to an objective standard rather than the performance of others (Schloss, Smith, & Schloss, 1995). The instructional assessment procedures described in this chapter are criterion-referenced assessments, since they derive from the student's instructional objectives and have very well defined criteria or standards by which the student's performance is evaluated. Criterion-referenced assessment and curriculum-based assessment (Tucker, 1985) are often used interchangeably, i.e., both rely heavily on direct behavioral observations of the student's performance in relation to the demands of the curriculum in general and his or her IEP in particular. Criterion-referenced assessment is used primarily for formative evaluation purposes, i.e., to monitor student progress and plan remedial instruction as needed.

This chapter addresses criterion-referenced assessment strategies used for formative assessment purposes. These instructional assessment procedures are consistent with a behavioral assessment model, as defined by Mash (1979):

> Behavioral assessment is characterized at a conceptual level by a view of human behavior as predominately under the control of contemporaneous environmental variables rather than determined by underlying intrapsychic mechanisms or inferred personality traits. (p. 24)

These behavioral assessment procedures are applicable to a wide range of academic and community functioning behaviors and involve several direct observation behavioral assessment methodologies. The model of instructional assessment recommended in this chapter adheres to the following principles (Mash & Terdal, 1997).

- Assessment should focus on observable behavior rather than global underlying traits or dispositions.

- Assessment should focus on the individual's behavior rather than norm group comparisons.
- Assessment should focus on situational influences on behavior rather than non-contemporaneous historical experiences.
- Assessment should contribute to the development of more effective intervention strategies.
- Multiple direct assessments conducted in natural contexts may be needed to better understand the functional relationship between a student's behavior and the situation.

Key Question #2: What are socially significant instructional objectives?

The direct behavioral observation assessment methodology recommended in this chapter to be used as part of a dynamic data-based decision-making process begins by establishing the social significance of instructional objectives, including both those behaviors targeted for strengthening and those targeted to be weakened. The social significance of behaviors targeted to be enhanced is determined in a variety of different ways, including person-centered planning (Miner and Bates, 1999), community-referenced curriculum development (Brolin, 1991; Brown et al., 1979), and high stakes standards based assessment (Thurlow, Elliott, & Ysselydyke, 1998).

As described previously in this text (Chapter 1), person-centered transition planning is a collaborative process that assists planning teams to prioritize instructional objectives based on the unique preferences and interests of each student and family. These personal preferences and interests should be considered in relation to environmental demands. Environmental demands refer to the skills needed to function more autonomously in a wide variety of curriculum domain areas, including school, community, vocational, domestic, and recreation-leisure domains.

Within the school domain, environmental demands include both curricular standards and extracurricular or "hidden curriculum" demands associated with school success (Archer & Gleason, 1989). The academic curricular demands of school environments, as determined by the learning standards and benchmarks adopted by many states, reflect the academic priorities for instructional assessment. An emphasis on these academic priorities is evident in federal education legislation such as the 1994 Goals 2000: Educate America Act (PL 103-227). This school reform legislation encouraged individual states to establish "high stakes" learning standards and assessment procedures to monitor student attainment of these academic priorities.

More recently, the Individuals with Disabilities Education Act was amended and reauthorized to include specific language related to the involvement of students with disabilities in the general education curriculum and related accountability assessments. This includes alternative assessments for those students not able to participate in the standardized assessments (PL 105-17). Taken together, these federal laws endorse educational accountability for all students. The general education curriculum and related learning standards provide a set of socially significant target behaviors that should be considered in relation to the individual's preferences and interests, and addressed with the instructional assessment strategies presented in this chapter.

Key Question #3: What is an ecological inventory and how might it contribute to the selection of socially significant instructional objectives?

The ecological inventory (Brown et al., 1979) is an excellent environmental assessment procedure for identifying the wide variety of skills and activities associated with community functioning in nonacademic domains. Once a curriculum domain of interest is identified, relevant environments within that domain are delineated. These environments are then further analyzed to determine sub-environments within them and specific skills/activities associated with each.

For example, within the community domain, relevant environments include grocery stores, restaurants, banks, pharmacies, and department stores. As part of an ecological inventory assessment, these community environments are further analyzed into their sub-environments (entry way, produce section, and checkout lane within the grocery environment) and specific skills and activities within each sub-environment are identified.

The social significance of behaviors targeted for reduction is determined in a similar manner by initially addressing the individual's preferences and interests, as expressed within his or her person-centered planning activities. In addition to the individual's preferences and interests, other evidence that should be considered in assessing the social significance of challenging behavior include concurrence among several people that a problem exists, documented attempts to resolve the problem through direct and informal means, and support from significant persons to proceed with more formalized assessment and intervention activities (Sulzer-Azaroff & Mayer, 1977).

For behaviors targeted for reduction, one should use a more complete functional assessment preceding more focused direct behavioral observations. Those interested in functional assessment should access procedural manuals that comprehensively address these practices. (See O'Neill, Horner, Albin, Storey, & Sprague, 1990.)

Key Question #4: What is social validation assessment and how does it contribute to determinations regarding social significance?

For both increase and decrease instructional objectives, social validation assessment plays a prominent role in the determination of social significance. Social validation assessment refers to a three-part process for determining the social significance of program goals, acceptability of intervention practices, and the acceptability or value of program results (Kazdin, 1989). Social comparison and subjective evaluation are two of the most commonly used methods for determining social significance. With social comparison, an individual's behavior is compared to a reference group and noted discrepancies are targeted for intervention.

For example, nondisabled adults who are leading productive, independent, and integrated lives within their home communities would be an appropriate comparison group for the identification of career development competencies. On the other hand, the norm group used to establish academic performance standards for high school students would be an appropriate comparison group for evaluating the attainment of secondary academic competencies.

In other cases the comparison group could be the norm group for standardized testing of high school competencies. Such a comparison might lead to a focus on academic related competencies. With subjective evaluation, significant others in the student's life provide input to curriculum prioritization decisions (Wolf, 1978). These subjective decisions are influenced by the values and priorities of the significant other. Specifically, those coming from a perspective that values academic performance may lean in the direction of supporting academic priorities; those coming from a perspective that favors a community-referenced curriculum may support more functional target behaviors.

Historically, the concept of social validation and its accompanying decisions regarding the social significance of target behavior selection and outcomes have been made independent of the perspective of the individual with disabilities. With the advent of transition language in IDEA that emphasizes student preferences and interests as legitimate priorities, the concept of social validation must be broadened to more fully embrace the student perspective in this process. As students assume more direct control over their own program planning, it is likely that their opinions will be more fully reflected in their instructional priorities and related assessment practices. Consequently, instructional assessment will need to address those target behaviors of highest priority to the individual with disabilities. The direct behavior observation strategies described in this chapter should be conducted with the endorsement or consent of the individual with disabilities and should be reserved for socially significant target behaviors.

Key Question #5: What are the characteristics of a "quality" instructional objective?

Once socially significant target behaviors have been identified, these behaviors should be incorporated within instructional objectives that conform to recommended guidelines (Billingsley, Burgess, Lynch, & Matlock, 1991). Specifically, these instructional objectives should identify functional target behaviors, be written in a technically adequate fashion, and include maintenance and generalization considerations.

Functional behaviors are those socially significant skills that have immediate or future usefulness to the individual. Technically adequate objectives are written to include conditions of performance, a measurable target behavior, and a criterion by which mastery can be evaluated. Maintenance and generalization conditions specify opportunities for ongoing performance and assessment of the target behavior under more naturalistic circumstances. Collectively, these characteristics of a "quality" instructional objective provide guidance for both instructional assessment and program design.

Key Question #6: What are some of the issues involved in selecting an appropriate direct observation assessment methodology for an instructional objective of interest?

The behavioral assessment methodology best suited for particular instructional objectives is best determined by the conditions of assessment, characteristics of the target behavior, and the performance criteria. Specifically, it is much easier to select an appropriate direct observation assessment methodology when the behavioral objective involves a functional, socially significant target behavior that is presented in a technically adequate fashion with a measurable criterion and well specified maintenance and generalization conditions (Billingsley, Burgess, Lynch, & Matlock, 1991; Davis & Bates, 1997).

In addition to considerations related to the nature of the behavior, its conditions and criteria, specific issues that must be addressed when designing an appropriate instructional assessment include decisions regarding: a.) the time and place for assessment, b.) who will conduct the assessment, c.) design of data recording forms, d.) whether or not inter-observer reliability assessment will be assessed, e.) how often assessment will be conducted, and f.) how data summaries will be prepared and used as part of a data-based decision-making process. There are far more direct behavioral observation assessment methodologies than can be addressed in this text. However, a few of the more commonly used and versatile assessment procedures are described in this chapter, with case study examples to illustrate their application with a wide variety of socially significant behavior in both school and community settings. These include task analytic assessment, frequency assessment, duration/latency assessment, and interval recording assessment.

Key Question #7: What is task analytic assessment and when should this methodology be chosen?

Task analytic assessment is best suited for direct observation of target behaviors that involve the performance of a series of component steps in a consistent skill sequence. Although academic competencies and related learning strategies lend themselves nicely to task analysis of their component skills, this method of assessment has most commonly been applied to functional community living task sequences (Storey, Bates, & Hanson, 1983: Test, Spooner, Keul, & Grossi, 1990). The following questions must be addressed when designing and conducting task analytic assessment:

- What natural cue (if any) should be present to initiate the start of an assessment trial?
- What instructor or evaluator cue (if any) should be used to occasion the assessment trial?
- How much time will students be allowed to initiate performance of each step of the task analysis prior to that step being scored minus (-)?
- What will you do when the student commits an error?
- What will you do when the student successfully performs a step?
- What will you say to the student during the assessment?
- What will you say when the task is completed?
- How will you record student performance?
- How often would you assess inter-observer reliability?
- How many assessment trials will you conduct as part of baseline?
- How often will you conduct task analytic assessment during instruction?
- How will your assessment practices differ during baseline and instruction?
- How will you summarize the results of baseline and instructional assessments?
- How often will you review your data summaries and consider instructional program changes/modifications?

Window to the World
Christine: Task Analytic Assessment

The assessment situation for a task analytic assessment should be as similar as possible to the ultimate performance conditions. For example, Christine is a twenty-year-old student with moderate mental retardation in her final year of public school eligibility. As part of her person-centered transition planning, she has expressed an interest in becoming a cook's helper at a local restaurant. Christine's vocational supervisor commented that her only concern regarding this goal was Christine's personal hygiene skills, particularly her hand washing after using the restroom facilities. As a result of Christine's interest in food service employment and the importance of personal hygiene to this goal, her IEP included the following behavioral objective:

After using the toilet facilities at school, Christine will wash her hands (see task analysis for detail) with 100% independence across five consecutive opportunities. After meeting criterion, Christine will demonstrate this skill to the same criterion in her food service job experience and maintain this skill at the same level when assessed one time per week for the remainder of the year at school, at home, and at work in the presence of her teacher, parent(s), and job coach, respectively.

One approach to assessing this skill would be for the instructor to follow the student into the restroom, wait until she finishes using the facilities, and then assess what steps of the task are completed independently and what steps are either attempted or completed incorrectly. The natural cue for this assessment would be the bathroom setting and the completion of using the facilities. In addition to these natural cue conditions being present, the evaluator may choose to initiate the start of an assessment trial with a more formal task demand, such as "Wash your hands." In some cases, the evaluator may choose to provide an explanation to the student regarding the skill to be assessed and the purpose of such an assessment. For example, the instructor could say: "Christine, we've talked about how important it is to wash your hands after using the toilet. You've just finished using the toilet. Now I'd like for you to wash your hands. I want to see how much you can do on your own without any help. Later, we'll work on this together. Do your best."

After deciding how the assessment trials will be initiated, the evaluator should decide on a standard amount of time (typically three to ten seconds) that will be allowed for the student to initiate each. For example, if the evaluator decided to allow five seconds for Christine to initiate the first step, "Turn on water," she would wait five seconds following the formal task demand for Christine to turn on the water. If Christine would successfully turn the water on within five seconds, the evaluator would record a (+) for step one; if she failed to initiate the step within five seconds or made an error, the evaluator would record a (-). Successfully performed steps are followed by another five second opportunity to initiate the subsequent step of the task analysis. For steps that are either not initiated within five seconds or performed incorrectly, the evaluator would score the step(s) (-) and intervene if necessary to arrange the task for evaluation of the next step. For example, if a student failed to "Turn on the water," it would be impossible to do step

Figure 1
Task Analytic Assessment Data Recording Form

Name of Student: Christine   **Teacher/Evaluator:** Ms. Sanders

Setting(s): Classroom Bathroom   **Target Behavior(s):** Hand Washing

Steps of Task Analysis	Baseline							Instruction Assessment Probes							
1. Turn on water	-	-	-	-	-	-	-	+	+	+	+	+	+	+	+
2. Wet hands	+	+	+	+	+	+	+	+	+	+	+	+	+	+	+
3. Pick up soap	-	-	+	+	+	+	+	+	+	+	+	+	+	+	+
4. Soap palms	-	+	+	+	+	+	+	+	+	+	+	+	+	+	+
5. Put soap down	-	-	-	-	-	-	-	-	-	+	+	+	+	+
6. Soap backs of hands	-	-	-	-	-	-	-	-	-	-	-	+	+	+
7. Rinse hands	-	-	-	-	-	-	-	+	+	+	+	+	+	+	+
8. Turn off water	-	-	-	-	-	-	+	+	-	+	+	+	+	+	+
9. Pull paper towel	-	-	-	-	-	-	-	-	-	-	+	+	+	+	+
10. Dry hands	-	-	-	-	-	-	-	-	-	-	-	-	-	-	-
11. Throw towel away	-	-	-	-	-	-	-	-	+	+	+	+	+	+	+
# of Steps Independent	1	2	3	3	3	3	4	6	6	7	9	9	10	10	10
Assessment Trials	1	2	3	4	5	6	7	8	9	10	11	12	13	14	15

two, "Wet hands." In this case, the evaluator needs to intervene by turning on the water for the student. However, for steps that are not essential for subsequent performance, e.g., turning off water is not essential for the student to ultimately dry hands, such evaluator intervention is unnecessary. Whenever the evaluator intervenes, she should do so in as unobtrusive manner as possible and without drawing too much attention or providing too much assistance. The purpose of this intervention is to allow each step to be evaluated rather than to provide instructional assistance to the student.

Typically during a task analytic assessment, the instructor would refrain from providing contingent social reinforcement and would instead provide more generic statements of encouragement such as "try your best" or "keep going." It is important to remember that the purpose of assessment is to find out what the student can do on his or her own; instruction will provide the cues, corrections, and reinforcement needed to learn the skill. When each task analytic assessment trial is completed, the instructor should thank the student for his or her effort rather than comment on how well the student has done.

During instruction, ongoing assessment is needed to monitor student performance for the purpose of making needed program modifications to assure success. For example, periodic assessment probes, identical to baseline, could be conducted weekly to determine whether or not satisfactory progress is being made. These ongoing assessments could include additional information regarding prompt levels needed to occasion student performance on specific steps of the task analysis. Regardless of the method of ongoing assessment chosen, these assessments should provide comparable data from which program improvements can be evaluated. The development of graphic summaries of instructional assessment is one of the very best ways to make data-based decisions. Figure 1 provides an example of a completed task analytic assessment data sheet for the hand washing instructional objective presented previously for Christina.

Key Question #8: What is frequency assessment and when should this methodology be chosen?

One of the most common direct observation methods is frequency recording. With frequency recording, the observer records the number of responses emitted in a particular observation period. Frequency recording is appropriate when the target behavior has a distinct start and stop, and is of relatively consistent duration. For example, the number of trays cleaned by a kitchen worker could be assessed with frequency recording, but the number of times the person left the immediate work area might not be assessed appropriately with frequency recording if the amount of time of each occurrence varied drastically. Frequency measures have been used for behaviors that leave relatively permanent evidence of their occurrence (problems completed on a worksheet, words or sentences in an essay, assemblies completed, and pencils broken) and for behaviors that are relatively transient in nature (oral answers to questions in class discussion, social greetings, peer requests for assistance, and swearing).

Frequency recording, like all direct behavioral observations, is dependent on having a clearly defined operational (measurable) definition of the target behavior(s) of interest. Once the target behavior is defined, a frequency recording data sheet (See Figure 3.) should be constructed to allow the observer to record the dates, times, and frequency tallies. Frequency recording should be conducted by someone in the setting who positions him or herself so that they are in a position to see the individual throughout the designated observation period. As the student does the behavior, the observer makes a tally mark in the box corresponding to the day and times of the observation. At the completion of each day's observations, the observer adds the tally marks and enters a total frequency count.. If the observation periods vary in length, these frequency counts should be converted to rate per minute to provide a more accurate and comparable record of behavior strength.

Window to the World
Shane: Frequency Assessment

For example, during Shane's person-centered transition planning discussions, he said he wanted to improve his grades in his academic content classes because he would like to pursue post-secondary education at his local community college. His general education English teacher commented that she would be willing to give Shane extra credit whenever he contributed to class discussions, i.e., answered questions appropriately or made an on-task comment relevant to the discussion topic. By collecting frequency data regarding these contributions, Shane's teacher would have a consistent record of his performance from which she could award extra-credit and evaluate the instructional objective. Figure 2 provides an example frequency data sheet for recording Shane's contributions to class discussions.

In English class, Shane will contribute an average of three times per day to class discussion across two consecutive weeks. Shane will maintain this level of participation in English class for the remainder of the school year and will contribute this often to class discussions in his history class as well, when assessed by his resource teacher one time per week for the remainder of the semester.

Figure 2
Frequency Assessment Data Recording Form

Name of Student: Shane		Teacher/Evaluator: Dr. Howell_____				
Setting(s): English Class- Third Hour						
Target Behavior(s): Contributions to Class Discussion						
Date	Start Time	Frequency Tally	Stop Time	Freq. Total	Time Total	Rate Per Min.
Sept. 18	10:30		11:15	0	45 min.	0
Sept. 19	10:30	/	11:15	1	45 min.	0.02
Sept. 20	10:30		11:15	0	45 min.	0
Sept. 21	10:30		11:15	0	45 min.	0
Sept. 22	10:30		11:15	0	45 min.	0
End of Baseline: Beginning of Instruction						
Sept. 25	10:30	///	11:15	3	45 min.	0.07
Sept. 26	10:30	//	11:15	2	45 min.	0.04
Sept. 27	10:30	////	11:15	4	45 min.	0.09
Sept. 28	10:30	///	11:15	3	45 min.	0.07
Sept. 29	10:30	///	11:15	3	45 min.	0.07
Oct. 2	10:30	////	11:15	4	45 min.	0.09
Oct. 3	10:30	///	11:15	3	45 min.	0.07
Oct. 4	10:30	///	11:15	3	45 min.	0.07
Oct. 5	10:30	////	11:15	4	45 min.	0.09
Oct. 6	10:30	////	11:15	4	45 min.	0.09

Key Question #9: What is duration assessment and latency assessment and when should this assessment methodology be chosen?

Duration/latency recording refers to time-based measures of behavior strength. Specifically, duration refers to how long a target behavior or behavioral episode lasts, while latency refers to the amount of time that elapses from a cue or signal for the behavior to occur and the initiation of the behavior. Duration recording has been used for behaviors such as in-seat, on-task, engagement in leisure activity, and time required to complete specific work assignments. Latency recording has been used to measure how long it takes people to comply with teacher/supervisor directives, how long it takes someone to be "ready to learn" following the bell, and how much time elapses between a peer's social request and the individual's response. Since precise start and stop times are needed for duration/latency recording, these observations are more reliable when these times are easily defined. Also, this type of assessment requires continuous attention by the observers and the aid of a stopwatch for more precise measurement.

Window to the World
Carol: Duration and Latency Assessment

Carol is a senior in high school who is participating in a paid work experience as a housekeeper with a major hotel chain. Carol has learned the sequence of skills required to clean individual hotel rooms, and she is interested in a full-time job at this hotel following graduation. The employer is interested in hiring her, but the supervisor of housekeeping wants her to finish rooms in about the same time as her other employees and not to waste so much time between rooms. Currently most housekeepers are able to clean individual rooms in twenty to thirty minutes and take between one and two minutes between rooms. Carol's IEP objective is as follows: At her job site as a hotel housekeeper, Carol will clean all of her assigned rooms in less than thirty minutes, taking no more than two minutes between rooms for five consecutive work days. After meeting criteria, Carol will maintain this skill across longer work days and for the remainder of her assigned work experience.

Figure 3 provides an example Duration/Latency Recording Form for recording the duration of Carol's room cleaning time and the latency of her time between rooms. Her duration data are recorded by identifying the start and stop times for each room that she cleans. Carol's start time is determined to be the time that she opens the door to begin cleaning the room and the end time is the time she exits the room after completing the cleaning.

Figure 3
Duration/Latency Data Recording Form

Name of Student: Carol				Teacher/Evaluator: Mr. Faw			
Setting(s): Hampton Inn Hotel							
Target Behavior(s): Duration Cleaning Rooms; Latency Between Rooms							
Duration Data Recording				**Latency Data Recording**			
Date of Observation	Start	Stop	Duration	Date	Start	Stop	Latency
Nov. 6	8:20	8:58	38.0 min	Nov. 6	8:58	9:02	4.0 min
Nov. 6	9:02	9:42	40.0 min	Nov. 6	9:42	9:46	4.0 min
Nov. 6	9:46	10:25	39.0 min				
Nov. 7	8:15	8:55	40.0 min	Nov. 7	8:55	9:00	5.0 min
Nov. 7	9:00	9:45	45.0 min	Nov. 7	9:45	9:50	5.0 min
Nov. 8	8:15	8:52	37.0 min				
Nov. 8	8:56	9:40	44.0 min	Nov. 8	9:40	9:45	5.0 min
Nov. 8	9:45	10:30	45.0 min				
End of Baseline; Start of Program							
Nov. 9	8:15	8:55	40.0 min	Nov. 9	8:55	9:00	5.0 min
Nov. 9	9:00	9:42	42.0 min	Nov. 9	9:42	9:47	5.0 min
Nov. 9	9:47	10:30	43.0 min				
Nov. 10	8:20	9:00	40.0 min	Nov. 10	9:00	9:05	5.0 min
Nov. 10	9:05	9:45	40.0 min	Nov. 10	9:45	10:00	5.0 min
Nov. 10	10:00	10:45	45.0 min				
Nov. 13	8:15	9:00	45.0 min	Nov. 13	9:00	9:06	6.0 min
Nov. 13	9:06	9:50	44.0 min	Nov. 13	9:50	9:56	6.0 min
Nov. 13	9:56	10:45	49.0 min				

To conduct duration recording, the observer typically would have a duration/latency recording form on a clipboard, a stopwatch, and a pen or pencil. When Carol would enter each room, the observer would start the stopwatch and record the approximate time on the data sheet. Once Carol completes cleaning the room, the observer would stop the stopwatch, record the approximate actual time on the data sheet, and record the elapsed time from the stopwatch in the duration column of the data sheet. Latency recording for time elapsed between rooms is recorded in virtually an identical fashion as duration data. When Carol exits a room, a second stopwatch is started and when she enters the next room, the stopwatch is stopped. This elapsed time is recorded on the latency data sheet. With latency data, it is optional to record the actual start and stop times. The actual elapsed time from the stopwatch is sufficient.

Key Question #10: What are the different interval assessment procedures and under what conditions might you choose each of these methodologies?

Interval recording methods are often chosen when the target behaviors are not easily counted due to the uncertainty of their start and stop times, or there are logistical concerns regarding the feasibility of continuous observation. Examples of behaviors of interest that may pose problems for observers to reliably count or measure the exact time of occurrence include attending, eye contact, and smiling. Logistical concerns may make it impractical for an observer to maintain continuous observation required to obtain an exact frequency count or duration measure.

Since interval recording methods are applicable to a wide variety of target behaviors and produce a reasonable estimate of a behavior's frequency or duration, they provide a reasonable alternative in many cases to the more demanding frequency and duration measures. With interval recording, an observation period is divided into a series of equal length intervals and the observer makes a judgment regarding the occurrence (+) or nonoccurrence (-) of the target behavior in each interval. Commonly used interval recording methods include partial interval recording, whole interval recording, and momentary interval recording or time sampling. Instructional objectives that would be assessed appropriately by these three methodologies are presented and used to illustrate the proper use of each.

Window to the World
Case Study of Interval Recording Assessment

Shanthi is a seventeen-year-old junior in high school. As part of her person-centered transition planning activities, Shanthi and her parents expressed their interests in her becoming involved in the jointly sponsored tech preparation programs from her high school and the local community college. Specifically, Shanthi would like to enroll in the clerical software applications class.

In response to these interests, her special educator and the tech prep coordinator voiced concerns that Shanthi has been somewhat disruptive in previous general education classes and has not worked independently on the in-class homework assignments. These in-class disruptions have consisted of loud self-deprecating comments such as "I'm stupid," banging the desk, and

kicking her chair. In response to Shanthi's and her parents' interests in the tech prep class and her teachers' concerns regarding her past behavior in general education classes, the following objective was developed:

While attending the software applications class, Shanthi will be on-task 90% of the time and will refrain from engaging in disruptive behavior (negative self-statements, banging desk, kicking chair, etc.) in 90% of the observation intervals across ten consecutive class sessions. After meeting criterion, Shanthi will extend these behavioral improvements to a second general education class and maintain this level of performance for the remainder of the semester when assessed one time per week.

For this behavioral objective, partial interval recording provides a relatively reasonable estimate of the frequency of disruptive behavior without having to record each and every behavioral event. For example, a twenty-minute observation period within the software applications class could be divided into twenty one-minute intervals. Within each interval, a response is recorded as occurring (+) when a single instance of the behavior is observed. Intervals in which no occurrences of the behavior are observed are recorded (-). Partial interval recording is appropriate for behaviors that are brief in duration or occur in fleeting, but high frequency, moments in which individual frequencies would be difficult to discriminate. Since a single instance of a target behavior within an interval results in an entire interval being scored as an occurrence, this method yields an overestimate of target behaviors and might be used best for instances such as Shanthi's when you are interested in assessing undesirable behavior(s). Economical advantages of this assessment method are that the observer does not need to continue observation within an interval following the first occurrence of the target behavior and does not need to count every instance of the behavior.

Momentary interval recording or momentary time sampling is an appropriate assessment methodology for estimating behavior strength of target behaviors that persist for long periods of time or are expected to occur quite frequently. Momentary interval recording of Shanthi's on-task behavior, for example, is a very economical way to obtain a reasonably accurate estimate of this behavior. The percentage of intervals scored as on-task (+) in each observation would be computed by dividing the sum total of occurrences into the total number of observations. Figure 4 provides an example of momentary interval recording of Shanthi's on-task behavior.

Target behaviors that might lend themselves nicely to this assessment method include studying, engagement in leisure activity, and on-task behavior at work or school. The major advantage of momentary interval recording procedures is that the observer is free to do other things during the interval and only has to attend specifically to the student's target behavior at the end of each interval. With interval lengths of one to two minutes, this allows the observer to maintain consistent measurement with minimal disruption of other activities.

Whole interval recording requires the behavior to persist for the entire length of an observation interval in order for the interval to be scored as an occurrence (+). As a result, this method requires the observer to maintain continuous observation throughout each interval until the person ceases to engage in the target behavior. Once the behavior stops, the observer records a nonoccurrence (-) for that interval and does not begin to observe again until the next interval begins.

Figure 4
Interval Recording Assessment Data Sheet

Name of Student: Shanthi   **Teacher/Evaluator:** Mr. Roth
Setting(s): Computer Software Applications Class
Target Behavior(s): On-Task Behavior   **Interval Length:** 60 Seconds
Type of Interval Recording: ⊗ Momentary   ○ Partial   ○ Whole
Observation Code: Occurrence: + ; Nonoccurrence: -

Observation Intervals

Date	Time	1	2	3	4	5	6	7	8	9	10	11	12	13	14	15	16	17	18	19	20	#+	%+
11/27	9:00	+	+	-	-	-	-	+	-	-	-	+	-	+	-	-	+	-	+	+	-	8	40
11/28	9:00	-	+	-	+	-	-	+	-	-	+	-	+	+	+	-	-	-	+	+	-	9	45
11/29	9:00	-	-	+	+	-	-	-	+	-	+	-	-	+	-	+	-	+	+	-	-	8	40
11/30	9:00	-	-	-	-	-	-	+	+	+	-	-	-	-	+	+	+	-	-	-	+	7	35
12/1	9:00	-	-	-	-	-	-	+	-	-	-	-	-	+	+	-	+	-	+	+	-	6	30

End of Baseline Assessment; Beginning of Graphic Feedback Program

Date	Time	1	2	3	4	5	6	7	8	9	10	11	12	13	14	15	16	17	18	19	20	#+	%+
12/4	9:00	+	+	-	+	+	-	-	+	-	-	-	+	-	-	-	+	+	-	+	+	10	50
12/5	9:00	+	-	+	+	+	-	-	+	-	-	+	-	+	-	+	+	+	+	-	+	12	60
12/6	9:00	+	-	+	-	+	-	+	+	+	+	-	-	+	-	+	-	-	+	-	+	11	55
12/7	9:00	+	+	+	+	-	+	-	+	+	-	+	-	+	-	+	-	+	-	+	+	13	65
12/8	9:00	+	+	-	+	-	+	-	+	+	+	-	+	-	+	+	+	+	+	-	+	14	70
12/11	9:00	+	+	+	+	+	-	-	+	+	-	-	+	-	+	+	+	+	+	+	+	15	75
12/12	9:00	+	+	+	-	+	-	+	+	+	-	+	+	+	+	-	+	-	+	+	+	15	75
12/13	9:00	+	+	+	+	+	+	+	+	-	+	-	-	+	+	+	+	-	+	+	+	16	80
12/14	9:00	+	+	+	+	+	+	+	-	+	+	+	-	+	-	+	+	-	+	+	+	16	80
12/15	9:00	+	+	+	+	+	-	-	+	+	+	-	+	+	+	+	+	+	+	+	+	17	85

This approach should be reserved for behaviors that are expected to occur for long periods of time without interruption and for situations in which observer time is not limited. Since any interruption of the target behavior results in an entire interval being scored as a nonoccurrence (-), this method yields a conservative estimate of a target behavior's strength. However, given the relative comparability of the purposes and estimates of behavior strength obtained from momentary interval recording and whole interval data, this author finds momentary interval recording methods to be advantageous due to their economical advantage over whole interval methods.

Key Question #11: What is inter-observer reliability?

The effectiveness of data-based decision-making is dependent on reliability of measurement. With direct behavioral observation data, reliability refers to the degree of agreement obtained when two observers independently assess the same behavior with the same observation method(s). Each of the instructional assessment procedures described in this chapter have slightly different methods for computing inter-observer reliability. In general, inter-observer agreement is calculated by determining the percentage of agreement between the primary and secondary observer. For those interested in a more complete explanation of inter-observer agreement methods, Alberto and Troutmanís (1999) *Applied Behavior Analysis for Teachers* is an excellent resource.

Key Question #12: What is procedural reliability?

Behavior change is a function of the relationship between independent variables (the practices, procedures, and environmental events that we manipulate or control in one way or another) and dependent variables (socially significant target behaviors that we assess or measure). The certainty of our conclusions about these relationships is predicated on our confidence in the integrity of both sets of variables.

However, instructional assessment has focused almost exclusively on interobserver reliability and virtually ignored procedural reliability. Procedural reliability has been referred to as treatment integrity or treatment fidelity. These terms, which have been used virtually interchangeably, refer to the consistency by which a program or set of procedures is implemented. Treatment protocols should be developed and evaluated periodically by independent observers to assure that instructional programs are being implemented appropriately. If we are unsure whether or not a program was implemented appropriately, it is virtually impossible to make data-based decisions regarding program effectiveness and program modifications. Instructional assessment needs to address both the consistency of measurement of student behavior and the consistency of program implementation.

Key Question #13: What is the purpose of data-based decision-making?

The development of graphic summaries of instructional assessment is one of the very best ways to make data-based decisions. Some of the more common data-based decisions related to instructional assessment include length of baseline, adequacy of progress, need to modify program, and attainment of criterion. Although the trend lines within a graphic display provide useful visual information regarding student progress, the actual data sheets should be maintained and reviewed for more precise understanding of the instructional assessment data. Graphic summaries of the previously presented instructional assessment data (Figures 1-4) follow to illustrate how visual representations of data can be used to make programmatic decisions.

Prior to implementation of an instructional program, baseline assessment of the individual's target behavior should be conducted in as naturalistic a setting as possible to determine initial behavior strength and to have a record of performance from which program effectiveness can be judged. Without a valid understanding of baseline level of student performance, it is difficult to know where instruction needs to begin and impossible to fairly and objectively evaluate progress for the purpose of making program modifications.

Baseline assessment should result in a stable record of student performance. Typically a minimum of three assessment trials is needed to determine behavioral stability. However, it is important to realize that the length of baseline assessment is more related to the stability of the student's behavior than it is to a set number of assessment trials, i.e., baseline assessment should be conducted until the evaluator is confident about what the student can and cannot do.

Figure 5 provides a graphic summary of Christine's task analytic assessment data for hand washing. (See Figure 1.) In this example, more than three baseline assessments were needed to establish a stable picture of her skills prior to program implementation. Once a stable baseline was obtained, Christine acquired ten of the eleven steps through systematic instruction. Inspection of Figure 1 provides evidence that Christine has been unable to independently dry her hands adequately. This lack of improvement may necessitate further breakdown of this step into its subcomponents, i.e., dry palms, dry back of one hand, and dry back of other hand.

Figure 6 provides a graphic summary of Shane's frequency assessment data for contributions to English class discussions. (See Figure 2.) Visual inspection of this figure confirms his lack of participation in class during baseline and the success of the bonus points intervention program. This graphic summary indicates that Shane has met criterion on this instructional objective and that pro-

Figure 5
Task Analytic Assessment Summary
Christine's Hand Washing Program

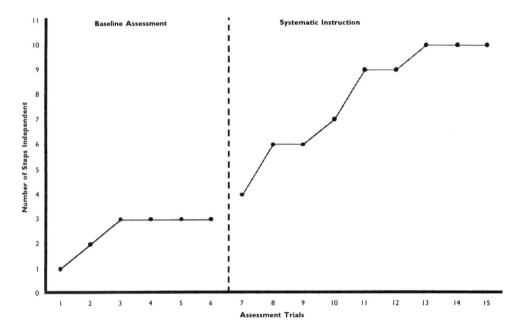

grammatic attention needs to shift toward maintenance and generalization of this behavior.

Figure 7 provides a graphic summary of Carol's duration data for cleaning hotel rooms. (See Figure 3.) After a stable baseline, a goal setting criterion was established at thirty-six minutes per room. Carol's lack of progress in this program suggests that her program needs to be modified. Perhaps the thirty-six-minute criterion was too stringent and she is getting discouraged or she needs more direct instruction within each hotel room to assist her in more efficiently cleaning the rooms. These possibilities should be pursued with continued data collection to evaluate their effectiveness.

Figure 8 provides a graphic summary of Shanthi's momentary interval assessment data for on-task behavior. (See Figure 4.) Based on this summary, the graphic feedback and goal setting intervention appear to be effective and should be continued. Shanthi is making consistent progress toward her goal of 90% on-task behavior.

Figure 6
Frequency Assessment Data Summary
Shane's Contributions to Class Discussion

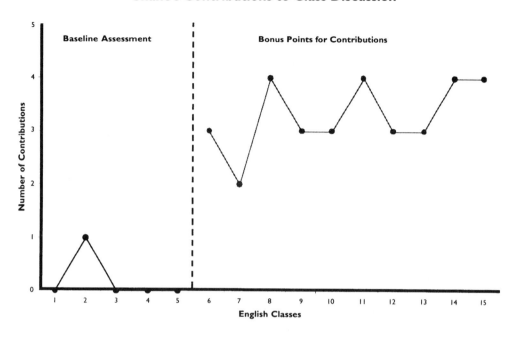

Figure 7
Duration Assessment Data Summary
Carol's Goal-Setting Program

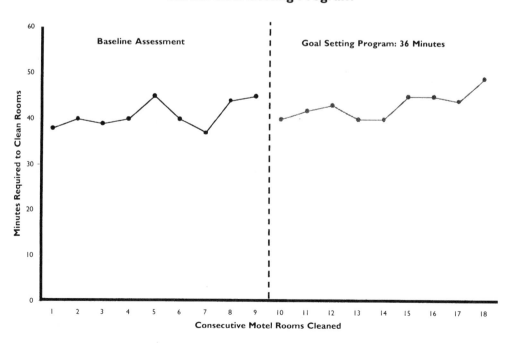

Figure 8
Momentary Interval Recording Assessment Data Summary:
Shanthi's On-Task Time

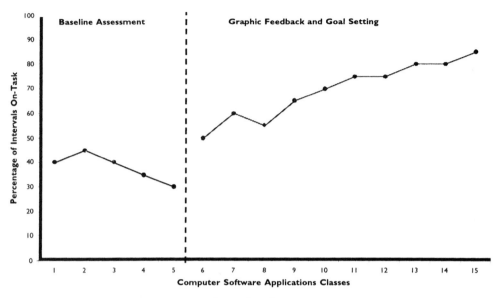

Conclusion

The instructional assessment practices described in this chapter are applicable with individuals who experience a wide variety of disabling conditions, from mild to severe. These practices have proven useful with academic and functional living skills in both school and community settings. The primary purpose of instructional assessment is to generate information from which more effective program decisions can be made, i.e., decisions that enhance student performance of valued skills. For this reason, graphic summaries of assessment information are recommended as part of an ongoing program review and data-based decision-making process.

Recent educational reform initiatives have placed a premium on educational accountability and have identified instructional assessment as a national priority. Although these initiatives have included all students, they have relied extensively on standardized, norm-referenced testing used for summative assessment purposes. For many students with disabilities, these standardized tests are inappropriate, and an alternative form of instructional assessment is needed. The direct behavioral observation methodologies and formative assessment practices described in this chapter should play a prominent role in alternative assessment and instructional accountability for students with disabilities. For example, an assessment portfolio consisting of multiple direct observation instructional assessments could be developed and maintained as an alternative to student participation in district-wide standardized testing.

Best Practice Recommendations

1. Select socially significant target behaviors for more in-depth instructional assessment.
   a. Use person-centered planning to identify preferences and interests of the individual.
   b. Conduct environmental analyses, e.g., ecological inventories, to identify the environmental demands for community adjustment.
   c. Examine general education learning standards to identify benchmarks within the curriculum that are related to the individual's preferences and interests and community demands.
2. Develop instructional objectives that conform to the following criteria:
   a. Target behavior(s) is functional to the individual, i.e., meets the test of social validity.
   b. Conditions of performance (and assessment) are described.
   c. Target behavior is operationally defined, i.e., is measurable.
   d. Assessment criteria address socially valid expectations for competence.
   e. Maintenance and generalization conditions are included.
3. Select a direct observation methodology for assessing the target behavior(s) of interest.
   a. Use task analytic assessment for behaviors that can be reduced to a sequence of component steps.
   b. Use frequency assessment for behaviors that have a relatively constant duration, have a distinct start and stop, or produce a measurable permanent product.
   c. Use duration assessment for behaviors in which length of occurrence is important and that have relatively clear start and stop times.
   d. Use latency assessment for behaviors in which the length of elapsed time between a well defined cue or signal and their initiation of occurrence is important.
   e. Use interval recording methods when continuous direct observation is impractical and it is permissible to obtain an estimate of a behavior's frequency or duration strength.
4. Establish the inter-observer reliability of the selected direct observation assessment methodology.
5. Conduct baseline assessment to determine the stability or consistency of an individual's performance prior to more formalized instruction.
6. Conduct ongoing instructional assessment to determine whether or not satisfactory progress is being made and what, if any, program modifications should be made.
   a. Develop and maintain graphic displays of baseline and instructional assessment information for data-based decision-making purposes.
   b. Meet regularly to review student assessment information and make corresponding program adjustments to assure acquisition, maintenance, and generalization of the individual's instructional objectives.

Future Research Issues

1. How often should instructional assessment information be collected and reviewed for effective data-based decision-making purposes?
2. What is the optimal length and number of intervals required to collect valid measures of behavior strength using interval recording instructional assessment procedures?
3. Does ongoing instructional assessment improve student achievement for students of varying ability levels in both academic and community living skills curriculum areas?

Discussion Questions

1. In what ways do you see new and improving technologies being of value in instructional assessment and its related data-based decision-making?
2. How important do you feel it is to involve students directly in selecting their target behaviors and collecting ongoing instructional assessment information?
3. How often do you feel teachers should collect instructional assessment information?

Community-Based Activities

1. Develop a task analysis for a computer software application of your choosing and conduct an assessment of one of your classmates or peers who is not knowledgeable about this application.
2. Develop an operational definition of any socially significant target behavior of your choosing, select an appropriate instructional assessment procedure, conduct a minimum of five baseline assessment trials, and graph the results.
3. For the socially significant behavior identified in Activity #2, implement an instructional program, conduct a minimum of five additional assessment trials, graph the results of baseline and instruction, and provide a rationale for any data-based decision, if any, that you would make.

References

Alberto, P. A., & Troutman, A. C. (1999). *Applied behavior analysis for teachers* (5th ed.). Upper Saddle River, NJ: Merrill/Prentice Hall.

Archer, A. L., & Gleason, M. M. (1989). *Skills for school success*. Boston, MA: Curriculum Associates.

Billingsley, F. F., Burgess, D., Lynch, V. W., & Matlock, B. L. (1991). Toward generalized outcomes: Considerations and guidelines for writing instructional objectives. *Education and Training of the Mentally Retarded, 26,* 351-360.

Brolin, D. E. (1991). *Life-centered career education: A competency-based approach* (3rd ed.). Reston, VA: Council for Exceptional Children.

Brown, L., Branston-McLean, M. B., Hamre-Nietupski, S., Pumpian, I., Certo, N., & Gruenwald, L. (1979). A strategy for developing chronological age appropriate and functional curricular content for severely handicapped adolescents. *Journal of Special Education, 13*(1), 81-90.

Collins, B. C., Hall, M., & Branson, T. A. (1999). Teaching leisure skills to adolescents with moderate disabilities. *Exceptional Children, 63*(4), 499-512.

Davis, P. K., & Bates, P. (1997). Transition-related IEP objectives: Ensuring their functionality, technical adequacy, and generality. *Exceptionality, 7*(1), 37-60.

Individuals with Disabilities Education Act Amendments of 1997, 20 USC § 1400 et seq.

Kazdin, A. E. (1989). *Behavior modification in applied settings*. Pacific Grove, CA: Brooks/Cole.

Mash, E. J. (1979). What is behavioral assessment? *Behavioral Assessment, 1,* 23-29.

Mash, E. J., & Terdal, L. G. (1997). *Behavioral assessment of childhood disorders.* (3rd ed.). New York: Guilford Press.

Miner, C., & Bates, P. (1997). The effect of person-centered planning activities on the IEP/transition planning process. *Education and Training in Mental Retardation, 32,* 105-112.

O'Neill, R. E., Horner, R. H., Albin, R. W., Storey, K. & Sprague, J. R. (1990). *Functional analysis of problem behavior: A practical assessment guide.* Sycamore, IL: Sycamore Press.

Overton, T. (2000). *Assessment in special education: An applied approach.* Upper Saddle River, NJ: Merrill.

Schloss, P., Smith, M. , & Schloss, C. (1995). *Instructional methods for adolescents with learning and behavior problems.* Boston, MA: Allyn & Bacon.

Storey, K., Hanson, H., & Bates, P. (1984). Acquisition and generalization of coffee purchase skills by adults with severe disabilities. *Journal of the Association for Persons with Severe Handicaps, 9,* 1978-1985.

Sulzer-Azaroff, B., & Mayer, G. R. (1977). *Applying behavioral analysis procedures with children and youth.* New York: Holt, Rinehart, and Winston.

Thurlow, M. L., Elliott, J. E., & Ysselydyke, J. E. (1998). *Testing students with disabilities: Practical strategies for complying with state and district standards.* Thousand Oaks, CA: Corwin Press.

Tucker, J. A. (1985). Curriculum-based assessment: an introduction. *Exceptional Children, 52* (30, 199-204.

Wolf (1978). Social validity: The case for subjective measurement or how applied behavior analysis is finding its heart. *Journal of Applied Behavior Analysis, 11,* 203-214.

Chapter 3
Systematic Instruction:
Developing and Maintaining Skills that Enhance Community Inclusion

Keith Storey

Chapman University

Key Questions
1. **How are skills best taught?**
2. **What is the difference between cues and corrections?**
3. **What is the best way to break down a task for instruction?**
4. **What do you do if the learner is having difficulty learning steps of the task analysis?**
5. **How does reinforcement influence learning?**
6. **Can learners generalize what they have learned?**

The accurate instruction of learners with disabilities in community settings is of decisive importance. It is with this instruction that skills necessary for community living are learned. Without good instruction, it is doubtful that community living will be successful. Independence, productivity, and integration are all based upon individuals having the skills necessary to be competent in specific situations, including shopping for groceries, interacting with co-workers, and cooking meals. In other words, the emphasis of instruction is to develop competence for individuals (Gold, 1980).

Key Question #1: How are skills best taught?

Behavior is what a person does, such as getting on a bus, greeting a co-worker, or cooking a meal. These behaviors are shaped and maintained by stimuli in the environment. These stimuli (technically known as discriminative stimuli or SDs) also may be thought of as cues, or clues for what to do. For example, in front of an elevator, the opening of the doors is the discriminative stimulus to get on the elevator. A teakettle whistling is the discriminative stimulus to pour the boiling water into the teacup. So the point of instruction is to get the learner to respond appropriately to the naturally occurring stimuli in the environment.

We often mistakenly think that the purpose of instruction is to get the person to do what they are supposed to do. However, the real purpose is to get the person to respond appropriately to the stimuli so that they can perform skills independently. For example, if I am teaching someone how to ride a bus and the bus pulls up and the doors open, I could give a verbal cue, "Get on the bus" and the person would be likely to get on the bus. However, they might be responding only to my verbal cue, and without my presence and cue, are unlikely to be able to get on the bus independently.

But if I were to give a cue that highlights the discriminative stimulus, "The doors are open, what do you do now?," then the person is more likely to be able to respond independently to the discriminative stimulus of the open doors in the future. Thus, instruction is giving the person information so that they can perform the behavior when it is appropriate to do so.

Key Question #2: What is the difference between cues and corrections?

Cues and corrections are two different things. A cue refers to initial information provided to a learner before a behavior is performed. A correction procedure refers to supplementary or corrective information to communicate to a learner that a response already performed is inappropriate or that a different response is needed.

Cues

Cues (also known as prompts) are an added antecedent stimulus which increases the probability of a correct response. The logic of cues is that they occur before the behavior should happen and thus increase the likelihood of a correct response so that you can reinforce that response. The purpose of cues is to assist the learner in performing behaviors (skills) in response to naturally occurring discriminative stimuli. The learner is thus: a) alerted to important natural signals that provide information about behaviors to emit and b) able to respond appropriately. As Steere and Pancsofar (1995) have written "The cue is the clue to do something new."

There are different types of cues that may be used to provide information to learners, and they may be used in different ways.

Verbal Cues

These are statements or questions uttered by an instructor that draw attention to the natural cue. Verbal cues may state specifically what the individual should do, such as "Spread the peanut butter on the bread" or "Here comes Tom Rover. Be sure and say hello to him when he gets to you." Verbal cues also may be nonspecific questions (i.e., indirect verbal cues) that alert the learner that something should be noticed such as "What do you do after you have the peanut butter on the knife?" or "Here comes Tom Rover,. What should you do when he gets to you?" Specific verbal cues provide more information than nonspecific verbal cues.

Modeling

The instructor does the task to show the learner how to perform the task. For example, the instructor could spread some peanut butter on the bread and then hand the knife to the learner.

Gestures

These are movements made by the instructor to draw attention to natural cues. Pointing, motioning, or shadowing movements are examples. For example, the instructor could point to the bread where the peanut butter is to be spread.

Physical Guidance

This involves physical contact between the instructor and the learner. It may involve full physical prompting (hand over hand) to direct the learner's movements, or just a light touch. For example, to spread peanut butter, the instructor could hold his or her hand over the hands of the learner and help them move the knife with the peanut butter across the bread.

Remember that cues: a) are sources of information, b) provide the minimal amount of information needed to get the correct responses, and c) ideally focus attention on natural discriminative stimuli. You want to provide cues just before or at the time of the natural discriminative stimulus. For example, "See the bakery on the corner. Here comes our stop. When the bus stops and the doors open we get off." Be sure and reinforce the learner for responding correctly (e.g., "That was great the way that you stood up and got right off the bus when the doors opened.").

It helps if you label why the person is getting reinforced so that he or she clearly understands the connection between the behavior and the reinforcer. Use the minimally intrusive cue to obtain the correct performance. You do not want the cue to control the learner's behavior rather than the natural discriminative stimulus. This is known as "prompt dependency" or "learned helplessness," where the learner passively waits to be told what to do.

Correction Procedures

The basic assumption should be that errors are a function of the instructional approach, not inherent to the learner because of a disability label. Errors are not random. Few learners perform with unpredictable error patterns. The two most common errors are due to prior history (where the person has learned an inappropriate response to an discriminative stimulus) and incomplete instruction (Horner, Bellamy, & Colvin, 1984).

First, collect information on incorrect performance as well as correct performance. Errors are of equal, if not greater, importance for instructors to attend to (Horner, 1984). Second, design instruction to minimize errors. You can do this by following the general case programming and other guidelines in this chapter. Third, correct errors as soon as they are made. Finally, collect data that documents error patterns.

When a learner makes an error, stop the learner immediately. It is important to interrupt the learner as soon as an error is initiated or observed and interrupt in a non-punitive manner. Second, recreate the situation in which the error occurred. Third, have the learner repeat the step using enough assistance to assure success. Be sure to deliver praise for the correct response. Finally, repeat the step again using less assistance.

There are three types of errors that a learner may make: initiation errors, discrimination errors, and response errors.

Initiation Errors

An initiation error is when the learner fails to initiate a behavior in response to the discriminative stimulus in the environment. For example, in making a peanut butter sandwich, an initiation error occurs when the learner stops after opening the jar of peanut butter and fails to initiate the next step of picking up the knife. Respond to initiation errors by:

1. isolating preceding two steps and difficult step
2. identifying cues to ensure correct responding
3. pairing cue and task stimuli
4. fading cues
5. immediately reinforcing self-initiations
6. fading reinforcement

Discrimination Errors

These are errors where the learner responds to the wrong discriminative stimulus in the environment. For example, in making a peanut butter sandwich, picking up a jar of pickles on the counter rather than the jar of peanut butter would be a discrimination error. Respond to discrimination errors by:

1. increasing intensity and frequency of reinforcer
2. highlighting the relevant dimension of stimulus
3. presenting examples with very similar stimulus
4. fading reinforcement

Response Errors

These are errors where the learner makes an incorrect response. For example, the learner could put the jar of peanut butter away in the freezer instead of in the refrigerator. Respond to response errors by:

1. increasing intensity and frequency of reinforcer
2. identifying cues to ensure correct responding
3. presenting examples in cumulative sequence

Key Question #3: What is the best way to break down a task for instruction?

For instructional purposes, a task analysis is the key to building instruction. The more thorough you are, the more successful the person is going to be. A task analysis is a process of breaking a task into its required component responses, and listing these responses in an appropriate sequence (Bellamy, Horner, & Inman, 1979). In other words, it is a complete description of each and every behavior needed to accomplish a specific activity.

The purpose of task analysis is to facilitate instruction by focusing the instructor's attention on the specific demands of a task and by providing a method for gathering data during instruction about the acquisition of the task by the learner. The teaching of complex tasks proceeds most efficiently if the tasks are shaped by successive approximations. People learn simpler component responses and chain them together ultimately to perform the complex target behavior (Cuvo, 1978).

A task analysis is a tool for the person who will be teaching the person with disabilities. Construction of a task analysis before instruction begins meets three instruction needs: a) it increases the likelihood that the instructor has a thorough understanding of the task in question, b) the task analysis provides the basis for a system for data collection, and c) it identifies natural cues from which to direct instructional strategies.

In developing a task analysis, consider the following points:

1. The specific objective for the task should be identified and recorded.
2. The person who will be doing the teaching should perform the task several times before constructing the task analysis (this is important because there are often more than one method of completing a task, such as putting on a coat).
3. The person who will be doing the instruction should analyze the task and construct the task analysis.
4. The tasks should be broken down into response units small enough to instruct the learner successfully.
5. The steps in the task should be sequenced in exactly the order in which they will be performed.
6. Mandatory steps in the task analysis should be identified (certain steps in the task analysis which are considered essential). If these steps are not performed or are performed incorrectly, the terminal goal is not achieved successfully.
7. The discriminative stimulus for each step should be identified (Cuvo, 1978; Gold, 1976; Mank & Horner, 1988; Powell, Pancsofar, Steere, Butterworth, Itzkowitz, & Rainforth, 1991).

Chains of Behavior

The task analysis represents a chain of behavior, or the sequence of what the learner must do. Once a task analysis has been developed there are three strategies for using the task analysis for instructional purposes: forward chaining, whole task chaining/concurrent chaining, and backward chaining.

Forward Chaining

This is a teaching procedure in which a sequence of responses is developed by first reinforcing the initial step in the task analysis, then reinforcing the addition of the second step, and so on until the entire activity has been learned. It is a cumulative process; only the first step is taught initially and then additional steps are added one at a time. For example, in teaching a person to put on pants, the instructor would teach the first step "put foot into the pant leg," and then stop the instruction until the learner can independently perform that step.

Whole Task Chaining/Concurrent Chaining

This process is where all steps of the task analysis are taught simultaneously in a forward sequence from the initial step in the task analysis to the last step, all in one session. For most community activities, whole task chaining is the preferred method of instruction because the learner is performing the whole activity in the context in which it must occur.

Backward Chaining

With backward chaining, the last response in the task analysis is taught first, then the response that precedes that, and so on until the first response in the sequence is taught. The advantage of backward chaining is that the response closest to the terminal reinforcer is taught first. An example of backward chaining when teaching a learner to put on pants is to set up the activity to the last step by putting the pants on the learner and getting them ready to button or physically assist the learner up until the last step (the last step in the task analysis, put button through the button hole, would be taught first) and then provide cueing procedures. Backward chaining is an efficient way to teach a task but is often difficult to use in community settings.

Key Question #4: What do you do if the learner is having difficulty learning steps of the task analysis?

No matter how well one teaches, there will be individual steps of some tasks that prove problematic. A learner may perform most of a task accurately yet make consistent errors or require a consistent level of assistance on a few remaining steps. With these steps, modifying the kind, type, and amount of assistance and manipulating the kind and amount of reinforcement may not be effective in improving learner performance. A person's consistently poor performance on such steps functionally defines them as "difficult steps."

1. Provide Massed Trials

With massed trials, the learner doesn't practice the whole chain but performs the same step many times providing extra practice on the step that is difficult and maximizes the effect of training and feedback. This prevents other steps from occurring between feedback on one trial and the performance of the next trial. Naturally occurring tasks are preferable over unnatural tasks (i.e., emptying all wastebaskets in an area versus putting on and taking off the same wastebasket bag).

For example, in learning how to empty wastebaskets, a learner is having trouble learning the step of shaking the trash bag open. The instructor could then have the learner open up bags before doing the rounds. Since it is a short task, find a location where there are multiple wastebaskets (such as an office) and provide many trials.

First, provide a discriminative stimulus for the step ("open the trash bag" or the natural discriminative stimulus of having the bag in hand while standing in front of trash can). Second, have the learner perform the step with or without assistance. Third, provide the learner with immediate feedback on performance. And finally, repeat the discriminative stimulus and the process.

2. Manipulate the Demands of a Step to Ensure Learner Success

One can reduce the difficulty for the learner by manipulating the task and need for assistance. It should be set up so the learner is performing correctly on 75% of the trials. This will help minimize uncooperative behavior and focus the training on what the learner can do instead of what he or she can't do.

The learner should not experience repeated failure. You are trying to facilitate the performance of the response required or maximize the effect of the natural cue for breaking the sequence down in an easy-to-hard continuum. For example, open the bag part way if the learner is having trouble opening the bag.

3. Increase the Level of Reinforcement during Massed Trials Training

Although you might have increased the opportunity for reinforcement, since the step is difficult for the learner it still will require more effort to perform correctly. Increase the level of reinforcement to a level above that normally used when training the steps together. This is a step that has been frustrating for the learner. Massed trials should not be punishing or aversive. For example, when doing massed trials on bag opening, increase the amount of verbal praise. Or, if the learner particularly likes some part of a task, you may want to do that after massed trials.

4. Conduct Massed Trials in Short Time Blocks

Keep massed trials shorter than normal training sessions (maybe ten to fifteen minutes long, two to three times per day). Give the learner access to the task but end before the learner begins to get bored by the task. For example, in using massed trials to teach a learner how to shake open the trash bag for emptying a wastebasket, go to an office with a lot of trash cans several times a day.

5. Systematically Include Mastered Steps in the Chain of the Task

It is of little use if the learner can do the difficult step in a mass trial session but can't integrate it back into the natural chain. Adding the previous step in the chain during the practice sessions as the learner becomes more competent in the difficult step can accomplish this. Then require the step immediately preceding the learned difficult step in the chain. Always perform the difficult step or isolated skill with the natural chain and context. This is the true test of learner performance as this is where the learner will need to use it. For example, if after many massed trials the learner has finally mastered the step of shaking the trash bag open, add this step(s) back.

6. Systematically Fade Your Assistance

Before providing any type of assistance, decide how you are going to fade it. It is easy to add something that will help the learner and then not be able to fade it and the learner becomes dependent upon the cue. Verbal directions are very difficult to systematically fade. You usually have to say it or not say it. For example, if you are assisting the learner by partially opening the bag, open it less and less during the massed trials as the learner acquires the skill.

Key Question #5: How does reinforcement influence learning?

Technically defined, positive reinforcement is an event presented after a response has been performed that increases the frequency of the behavior it follows (Kazdin, 1989). In other words, positive reinforcement is a process. You can see that reinforcement has happened only when you see change. An individual's behavior should increase following the delivery of the reinforcer. If the behavior doesn't increase, it isn't a reinforcer.

Not all items or events are reinforcers for everyone. One person may like Ian Hunter, another the Rolling Stones. One person may like ice tea, another soda. Another way to analyze reinforcement is to see it as arranging conditions under which someone gets things. Though reward and reinforcement are sometimes used interchangeably, an important distinction to recognize is that people are rewarded, but behavior is reinforced. Reinforcement can be used to teach new behaviors or to strengthen behaviors that the person already has.

General Guidelines for Using Reinforcement

1. Only reinforce correct responses. Reinforcement strengthens the behavior that it follows, so don't inadvertently reinforce incorrect performance.
2. If you provide assistance, also provide reinforcement. Reinforcement strengthens the response, so make sure that you deliver the reinforcement after the person performs the response correctly. It is okay to provide assistance but make sure that the reinforcement comes after the assistance and after the correct performance.
3. Use a positive tone.
4. Be brief. Do not interrupt the person and take them off-task.
5. Vary what you say. You don't always have to say "good job." It is easy to get in a rut of saying the same word or phrase.
6. Make sure you are reinforcing. You want to be pleasant and positive so that the person you are working with will want to interact with you and receive instruction from you. This will make praise from you reinforcing and other reinforcers less necessary. So be nice!
7. Do not reinforce simply attending to the task. It is correct performance (i.e., outcome) that you want to reinforce. Reinforcing attending to task (i.e., process) may not increase output.

Types of Reinforcers Useful in Community Environments

Participation and instruction in school and community settings are often activity-based. Activity-based means that a chain or sequence of behaviors are performed that produce an outcome that is functional for the individual (e.g., the sequence of behaviors for eating at a restaurant include entering, waiting to be seated, ordering, eating, and paying.). The focus should be on activities rather than brief skill sequences because activities are outcome based and more likely to have a positive impact on the person's lifestyle (Wilcox & Bellamy, 1987). You will be out in the real world teaching skills that are functional and usually require a long chain of behavior sequences, so reinforcement must be used in the sequence and especially at the end of the sequence.

Selecting Reinforcers

1. One simple way to find out what a person likes is to ask! However, it may not always be that easy and you may need a more structured interview to help the person think about the different reinforcers available.
2. If the person is not able to easily tell you what he or she likes, someone else who knows the person well might be able to. Family members, friends, roommates, significant others, or co-workers might be good resources. Each one might give a different perspective on what the person likes in different situations, such as at work versus at home.
3. Direct observations are very useful in assessing reinforcement preference. These include recording foods the person prefers, the type of activities engaged in, or with whom the person prefers to interact.
4. If people with disabilities have had limited exposure to activities and

reinforcers in the community, they might not know what they like. Thus persons with disabilities should take part in many community activities so that they are more likely to make an informed choice concerning reinforcers.

Considerations in Using Reinforcers
Age Appropriate

The reinforcer should be age appropriate for the person. Age appropriate means chronological age, not mental age. For example, a twenty-one-year-old should not be given stuffed animals as a reinforcer. Stuffed animals are age appropriate for someone around six years of age. Age appropriate reinforcers for a twenty-one-year-old might include going to a concert, having a drink in a bar, having a snack, going on a date, playing softball, eating in a restaurant, or having friends over for dinner.

When using reinforcers, consider the impact that they will have on other people in addition to the person being reinforced. How would employees in a factory view a forty-year-old co-worker with cerebral palsy being given a "smiley face" sticker for completing a task? That employee would be stigmatized and co-workers would be likely to value him or her less as a fellow adult and more as a child. If you are not sure if a reinforcer is age appropriate or not it is probably best not to use it and to come up with a different reinforcer. Better to be safe than to stigmatize the person you are working with.

Health Appropriate

When using edible reinforcers, it is important to consider if they are good for the person's health. If edible reinforcers are necessary and appropriate, raisins, pieces of fruit or vegetable, or juice are good alternatives to things like candy, cereal, or cookies. Also be aware of the person's medical history concerning allergies or special diets.

Ease of Delivery

Be sure that the reinforcer can be delivered easily. One nice thing about using praise as a reinforcer is that it can be delivered quite easily and efficiently and you don't have to interrupt what the person is doing to deliver it. If you are using reinforcers such as tokens or food, the delivery may not be so easy. For instance, if a person is working as a bus person in a restaurant, and you want to deliver a piece of fruit as a reinforcer, you must stop the person on the job. He or she might have to set down some dishes or a tub and wash hands before you can offer the piece of fruit and praise for clearing the table. The person will eat it and then go back to work. This is not very efficient and not typical for the workplace. It could stigmatize that person in front of co-workers, the employer, and customers.

Time of Consumption

Not only do you want to deliver the reinforcer quickly, you want the person to consume it within a reasonable amount of time. Giving someone taffy as a reinforcer would probably not be a good idea if the person is working at a job where he or she needs to use hands.

Satiation

If even you like salted pretzels a lot, would you want to eat them all day long? After fifty pretzels you would probably not want any more. This is known as satiation. At this point something to drink would probably be more reinforcing than another pretzel. It is important that you use different reinforcers and mix them so that the person doesn't satiate on one reinforcer.

Some ways to prevent satiation are:

1. Have different reinforcers available for different tasks.
2. Alternate reinforcers during instructional sessions.
3. Gradually decrease the size or amount of the reinforcer.
4. Be sure that the reinforcer you are using is not something the person has easy access to throughout the day.
5. Change the pool of reinforcers that the person has to choose from so he or she can't always pick the same reinforcer and possibly become satiated.

Contingency

Contingency means that when the person does a certain behavior (such as correctly bussing a table), they get a specific reinforcer (i.e., praise from the job coach). If the person don't bus the table, he or she doesn't get the praise. This is probably the most important consideration for delivering reinforcement—is the reinforcement contingent on what the person does? If it isn't, you've got problems. One way to help make the connection between the reinforcement and the behavior is to label reinforcement contingencies. In other words, tell the person why he or she is being reinforced. For example, if a person pays correctly when getting on a bus, you could say "That was a great job of putting your dollar in the slot. Way to go!"

The person needs to be reinforced for what he or she does. A common mistake is when the instructor makes it too difficult for the person to get the reinforcer. What usually happens is that the person becomes frustrated or angry because of not being reinforced, so he or she doesn't do what the instructor expects. So be sure that you are delivering reinforcement often enough.

When to Reinforce in Behavior Chains

If you deliver reinforcement only at the end of a behavior chain, not all responses in the chain are equally affected. The reinforcer has a greater effect on responses later in the chain. The longer the chain is, the less likely a reinforcer at the end of the chain will maintain performance of early responses (Bellamy et al., 1979). So you must take into account the number of responses within a chain when deciding on a reinforcement schedule. You may want to deliver reinforcement at several points in the chain.

Suppose that George is learning how to clean an office. He might be responsible for emptying recycling and wastebaskets, vacuuming, sweeping, wet and dry dusting, and removing trash. If you wait till George completes all the tasks the reinforcement schedule might be too thin and he might slow down or stop working.

However, a reinforcer delivered at the end of a chain does reinforce all responses in the chain, though not equally, as pointed out. So if George makes a mistake in the chain and still gets reinforced at the end, he might be more likely to make the same mistake again. Thus, if George does make a mistake, stop him, provide feedback (i.e., "the recycling goes in the blue bag"), have him do it the right way, and then reinforce him. As reinforcement increases the probability that in the future the person will behave in the same manner, you want to be sure that you are reinforcing only correct responses. The opportunity to perform each subsequent step in the task analysis will effectively reinforce the learner's behavior only if the series of behaviors ultimately produces reinforcing events. For example, you might want to reinforce George with a snack break following completion of tasks.

Key Question #6: Can learners generalize what they have learned?

If a person learns how to purchase an item in a specific grocery store, it does not necessarily mean that he or she will be able to purchase the same item in a different grocery store. People with disabilities often have difficulty generalizing what they learn. Generalization is demonstration of skills in situations other than those in which the original instruction occurred. Generalization can be across time, persons, settings, and behaviors (Stokes & Baer, 1977). From an instructional standpoint, generalization doesn't just happen, it must be planned for. Trainers need to make generalization part of most, but not all, instruction (a person probably needs to know how to operate only one set of washer and dryers, not all washers and dryers). There are a number of strategies for facilitating generalization.

Setting
Train in the Natural Setting

Teaching is conducted directly in at least one type of setting in which the skills will be used. For example, in teaching how to set a table at a restaurant you could do the actual instruction at the restaurant.

Sequential Modification

Teaching is provided in one setting and generalization is probed in other settings. If necessary, teaching is conducted sequentially in more and more settings until generalization to all desired settings is observed. For example, one could teach bus riding to the work place, then to the aerobics studio and then to the grocery store.

Consequences
Introduce Natural Maintaining Contingencies

This involves:
1. teaching a functional skill that is likely to be reinforced outside instruction
2. teaching to a level of proficiency that makes the skill truly useful
3. making sure that the learner actually does experience the natural consequence
4. teaching the learner to solicit or recruit reinforcement outside instruction
5. teaching the learner to self-recruit feedback (Mank & Horner, 1987).
   Many environments ignore appropriate behavior and instead respond to inappropriate behavior (you cannot just assume that the behavior will be

maintained by the natural environment). Having the learner take a self-management data sheet to someone in the natural environment and recruiting feedback on how he or she performed could accomplish this.

Use Indiscriminable Consequences

If natural consequences cannot be expected to encourage and maintain generalization, artificial consequences might be used. It is best if the learner cannot determine precisely when those consequences will be available, and so must behave as if they always are available. An example is if you would use intermittent reinforcement (where the person receives reinforcement at different times or after so many "units") to maintain work performance.

Teach to Generalize

The learner is reinforced only for performing some generalized instance of the target skill. Performing a previously reinforced version of the response is no longer reinforced. For example, once a learner consistently does grocery shopping in one store, the instructor might provide reinforcement only for successful shopping in another store.

Program Common Stimuli

This requires selecting a salient, but not necessarily task-related, stimulus from the situation to which generalization is desired, and including that stimulus in the training program. For example, when teaching an individual exercise skills to participate in aerobics class, use the music from the class when teaching the skills outside of the aerobics class.

Sufficient Exemplars

This strategy, similar to sequential modification, involves sequential addition of stimuli to the teaching program until generalization to all related stimuli occurs. For example, in teaching how to put on a sweater, use a long-sleeved crew-necked sweater, then a V-necked sweater, then a short-sleeved sweater.

Multiple Exemplars

Several examples of the stimulus class to which generalization is desired are trained at the same time. For example, when teaching exercise skills, teach three types of skills and generalization might occur to untaught skills.

Other
Incidental Teaching

This also is called naturalistic teaching, non-intensive teaching, or minimal intervention. Settings, cues, prompts, materials, response definition, and other features of the training situation are purposely varied to avoid a ritual, highly structured program that might inhibit generalization.

Mediate Generalization

Teach a secondary behavior or strategy that will help an individual remember or figure out how and when to generalize, or which will dispel the differences between the teaching and generalization situations. An example is using picture prompts for cooking skills. Once Tom understands how to use picture prompts to cook a hot dog, he might be likely to successfully use picture prompts to pop popcorn or make a smoothie.

Use Self-Mediated Stimuli

This is the use of self-management strategies. Self-management may be broadly construed as giving the person more control over his or her own life. This control is given through teaching the person skills and providing specific strategies to control or modify one's own behavior. Self-management ideally involves:

- recognizing one's own problem
- translating problems into behaviors to be changed
- finding natural contingencies or contriving them to support change
- arranging the contingencies for change to occur.

General Case Programming

Representative examples of positive stimuli (stimuli in the presence of which the skill should be used), negative stimuli (stimuli in the presence of which the skill should not be used), and irrelevant stimuli (stimuli that should not effect skill use, but might inappropriately do so) are selected for teaching from the universe to which generalization is desired (Horner, McDonnell, & Bellamy, 1986).

General case programming is one of the most effective strategies for facilitating generalization. The steps to general case programming are:

1. Define the instructional universe.

    This involves defining the amount of behavior required by the activity and defining the variations in stimulus situations where the activity may occur.

2. Define the range of relevant stimulus and response variation in the instructional universe.

    This requires: a) defining the chain of generic responses; b) determining the generic discriminative stimulus for each response; c) documenting the variation in relevant stimulus dimensions across generic stimuli; d) documenting the topographical variation across generic responses; and e) identifying exceptions as potential errors.

3. Select examples from the instructional universe to use in teaching and probe testing.

    This involves: a) selecting the minimum number of training examples that sample the full range of stimulus and response variation in the instructional universe; b) selecting examples that will deliver equal amounts of new information to the learner; c) selecting examples that vary irrelevant stimuli; d) selecting examples that teach the learner what not to do as well as what to do; e) selecting examples that include significant exceptions; and f) selecting examples that are logistically feasible.

4. Sequence teaching examples.

    This is accomplished by: a) teaching multiple components of an activity within sessions; b) presenting multiple examples of an activity with individual sessions; c) juxtaposing maximally similar positive and negative examples; d) using cumulative programming; and e) teaching the general case before teaching exceptions.

5. Teach the activity.
6. Test with non-trained, probe examples.

This is completed by: a) conducting probe tests after the learner has learned some or all of the teaching examples; b) using probe tests to obtain information, not to teach; and c) identifying error patterns and modifying teaching examples to eliminate these error patterns.

Generalization Error Patterns
Irrelevant Stimuli Control the Target Response

To avoid this problem, use both positive and negative teaching examples. For example, if a person learns that the discriminative stimulus for crossing a street is initiation of crossing by another person, present the learner with situations in which another person crosses the street first and situations where nobody crosses in front of the learner.

Irrelevant Stimuli Control Irrelevant Responses

Following successful teaching, the learner does not perform the target behavior under novel conditions because irrelevant stimuli in the novel conditions exert more powerful control over irrelevant responses than the relevant stimuli exert over the target response. An example would be a learner who yells and grabs to obtain things even though he or she was taught to use sign language (but not in that setting). To avoid this problem, teaching should occur with a set of positive and negative examples that include those irrelevant stimuli that control irrelevant responses.

Since it may not be possible to conduct a general case analysis of all learning situations from an instruction standpoint, try using at least three examples for as many skills as possible. This involves conducting teaching in three different settings, with three different sets of materials, and three different teachers. This will increase the chances of successful generalization without having to take the time to conduct a general case analysis.

Window to the World
Cassie: Training to Increase Job Integration

Cassie was a twenty-seven-year-old woman with a developmental disability. Her labels included emotional and mental disturbances, moderate mental retardation, and sensory integration problems. She was employed at a restaurant where her job duties were to set and bus tables and sort silverware. Cassie needed to learn new job tasks and to be more socially integrated with co-workers. The use of natural supports (Storey & Certo, 1996), in this case having a co-worker teach Cassie new skills, was one way to increase integration on the job site. Assessment consisted of observing the frequency and type of interactions Cassie had with her co-workers.

One nondisabled co-worker was taught how to use instructional tactics of verbal instructions, modeling, practicing the step with corrective feedback, praise, and quality control checking (Likins, Salzberg, Stowitschek, Lignugaris, Kraft, & Curl, 1989). The co-worker was taught the skills during twenty-minute daily training sessions. The trainers listed the steps within the job task and proceeded to use the instructional tactics to model teaching the job task to the co-worker. After modeling the teaching of the job task, the co-worker then "taught" the job task to the trainers using the instructional procedures in a "tell-show-watch-coach" teaching sequence. These were the techniques that had just been modeled to her. While the co-worker was teaching the job task to us, we provided feedback to her.

Once the co-worker was effectively using the instructional tactics to teach each step with the job task, the co-worker started teaching Cassie the same job task. The training sequence involved the co-worker providing a verbal description, modeling a particular step, having Cassie practice the step, providing corrective feedback as necessary, and praising a correct response.

With co-worker instruction Cassie was able to learn new job tasks. However, for increasing her social interactions it was necessary to directly teach Cassie social initiation skills so that she was less dependent upon the initiations of others for social interactions.

Adapted from Storey and Garff, 1997

Window to the World
Sheila: Conversational Training

Sheila was a thirty-seven-year-old woman diagnosed with schizophrenia and mild mental retardation. She worked at a rehabilitation hospital where she helped prepare food in the kitchen. Sheila had good verbal skills and liked to interact with others. However, Sheila often engaged in inappropriate social interactions with co-workers and was in danger of losing her job due to these improper interactions. Two types of frequency and type of social interactions Sheila had with her co-workers were observed: conversations and question asking.

Data were collected concerning performance on a task analysis that involved the social interaction of having a conversation, including making an initiation, a continuation, and a termination statement. Training data and generalization data were collected at break times. The second data collection system involved recording whether Sheila initiated, made a response, expansion, or termination statement towards co-workers related to asking questions. Additional information was collected concerning if the interaction was appropriate and the topic of the interaction. Training data and generalization data were collected at break times.

For instruction on conversational script, we used procedures described by Breen, Haring, Pitts-Conway, and Gaylord-Ross (1985). This involved teaching initiation, sustaining, and termination conversational skills during break times. The skills were taught using a total task strategy when co-workers were not present, right before break time. Prompts, corrective feedback, modeling, and positive reinforcement were used to increase Sheila's skills. Sheila was instructed to ask a co-worker if they wanted a napkin or something to drink and complete the task if a co-worker said yes, make an initiating statement, make a continuing statement, and make a terminating statement at the end of break.

The second intervention was instruction on question asking. This involved role-playing a series of question-asking conversational exchanges appropriate to conversational context (Chadsey-Rusch, Karlan, Riva, & Rusch, 1984; Haring, Roger, Lee, Breen, & Gaylord-Ross, 1986). Question-asking was taught by:
1. giving a rationale for asking questions
2. modeling examples of different questions using socially validated topics
3. practicing asking questions by role-playing and corrective feedback
4. prompting question asking during training conversations
5. reinforcement of appropriate behavior

Sheila was instructed to ask initiating or expansion questions of co-workers or to make a response statement and to make a terminating statement at the end of break. Initially, initiation behaviors and topics of conversation were modeled. During instruction, the trainer waited thirty seconds for Sheila to initiate an interaction. If an interaction is not initiated in that time, a general cue (i.e., "What do we talk about?") was given.

Expansion training (Haring et al., 1986) was also used. This training involved producing a response that expanded upon the statement or interaction that just occurred. Using socially validated topics during role-playing sessions (co-workers were given a survey of topics that they liked to talk about), Sheila was prompted to ask questions that would initiate a new topic or expand the current topic. Instruction occurred immediately before break.

Sheila's social interactions with co-workers increased and were socially appropriate. In addition, her skills successfully generalized to other settings.

Adapted from Storey, Lengyel, and Pruszynski, 1997

Best Practice Recommendations

1. Skills are best taught by teaching the learner to respond to discriminative stimuli in the environment. The purpose of instruction is to give the learner information to perform skills.
2. Use cues to provide initial information to a learner before a behavior is performed. Use correction procedures to provides additional or corrective information to a learner that a response already performed is not correct or that a different response is needed.
3. A task analysis is the best way to break down a task for instruction.
4. If the learner is having difficulty learning steps of the task analysis, the general guidelines are to: a) provide massed trials, b) manipulate the demands of a step to ensure learner success, c) increase the level of reinforcement a learner receives during massed trials, d) conduct massed trials in short time blocks, e) systematically build a step back into the chain after it has been mastered, and f) systematically fade assistance.
5. Positive reinforcement plays a powerful influence in learning.
6. Persons with disabilities often have difficulty generalizing what they have learned across behaviors, settings, people, and time. While there are various methods of increasing generalization, general case programming is the most effective strategy.

Future Research Issues

We need a better understanding of how to best use cues for instruction. For instance, what type of cueing hierarchy is best? How do we teach cueing to instructors? The use of self-management and self-reinforcement strategies offer promising methodologies to help learners become more independent in community settings, but further research is needed in this area.

Discussion Questions

1. If a person is not learning a task, is it more likely that the task is not being taught correctly or that the person can't learn?
2. Can all people, no matter how severe their disability, be successful in community settings with appropriate supports?
3. How do support needs vary from person to person?

Community-Based Activities

1. Bring in materials for teaching a self-care/domestic task using a task analysis. Teach the task three times to someone, once using a concurrent (whole task) chain, once with a forward chain, and once using a backward chain. For the task analysis:

   a) List the natural cue and response for each step.

   b) Indicate which steps are mandatory.

   c) List the materials necessary to complete the activity.

   d) List three possible modifications/adaptations for relevant steps of the task analysis.

2. At an employment site, interview someone who is involved in training new workers on how to complete job tasks. Ask that person how they break down tasks and do the instruction.
3. Go to a community setting (such as a Laundromat) and observe the different ways in which people there complete a task. Determine which way would be most efficient for teaching a person with a disability you know and how modifications and adaptations might be useful.

References

Bellamy, G. T., Horner, R. H., & Inman, D. P. (1979). *Vocational habilitation of severely retarded adults: A direct service technology.* Baltimore, MD: University Park Press.

Breen, C., Haring, T., Pitts-Conway, V., & Gaylord-Ross, R. (1985). The training and generalization of social interaction during breaktime at two job sites in the natural environment. *Journal of the Association for Persons with Severe Handicaps, 10,* 41-50.

Brown, F., Evans, I. M., Weed, K. A., & Owens, V. (1987). Delineating functional competencies: A component model. *Journal of the Association for Persons with Severe Handicaps, 12,* 117-124.

Brown, L., Nietupski, J., & Hamre-Nietupski, S. (1976). Criterion of ultimate functioning. In M. A. Thomas (Ed.), *Hey, don't forget about me!* (2-15). Reston, VA: Council for Exceptional Children.

Chadsey-Rusch, J., Karlan, G. R., Riva, M., & Rusch, F. R. (1984). Competitive employment: Teaching conversation skills to adults who are mentally retarded. *Mental Retardation, 22,* 218-225.

Cuvo, A. J. (1978). Validating task analyses of community living skills. *Vocational Evaluation and Work Adjustment Bulletin, 11,* 13-21.

Gaylord-Ross, R., Haring, T. G., Breen, C., & Pitts-Conway, V. (1984). The training and generalization of social interaction skills with autistic youth. *Journal of Applied Behavior Analysis, 17,* 229-247.

Gold, M. W. (1976). Task analysis of a complex assembly task by the retarded blind. *Exceptional Children, 43,* 78-84.

Gold, M. W. (1980). *Did I say that? Articles and commentary on the try another way system.* Champaign, IL: Research Press.

Haring, T. G., Roger, B., Lee, M., Breen, C., & Gaylord-Ross, R. (1986). Teaching social language to moderately handicapped students. *Journal of Applied Behavior Analysis, 19,* 159-171.

Horner, R. H. (1984). The value of student errors. *Direct Instruction News, 3*(4), 13.

Horner, R. H., Bellamy, G. T., & Colvin, G. T. (1984). Responding in the presence of nontrained stimuli: Implications of generalization error patterns. *Journal of the Association for Persons with Severe Handicaps, 9,* 287-295.

Horner, R. H., McDonnell, J. J., & Bellamy, G. T. (1986). Teaching generalized skills: General case instruction in simulation and community settings. In R. H. Horner, L. Meyer, & H. D. Fredericks (Eds.), *Education of learners with severe handicaps: Exemplary service strategies* (289-314). Baltimore, MD: Paul Brookes.

Kazdin, A. E. (1989). *Behavior modification in applied settings* (4th ed.). Pacific Grove, CA: Brooks/Cole.

Lengyel, L., & Storey, K. (1995). Self-management strategies. In W. W. Woolcock & J. W. Domaracki (Eds.), *Instructional strategies in the community: A resource guide for community instruction for persons with disabilities* (99-107). Austin, TX: Pro-Ed.

Likins, M., Salzberg, C. L., Stowitschek, J. J., Lignugaris/Kraft, B., & Curl, R. (1989). Co-worker implemented job training: The use of coincidental training and quality-control checking procedures on the food preparation skills of employees with mental retardation. *Journal of Applied Behavior Analysis, 22,* 381-393.

Mank, D. M., & Horner, R. H. (1987). Self-recruited feedback: A cost-effective procedure for maintaining behavior. *Research in Developmental Disabilities, 8,* 91-112.

Mank, D. M., & Horner, R. H. (1988). Instructional programming in vocational education. In R. Gaylord-Ross (Ed.), *Vocational education for persons with handicaps* (142-173). Mountain View, CA: Mayfield Publishing Company.

Powell, T. H., Pancsofar, E. L., Steere, D. E., Butterworth, J., Itzkowitz, J. S. & Rainforth, B. (1991). *Supported employment: Providing integrated employment opportunities for persons with disabilities.* White Plains, NY: Longman.

Steere, D. E., & Pancsofar, E. L. (1995). Cues, prompts, and correction strategies. In W. W. Woolcock & J. W. Domaracki (Eds.), *Instructional strategies in the community: A resource guide for community instruction for persons with disabilities* (35-53). Austin, TX: Pro-Ed.

Stokes, T. F., & Baer, D. M. (1977). An implicit technology of generalization. *Journal of Applied Behavior Analysis, 10,* 349-367.

Storey, K. (1995). Reinforcement strategies. In W. W. Woolcock & J. W. Domaracki (Eds.), *Instructional strategies in the community: A resource guide for community instruction for persons with disabilities* (55-73). Austin, TX: Pro-Ed.

Storey, K., & Certo, N. J. (1996). Natural supports for increasing integration in the workplace for people with disabilities: A review of the literature and guidelines for implementation. *Rehabilitation Counseling Bulletin, 40,* 62-76.

Storey, K., & Garff, J. T. (1997). The cumulative effect of natural support strategies and social skills instruction on the integration of a worker in supported employment. *Journal of Vocational Rehabilitation, 9,* 143-152.

Storey, K., Lengyel, L., & Pruszynski, B. (1997). Assessing the effectiveness and measuring the complexity of two conversational instructional procedures in supported employment contexts. *Journal of Vocational Rehabilitation, 8,* 21-33.

Wilcox, B., & Bellamy, G. T. (1987). *A comprehensive guide to the activities catalog: An alternative curriculum for youth and adults with severe disabilities.* Baltimore, MD: Paul Brookes.

Author Notes

The completion of this chapter was supported in part by a grant (#H325H990101) from the US Department of Education. However, the opinions expressed herein do not necessarily reflect the position or policy of the US Department of Education, and no official endorsement should be inferred. I would like to acknowledge the influence of Rob Horner, Paul Bates, Hazel Bond, and Marc Gold for teaching me about what instruction is and isn't.

Chapter 4
Career Development
Developing Basic Work Skills and Employment Preferences

Margaret P. Hutchins
Illinois State University
Adelle Renzaglia
University of Illinois at Urbana-Champaign

Key Questions
1. What are commonly cited components of a career development program?
2. Why is a longitudinal approach beneficial in achieving vocational outcomes?
3. What does a community assessment entail?
4. What should an individual vocational assessment include?
5. How can vocational or career development opportunities be integrated into a young child's educational program?
6. How might work experiences be characterized for youth in middle school or early years of high school?
7. How might high school work experiences be selected?
8. What does the selection of a long-term employment experience entail?
9. What activities are critical when organizing effective vocational instruction in community-based sites?

Over three decades have passed since the President's Panel on Mental Retardation (1962) declared its support for vocational training and related services for all persons with mental retardation. This declaration launched the initiation of key legislation such as the Economic Opportunity Act of 1964, the Vocational Education Act of 1963, and the Rehabilitation Act Amendments of 1967 and 1968. These new laws emphasized the expansion of vocational programs and rehabilitation services, offered limited funding specifically targeted to enhance employment outcomes for persons with disabilities, and provided personnel training programs for rehabilitation service providers. However, implementation models during this time period focused primarily on adults and post-school services, and minimal preparation actually was occurring in programs for school-age children (Gajar, Goodman & McAfee, 1993; Rusch & Mithaug, 1980; Wehman, 1981).

Fortunately, the 1970s and 80s saw an increasing emphasis on career education and vocational services both within school programs and in the professional literature (Brolin, 1995). Professionals began to grapple with how career education and vocational services should be defined. In 1978 The Council for Exceptional Children (CEC) provided a definition of career education that was generally accepted among the professional community. Career education was defined as:

> *... the totality of experiences through which one learns to live a meaningful, satisfying work life ... career education provides the opportunity for children to learn, in the least restrictive environment possible, the academic, daily living, personal-social, and occupational knowledge and specific vocational work skills necessary for attaining their highest levels of economic, personal and social fulfillment.* (CEC, 1978)

Although this definition supports the overall quality of life for an individual, the importance of developing work skills also is clearly emphasized. As teachers within public school programs began to see the important role they could play by teaching students skills that would be necessary for successful employment, teachers assumed more responsibility for providing vocational instruction for their students (Hutchins, Renzaglia, Stahlman & Cullen, 1986; Moon, Goodall, Barcus, & Brooke, 1985).

Key Question #1: What are commonly cited components of a career development program?

The following components that define successful vocational or career development programs are commonly cited in the professional literature:

- a longitudinal approach that provides opportunities for students to acquire knowledge and skills from kindergarten through graduation
- an integrated curriculum, infusing vocational competencies within other academic and life skill areas
- a systematic inventory and analysis of the community job market and employment opportunities
- the use of vocational curricula that reflect the specific job demands of the local businesses
- opportunities for students to participate in work experiences and hands-on learning
- community-based instruction within local businesses and industries;
- an opportunity for students to acquire a job of choice prior to the completion of their school program
- increased parental involvement with decisions related to the employment future of their child
- the design and implementation of systematic instruction and evaluation strategies to enhance success

While most of these components have been identified for quite some time in the literature, professional efforts have continued to demand increased sensitivity and attention to the issues that serve as barriers to meaningful, integrated employment for individuals, regardless of their disability. Consequently, the past twenty years have witnessed an evolution of nontraditional vocational activities and strategies for promoting employment success. For example, supported employment was conceptualized as an alternative to a more typical vision of community-integrated employment (Bellamy, Rhodes, & Albin, 1986). This "employment vision" encouraged more flexibility and creativity within job development, training, and placement in order to optimize employment success for individuals who were often not viewed as "employable" (Bellamy, Rhodes, Mank, & Albin, 1988). In addition, increased successes and continued investigation has led to the development of new models that attempt to refine effective vocational services for school-aged individuals with disabilities, as well as, further define practices in areas such as job development, maintaining support on the job, and the use of assistive technology (Callahan, 1992; Hutchins & Renzaglia, 1990; Moon, Inge, Wehman, Brooke, & Barcus, 1990; Nietupski, Verstegen, & Hamre-Nietupski, 1992; Nisbet, 1992).

Career development programs today reflect a basic assumption that systematic and longitudinal methods must be used to ensure that instructional experiences and employment opportunities support the student's long-range career preferences and aspirations. Therefore, there is an increasing emphasis upon creating a vision for the individual in order to increase empowerment through choice (Ward, 1993; Wehman, 1993). That is, contemporary career development programs promote models and strategies that encourage informed choice, self-determination, a better quality of life, and a more carefully designed career path for the individual (Moore, Agran, & McSweyn, 1990).

Key Question #2: Why is a longitudinal approach beneficial in achieving vocational outcomes?

Students in general education are provided information concerning careers and career choices using a variety of materials and strategies throughout their elementary and secondary school years. Embedded within their curriculum are glimpses of occupational choices, in addition to specific activities such as participating in career orientation units, electives, and work-study programs. These provide unique experiences potentially related to vocational choices and career goals. Furthermore, once an employment goal is identified, a strategic series of activities including instruction, coursework, or other experiences is designed to optimize success in the choice and fulfillment of an occupation or career. It is reasonable to expect that individuals with disabilities will likewise benefit from a similar focus upon long-term planning in which progressive career-oriented employment will enhance opportunities for future career success.

A career development approach to providing vocational programs identifies individual needs over the entire school career of a student, rather than mere short-range solutions near the end of the student's transition years. Such a longitudinal approach promotes the development of long-term and self-determined decisions based upon a systematic review of experiences and instruction from the elementary grades through high school. Given such an approach, a plan is needed to explore career alternatives and continually reassess reasonable employment opportunities based upon current information. This information is obtained by developing an extended vocational plan that reflects individual preferences and proficiencies regarding many elements of work (e.g., job types, work environments, work tasks).

Additional proposed benefits of a career education or longitudinal approach (Brolin, 1995; Renzaglia, Hutchins, & Banks, 1995) include:

- providing learners with functional and meaningful skills to succeed in adult life
- encouraging relationships among schools, families, employers and the community
- offering learners a purpose for their education that allows them to experience outcomes
- providing an environment for practicing self-determination skills, thereby building learner self-esteem and empowerment
- promoting an overall curriculum and framework for service delivery that is sequential and competency-based, emphasizing learner preferences and proficiencies

Premises of a Longitudinal Career Education Model

The career education literature clearly articulates successful employment outcomes that easily can serve as the empirical underpinnings for the design and implementation of vocational programs. The four premises that are basic to the design of a longitudinal vocational service delivery model are discussed below.

Community Employment Prior to Graduation

PL 94-142 and its subsequent amendments ensure a free and appropriate education to all individuals with disabilities. During the educational process, there are opportunities for professionals and families to effectively design and implement vocational curricula that provide long-term employment options to graduates. Community employment is a viable and socially equitable outcome of the education process for students with disabilities. However, there are no mandated services for individuals with disabilities following their secondary school years, and no guarantees that programs can accommodate the employment goals of any individual. Adult service programs often struggle for funds and have access to fewer personnel resources to adequately address the individualized needs of interested consumers.

Consequently, school programs that terminate an individual's education suggesting he or she is "employment ready" are not facing the potential gap in services and the likely scenario that there is no one to effectively provide the necessary services to ensure and support long-term community employment. Therefore, schools must assist in accessing employment for motivated graduates with disabilities and facilitate the success of post-secondary transitions to specific work settings.

Systematic Selection of Sequential Experiences

Work experiences offer insights into an individual's skill proficiencies and preferences with respect to job types, work tasks, work environments, and social atmosphere. Providing a variety of vocational experiences is a facet of career education that is recommended throughout the literature (e.g., Brolin, 1995; Gajar et al, 1993; Hutchins & Renzaglia, 1990). Community employment options should be reviewed to identify a range and variety of potential work experience opportunities that can be sequenced systematically throughout each learner's vocational education. However, the sequence of these experiences must be carefully selected to systematically vary the factors that may affect skill proficiency and preference. Sampling diverse employment settings, co-worker interaction, supervision models, and job responsibilities assists in identifying the characteristics of a career or long-term employment opportunity that meets the needs, abilities, and "likes" of an individual.

Experiences Reflect Validated Community Employment Opportunities

One pitfall of many "prevocational" training models is the difficulty for individuals with disabilities to generalize skills to natural work environments. In many cases the skills being taught in school programs are not representative of those performed in the actual workplace. Furthermore, demonstrated competence on tasks taught in school programs does not assure success in community employment opportunities. Tasks must be relevant to specific community businesses and represent potential long-term employment opportunities.

However, equally important is to analyze job training opportunities carefully so that selected instructional tasks have social validity within the job market and represent meaningful or high priority work responsibilities relevant for future employment. Superficial analyses of many jobs may reveal simple tasks that are performed in a business (e.g., rolling silverware in a napkin in a restaurant setting). However, a more careful analysis may indicate that there are no opportunities for meaningful employment based upon that singular task (e.g., worker must also wait tables or serve as the cashier). Hence, these job tasks may represent only incidental pieces of a job. Needless to say, this does not result in a high probability of successful long-term community employment for persons with disabilities.

Family and Consumer Participation in the Decision-Making Process

Legal mandates have provided a basis for increased family and consumer involvement in the educational and transition process. Yet, specific strategies for enhancing and promoting a "team" approach to decision-making in all aspects of an individual's curriculum continue to evolve.

As an individualized career education plan is developed for a student, decisions are made regarding the types of experiences, their appropriate settings, and the amount of time to devote to instruction. It becomes critical to investigate individual learner needs, preferences, and concerns, as well as those of the family in order to create opportunities for active participation in the decision process. To value "individual choice" means to provide opportunities to communicate dreams and fears, likes and dislikes, and desires for the future. Data gathered early in a youth's education will offer insights into the program needs and supports to achieve an employment goal. Information regarding schedules, wages, transportation, and work preferences also must be assessed and discussed.

Longitudinal Career Education Model Overview

The remainder of this chapter describes the components of a longitudinal career education model and the implementation of activities providing vocational services to individuals with disabilities. The model includes a series of activities that involve systematic procedures for:

1. evaluating the employment opportunities available within a specific community

2. evaluating individual employment and job needs, preferences, and abilities

3. integrating the information about the community and the individual in order to sequence a series of work experiences that promote progressive evaluation of potential career choices

4. providing instruction and support during all phases of the career education program

5. evaluating individual performance within each work experience and the targeted long-term placement, as well as general program effectiveness

Key Question #3: What does a community assessment entail?

Research has shown that individual communities must be considered unique in terms of current and future employment opportunities. Therefore, the tasks and skills within a vocational training program must reflect the employment needs, job types, and performance demands in a specific locale (Hutchins & Renzaglia, 1990; Renzaglia et al., 1995).

To optimize success in community employment, service providers must establish procedures for initiating and conducting ongoing assessments of local community employment opportunities (Gajar et al., 1993; Hutchins, Renzaglia, Stahlman, & Cullen, 1986; Moon, Inge, Wehman, Brooke, & Barcus, 1990; Parent, Sherron, Stallard, & Booth, 1993). A thorough ecological assessment of community businesses and industries provides information for systematically selecting meaningful work experiences, designing appropriate vocational programs, and targeting specific long-term employment options. Activities for service providers include the following:

1. validating the types of employment options that exist within a community

2. contacting and communicating with employers in order to gather information on specific employment needs of the businesses, how the businesses are organized, and the management of relevant businesses

3. analyzing work sites to identify work performance demands, necessary work-related behaviors, and specific work site characteristics (Hutchins & Renzaglia, 1990; Renzaglia, Hutchins, & Banks, 1995)

Validating Community Employment Trends

An initial step in the analysis of community vocational opportunities involves assessing current and projected trends in the local job market (Patterson, 1996). Professionals in special education are likely to have a narrow and limited perspective of the community job market. They may be knowledgeable only in job types that are highly visible, cited as examples in professional literature, or mentioned by personal contacts within the community. As a result, vocational training programs for individuals with disabilities may tend to target work experiences that have few or no realistic or valid employment opportunities within the community, represent only a small percentage of the total number of job types that exist, or favor a single job type for employment or training.

Consequently, service providers must responsibly investigate the full range of community employment options and be aware of how these options may change over time. The collected data should contribute to decisions concerning further job development activities or choice of vocational experiences to offer learners. Several strategies have been suggested for validating employment trends and documenting community vocational opportunities that hold promise:

- Contact the local Chamber of Commerce for directories and membership lists to identify businesses and industries that are less publicized or familiar. A Chamber of Commerce directory often organizes businesses by the focus of the business and provides the number of employees. In addition, local trends in employment and business opportunities are often available.
- Local newspapers typically publish community business news that includes the introduction of new businesses in the area.
- Classified newspaper advertisements and "want ads" posted in windows of individual businesses offer insight into the types of positions available in a community. However, methods for effectively documenting valid employment trends across time require systematic records of advertised job types. Service providers should design a classification scheme that reflects specific job types in community businesses and industries and one or two times a month record the frequency of positions advertised in the Sunday paper. Longitudinal records of classified advertisements can reveal emerging trends, as well as unfamiliar or less visible opportunities.

Contacting and Communicating with Employers

A second step to assess community employment opportunities requires professionals to contact employers for specific information regarding a target business (Hagner & Vander Sande, 1998; Moon et al., 1990). Commonly recommended practices include writing letters of introduction to employers and telephoning and asking a few simple screening questions to schedule interview appointments as a follow-up to a written contact. Interviewing employers about the personnel needs, organization, and management of the business is next. A number of exemplary and replicable procedures for communicating with employers have been developed. These procedures include:

1. Using the contacts as a method for establishing relationships with employers. Direct and personal interviews seem to build more positive relationships than mailed surveys.
2. Establishing the purpose for an employer contact prior to that contact. Is the purpose to identify specific employment opportunities or training opportunities?
3. Emphasizing to employers the importance for gathering information about their specific businesses in order to provide more valid training opportunities to students and to more reliably recommend specific individuals for open positions.
4. Collecting as much information as possible early in the process to minimize interruptions of an employer's schedule. (See Table 1 for a list of recommended information to gather during initial employer contacts.)
5. Using employer contact procedures that are flexible in order to accommodate both large corporations and small businesses.
6. Establishing a system for documenting and recording employer contacts in order to limit such contacts to a reasonable minimum within the first week or two.

Table I
Recommended Information to Obtain During an Employer Interview

- Job Types and Descriptions of Work Responsibilities
- Number of Employees Hired for Job Types and Turnover Rate
- Working Hours and Schedule
- Benefits
- Employer's Previous Experience with Individuals with Disabilities
- Employer Interest in Participating in Work Experience/Job Placement Program
- Employer Receptivity to Alternative/Creative Employment Structures and Models

Job Task Skills	Work-Related Skills	Job Site Characteristics
• Identification of Job Task Components • Variations in Job Tasks and/or Materials • Frequency of Job Task Completion • Equipment and Tools Used • Position and Movement	• Mobility • Language • Hygiene and Self-Care • Social Skills • Academics	• Work Position • Mobility Requirements and Space • Physical Demands • Duration of Job Tasks • Problem Solving Requirements • Production Rate • Work Product Quality • Continuous Working Requirements • Co-Worker Presence • Social Atmosphere • Interactions with Public • Supervision Level • Staff Composition • Distraction Level • Comfort Factors • Equipment and Tool Maintenance and Safety

Analyzing Work Sites and Conducting Job Development Activities

After the initial contacts, if it appears training and placement opportunities are likely, more careful observations will be required. Generally, the information should reflect specific job demands and characteristics, and may be organized as work tasks and responsibilities, work-related tasks and behaviors, and job site characteristics.

Work Tasks and Responsibilities

These are those tasks that comprise the primary job description and define the specific position in a business. These tasks should be observable and easily analyzed. If a targeted job type or position includes some tasks that seem inappropriate for students receiving the vocational training services, discuss alternative accommodations (e.g., adaptations, job restructuring) during the negotiation stage with the participating business. Documentation of task expectations and performance should include materials and equipment necessary for task completion, frequency and duration of the task, and any variability in these parameters. Such information can influence decisions regarding the selection of work experiences or job placements.

Work-Related Tasks and Behaviors

Work-related tasks and behaviors refer to the competencies and adaptive behaviors that are not specified within the job description, but nonetheless contribute significantly to job success. Examples of work-related tasks and behaviors include grooming, using the restroom, eating, communication, money use, time telling, use of "break time", social skills, attendance, and compliance (Rusch & Mithaug, 1980). The importance of specific work-related tasks and behaviors varies across businesses, and assumptions should not be made regarding the importance of any specific task or behavior. Therefore, employer validation of mandatory work-related skills and behavioral expectations is particularly necessary. Reviewing expectations by inquiring about each task or skill within the work context is helpful (e.g., reading one's name to find a time card in the rack vs. reading short words or phrases). This also can alert the employer to alternative methods for achieving similar but not identical outcomes (e.g., highlighting the name on the time card with a yellow marker if the learner cannot read).

Job Site Characteristics

The specific characteristics of a job site greatly influence whether or not a particular site will be selected for work experiences and long-term employment opportunities (Renzaglia et al., 1995). Job site characteristics refer to an assortment of variables that should be observed or discussed as part of a thorough job analysis. These variables include physical features of the job tasks, productivity demands, the physical arrangement of the work area, the social climate, and the nature of supervision and management.

Key Question #4: What should an individual vocational assessment include?
Evaluating Individual Needs

A critical component of effective longitudinal vocational training is evaluating the needs of individual students. Traditionally, vocational evaluation has consisted of a variety of assessment procedures and strategies including:

1. assessment of basic skills
2. use of psychometric tests such as vocational interest inventories and abilities and aptitude tests
3. work samples
4. behavioral observation and situational assessment

However, in recent years the movement has been toward the use of authentic assessments that evaluate the individuals' interests, abilities, and aptitudes in natural contexts under real work conditions. This shift away from traditional vocational evaluation is supported by the poor employment outcomes for individuals with disabilities (Menchetti & Piland, 1998; Parker & Schaller, 1996). No longer are procedures that purport to measure an individual's employment potential using norm-referenced assessments considered the best predictor, or even a valid predictor of successful employment outcomes for persons with disabilities (Menchetti & Flynn, 1990; Parker & Schaller, 1996).

In addition, traditional vocational assessment techniques typically do not tap into an individual's preferences or proficiencies in specific work tasks or job positions within the local community (Agran & Morgan, 1991; Peterson, 1986).

Educators and employment specialists recommend using evaluation procedures that assess an individual's preferences, proficiencies, and specific accommodation needs relative to specific employment opportunities within the community (Banks & Renzaglia, 1993; Winking, O'Reilly, & Moon, 1993).

In addition to using authentic assessment procedures, person-centered planning is a process that establishes vocational goals and desired outcomes with and for an individual (Clark, 1998). Person-centered planning involves systematically identifying with the individual's life goals and significant others (e.g., family members, friends). Person-centered planning guides the authentic assessment of individual needs and interests and ensures that the vocational assessment is focused on the self-determined long-term goals of the individual.

The assessment process should include evaluating family and individual preferences and needs, individual physical capabilities and needs for adaptation, and individual performance on specific jobs. The use of such assessment strategies is an ongoing process for individuals participating in a longitudinal vocational training program. These strategies assist professionals in making valid and effective decisions at many points during an individual's training program and culminate in the identification of a specific long-term job placement.

Evaluating an Individual's Physical Capabilities

A primary consideration for selecting job training and placement opportunities is an individual's physical capabilities and limitations. The ability to perform specific movements can influence the choice of work experiences and long-term job placements. Specific strategies for optimizing job success commonly address the evaluation of an individual's physical capabilities and needs relative to job demands (Callahan, 1991; Sowers & Powers, 1989; Wehman et al., 1988). Information on an individual's motor abilities will help identify any necessary accommodations and the design of adaptations for successful job performance.

Demonstration of successful accommodations within community-integrated employment settings for individuals with physical disabilities has increased dramatically over the past ten years. Assessment procedures for evaluating an individual's reach, grasp, ability to apply force, and use of head and feet have been developed and piloted (Renzaglia, Hutchins, Koterba-Buss, & Strauss, 1994). A process designated as the Action Inventory describes specific and replicable methodologies for evaluating an individual's movement abilities and limitations within the framework cited above. The Action Inventory provides information to more effectively select work training opportunities and job placements. Additionally, the Action Inventory identifies technology that can be interfaced with an individual's movement abilities to enable access to a job. Frequently, such technology is not commercially available and must be designed specifically for an individual and the job requirements.

An assessment of every individual's physical capabilities and limitations may not be appropriate or necessary. However, if an individual has a physical disability, it is useful to conduct a careful movement inventory to generate adaptations or accommodations for enhanced job marketability.

Evaluating an Individual's Performance and Preferences

In a longitudinal vocational training program, an individual can experience a variety of work experiences within the community prior to a potential long-term job placement. Each experience should provide progressive insights regarding individual achievement and job satisfaction over the long term. To capitalize on this information, documenting each work experience and evaluating individual performance gains and job site behavior is imperative. One method for longitudinal documentation of work experiences is to complete an individual summary report across numerous variables upon job completion. The report should reflect those decision-making variables that will ultimately influence choices for further work experiences or job placement. Figure 1 is an example of such documentation of work experience histories.

Figure 1
Example of a Format for Documenting Work Experiences

Student _____				
Date:	3/02 to 9/02	_/_ to _/_	_/_ to _/_	_/_ to _/_
Work Site:	Leonard Rec Center			
1) General Job Types or Positions Experienced	Janitorial			
2) Job Tasks Experienced	1. sweep floors and activity room 2. clean sinks and mirror 3. mop locker room and bathrooms 4. vacuum			
3) Transportation - Community Mobility Training Experienced	N/A - could walk to site without crossing streets			
4) Work Position				
5) General Mobility				
6) Physical Demands - Gross Motor				
7) Physical Demands - Fine Motor				
8) Length of Work Tasks				
9) Variability of Daily Job Tasks				
10) Problem Solving Requirements				
11) Production Rate				
12) Work Product Quality				
13) Continuous Working Requirements				
14) Co-worker Presence				
15) Non-Task Social Contacts				
16) Social Atmosphere				
17) Interaction with Consumers				
18) Supervisory Contact				
19) Staff Composition	a.　　b. c.　　d.	a.　　b. c.　　d.	a.　　b. c.　　d.	a.　　b. c.　　d.
20) Distraction Level				
21) Comfort Factors				
22) Equipment/Tool Use				

Individual Performance

It is useful to maintain systematic records over time to record individual progress on job performance at each work site. Measures of progress and skill acquisition across jobs can contribute significantly to future placement decisions. In addition, keep documentation on the performance and acquisition of work-related behaviors within a specific training opportunity. Success in future jobs will be affected by an individual's work-related skills and his or her proficiencies demonstrated in training experiences. Specific communication and social skills are important in long-term job placement and success. Additional work site characteristics (e.g., degree of supervision provided, safety, production rate requirements) also may contribute in evaluating future job placement opportunities.

Individual Preference

Too often, vocational evaluation measures of individuals with disabilities ignore individual preferences for specific job tasks or working conditions. Preferences for tasks or working conditions can be measured to help identify an individual's preferred job choice in the context of actual work experiences or during situational assessments when students are provided varied vocational training opportunities. In order to effectively evaluate and utilize these variables, professionals must maintain records of individual performance and behavior across work settings. One should note any variation in work experiences through differing job types and work site characteristics to document discrepancies in job performance or behavior across settings. Report summaries provide the basis for identification of new experiences, further training, or job placements.

Inadequate communication skills and the lack of assessment techniques for "likes" and "dislikes" present challenges in assessing work preferences for some students. Certainly, opportunities for assessing an individual's pleasure or unhappiness are available without depending on verbal report. For example, Winking and her colleagues (1993) described a method to investigate nonverbal indicators of job preference. These indicators included specific behaviors such as eyes open/squinted shut to indicate preference/non-preference.

Evaluating Family Preferences and Concerns

Families are important participants in the development and implementation of individuals' longitudinal vocational training program. Their contribution may vary during an individual's life, but the information and perspective that they have to offer is invaluable to a professional (Ferguson et al., 1993; Wehmeyer & Davis, 1995; Yancey, 1993). The implementation of PL 94-142, the authorization of PL 101-476, the Individuals with Disabilities Education Act (IDEA), and the focus on transition planning all have provided the impetus for the collaboration of professionals with families in educational program planning and post-secondary outcomes for individuals with disabilities (Hosack & Malkmus, 1992; Turnbull, 1988).

Information from the family should include its hopes and dreams for the child as an adult, planned living arrangements and location, perceived obstacles to desired outcomes, financial security and needs, personal needs, preferences for working conditions and schedule, resources and family participation, preferred employment benefits, and any other issue that is of concern to the family.

Family input may significantly influence the direction and outcomes of vocational programming in areas such as:

1. parental expectations for post-school activities
2. prior work experiences (in and out of the home)
3. preferences for specific types of work
4. personal care needs, assistance, and medical concerns
5. mode of communication and concerns
6. family roles and support
7. preferred wages and benefits
8. transportation needs and issues
9. schedule and work hours
10. preferred method for obtaining feedback on learner job performance and related issues

Use of a family interview at critical times in the individual's educational program can maximizing family input into the employment decision-making process. The interview process can assess the family's initial expectations regarding vocational training, as well as changing family priorities and preferences with respect to available job opportunities. Intensive interviews should be completed assessing all aspects of vocational programming with the family when an individual enters middle school or junior high, again when the student transitions to high school, and finally when the individual participates in educational services geared toward post-secondary outcomes.

During the "in-between years," a less intense follow-up interview process should be conducted to update concerns and information previously provided by the family during the initial interview. Evaluating family priorities and concerns during the transition years (i.e., middle school, high school, young adult), coincides with a time when changes in the focus of an individual's vocational program will be considered. As suggested earlier in this chapter, during the early years an individual should be gaining experiences and training that contribute to making appropriate decisions in high school for narrowing the pool of vocational training opportunities.

Key Question #5: How can vocational or career development opportunities be integrated into a young child's educational program?

Although vocational training and work experiences are primarily targeted for youth and young adults, it is reasonable to evaluate vocational goals at even very young ages (Brolin, 1995; Clark, Carlson, Fisher, Cook, & D'Alonzo, 1991). Developing a work ethic that includes the demonstration of behaviors such as responsibility, task completion, and performance quality is a common objective of many elementary curricula. It may, in fact, be considered part of an initial introduction to a career orientation or exploration focus for learners without disabilities. Therefore, it is reasonable to consider methods for integrating vocational curricular content into an elementary educational program for young learners with disabilities.

There are several purposes for introducing a vocational component to the curriculum of young learners. First, adopting a longitudinal approach requires that all professional personnel have an awareness and interest in the future of their students. Even staff at the elementary level must be committed to the identification, selection, and implementation of instructional programs that will fulfill immediate and long-term goals of their students. In order to accomplish such an objective, teachers must promote the acquisition of skills that contribute to future employment success.

A second purpose for introducing vocational curricula to young learners is to offer the learner an opportunity to develop an awareness of career options. Many children in general education programs become aware at early ages of jobs, careers, and the world of work. Such awareness introduces the positive aspects of employment and offers the children a glimpse of the variety of jobs that people perform. Certainly it seems that learners with disabilities could benefit from such an awareness of employment opportunities.

Finally, an early introduction to vocational objectives promotes and encourages the development of positive work attitudes. Providing systematic instruction and reinforcement of successful work-related behaviors (e.g., social skills) promotes those behaviors often associated with a positive work attitude. Consistent long-term reinforcement of appropriate behaviors may enhance success in future work environments.

Considerations for Implementation

The primary focus of a vocational curriculum at a young age should not be the instruction of specific work tasks as they are performed in community businesses and industries (e.g., dust mopping with industrial mops, washing dishes using commercial dishwashing machinery). Likewise, instructional programs or work opportunities that target "traditional" prevocational tasks (e.g., sorting nuts and bolts, simple product assembly) will have little to do with successful adult employment. Rather, it is important to consider age appropriateness of those skills or behaviors that, if learned now, may assist each learner to be successful in an adult job.

School-Based Jobs

Many elementary classrooms and school communities identify a range of tasks in which learners participate (e.g., wash blackboard, water plants, take attendance to the office). These class or school jobs offer opportunities for the learners to assume responsibility for a task and contribute to the maintenance of the educational community. A recommendation, then, is to identify the jobs that do or could exist within the class or school that could be selected for all learners to perform. It is of no importance at this point in the learner's career if the job has long-term value or includes specific skills used in jobs within the local community. The focus of school-based jobs at young ages is to provide instruction to achieve independent performance and to focus on the more "affective" aspects of work, such as taking initiative to start the job, quality of performance, responsibility, and job completion.

Participation in school-based jobs also may reveal early preferences for a learner. Specific tasks may become more preferred due to the nature of the task (e.g., filing papers for the office secretary) or the context in which the task is completed (e.g., social atmosphere of the school office). Such information can contribute later in validating preferences of work experiences. In addition, the learner may learn to communicate a job preference in an appropriate manner.

Skills and Behaviors that Cross other Curricular Domains

A second consideration that can contribute to vocationally related experiences for young learners is the identification of skills and behaviors that cross other curricular domains (i.e., domestic, leisure, and community). Personal care skills (e.g., toileting, feeding, grooming), communication skills (e.g., indicating a need), and social skills (e.g., greetings, simple conversation) represent examples of desirable skills and behaviors for young children with disabilities that, if acquired, could certainly enhance employment opportunities in the future. Achievement of these skills at an early age will permit service providers of older learners to focus upon other skills specifically related to job success. That is, teaching work-related behaviors in age appropriate and meaningful contexts will minimize or even eliminate the additional time needed to acquire these skills as a young adult.

Additionally, the identification of objectives in other curricular areas that involve specific tasks and activities can provide another source of early vocational preparation (e.g., housekeeping tasks). Some objectives that are identified for individual learners in non-vocational contexts (e.g., domestic) may bear resemblance to selected work responsibilities in specific job types (e.g., sweeping). Instruction on these tasks may be germane to a future work environment and reduce the time spent in learning the required skills. For example, if a learner learns to wipe the snack table with a wet sponge in the elementary grades, the skill may generalize quickly to wiping tables in a dining hall during a subsequent work experience. Enhanced generalization then allows more time to be spent on acquiring novel skills (e.g., loading the dish machine) at the work site.

As with school-based jobs, early experiences with tasks relevant to actual employment situations also may provide a brief glimpse into preferred and non-preferred activities for the learner. For example, an individual may realize he or she does not prefer housekeeping after experiencing instruction on housekeeping tasks as part of a domestic skills curriculum. This information may contribute to a longitudinal perspective of preferred and non-preferred workplace activities.

Evaluation

A longitudinal approach to vocational instruction implies that there will be a deliberate attempt to provide work experiences over time and that systematic decision-making procedures will be utilized to select employment options and experiences. Therefore, the information that can be collected at young ages begins a learner's history of vocationally related experiences.

Maintaining accurate records of learner progress on all IEP objectives can serve to document acquisition of skills and behaviors related to vocational curriculum (i.e., work-related behaviors; school based jobs; domestic, leisure, and community activities). However, additional useful information may include notation of (a) preferred activities (e.g., how many times the learner requests to have a particular school job) and (b) the context or environment conducive to the learner's task success or preference (e.g., highly social atmosphere, likes to work with papers). Although this information may not be critical to the job the individual selects as an adult, it may help in the selection of initial early work experiences at the middle school or junior high level.

Key Question #6: How might work experiences be characterized for youth in middle school or early years of high school?

As learners enter the sixth grade and proceed through middle school or junior high, a vocational curriculum should be increasingly a part of the educational program (Banks & Renzaglia, 1993; Brolin, 1995). Specific vocational experiences can be introduced to youth with disabilities, and relevant vocational objectives can be targeted to ensure successful employment as an adult (McCarthy, Everson, Moon, & Barcus, 1985; Moore, Agran, & McSweyn, 1990). However, teachers and other related service providers must understand the importance of early work experiences, the planning for which must contribute to the ultimate goal of identifying long-term employment.

The purpose of an early work experience phase is twofold. First, it is important to give learners a wide range of work experiences. Secondly, task and work site characteristics should be as diverse as possible. During the adolescent years a diversity of job types and their associated skills can be introduced to develop learner's preferences and skill sets. The focus of this phase of a longitudinal vocational training program is to systematically evaluate each vocational training opportunity for maximum diversity from previous work experiences. In order to vary the range of vocational training experiences, several key considerations should be addressed. To provide varied work experiences, it is important to identify the range of jobs and job sites and their job characteristics.

Identifying a Range of Jobs

Jobs considered for early work experiences should reflect a variety of different job types (e.g., housekeeping, clerical, computer data entry, dishwasher, stock person). Job types may be labeled according to local convention and may represent unique job titles (e.g., city vehicle maintenance: washes all city police cars). However, it is also imperative that these job types represent realistic opportunities for employment in the community in which the learner plans to reside as an adult. There is no advantage to providing training on isolated job tasks or job types that do not or will not exist in the future (e.g., for example, training for work in fast food restaurants that are not within reasonable proximity of the learner's residence).

Finally, identifying job types for work experiences through commonalities in skills or job tasks (i.e., core skills) is useful. Many job types have similar responsibilities (e.g., bus person: bussing trays or tables, wiping tables, maintaining condiment areas, sweeping floors) although the positions exist within different businesses (e.g., university dining hall, hospital snack bar, finer dining, fast food restaurant). The use of job types that have core skills, common across a range of employment opportunities, enables students to learn skills that are useful in future job situations.

Identifying a Range of Sites

In conjunction with identifying a range of jobs, a range of vocational training sites must be identified to implement an effective program for youth with disabilities. To enhance program efficiency, several variables must be considered. First of all, federal laws must be observed regarding the age of the youth (e.g., the number of hours the students are allowed to work, time of day the students are allowed to work), the desired vocational experience, and any restrictions related to equipment and machinery on the work site. It is not appropriate to consider businesses with working conditions that are unsuitable for minors.

A second variable that may influence site selection is the distance that a learner may travel and the commute time. Individual service providers need to establish guidelines involving geographic location or transportation accessibility. A site is not recommended if commute time exceeds the time spent receiving job instruction. In addition, some businesses may engage in specific work skills at times that are not compatible with the student's school schedule. Many janitorial jobs occur at night or in early mornings. If the learner cannot receive initial instruction on those tasks at other times during the day, then another site with similar responsibilities and a compatible work schedule must be identified.

Finally, it may be beneficial to identify a few sites that contain different job types within the same business. A number of learners then can be served from the same place, instructional management may be arranged more efficiently, a variety of jobs are immediately available for experiences, and relationships with one employer may be more easily negotiated. A large hotel may have house-keeping, data entry, clerical, janitorial, and a number of food service job types in one location. Management responsibilities for the instructor are simplified compared to maintaining multiple sites. However, service providers should be cautious about having too many individuals with disabilities in one location, as well as restricting opportunities only to a single site, as it is unusual for one business to truly represent all potential employment options.

Selecting Experiences

A final consideration in implementing an early work experience phase, which focuses on sampling a variety of vocational opportunities, is the evaluation of selected variables (i.e., task, social, and environmental characteristics) that create differences across job types and potential training sites. Such variables can be categorized simply into task, social, and environmental characteristics.

Evaluation

Information collected on the student's experience and performance should include a summary of experiences in terms of task, social, and environmental variables. Historical information of each experience is helpful in assuring that the next experience will sample a different set of characteristics. In addition, information on student's experiences build a longitudinal perspective and can offer insights into task preference and proficiency for use during the selection of vocational experiences during high school. A sample format for maintaining a longitudinal record of experiences is provided at the end of this chapter (Renzaglia et al., 1995).

Key Question #7: How might high school work experiences be selected?

Vocational instruction has become commonplace at the secondary level for students with disabilities (Rusch & Chadsey, 1998). Many students are provided opportunities to sample work experiences to assist in identifying potential job placements upon graduation. However, if a longitudinal approach to vocational programming is adopted, then the focus of the experiences for high school students (i.e., ages fifteen to eighteen years) will entail more than just a random sampling of different job opportunities.

The primary purpose of the longitudinal approach at the secondary level is to collect in-depth information for informed decision-making regarding long-term employment opportunities. More specifically, the intent during this phase is to focus on those job types and work site characteristics that stand out due to student preference or proficiency. This phase identifies a more focused and limited range of employment possibilities with greater involvement in opportunities that were introduced earlier in the student's school program.

Considerations for Implementation

In order to offer a more focused sample of work experiences, two considerations dominate the decision-making process: the identification of the job types and the scheduling of the selected experiences. Previous information from the learner's vocational education program provides critical data for decision-making during this phase.

Identification of Jobs and Work Experiences

Selection of employment opportunities at the high school level should be based upon prior experience. Recommendations for focused experiences should be based upon learner preference, learner proficiency, and preference for certain social and environmental characteristics of the work site. (Refer to Table 2 for a list of variables to consider in selecting advanced work experiences.) Two to three experiences during the high school years will allow for additional vocational instruction within specific job types and, consequently, the opportunity for a more thorough follow-up on the potential of the job type for long-term employment.

It is not unusual for some work experiences to become accessible after a learner turns sixteen years of age or for new businesses in the community to reveal new and previously unexplored job types. Therefore, a novel job type or work experience may be identified for the student, expanding future opportunities beyond the scope of experiences acquired during the middle school or junior high years. Carefully review new experiences for job relevance and work site characteristics. The information then can be integrated into the longitudinal plan for providing instruction on the specific jobs during the learner's secondary years.

Identification of the Work Experience Schedule

After work experiences for the next several years have been targeted, the second consideration is the scheduling of these experiences. Service providers and families must decide whether to provide consecutive experiences, such as year to year or concurrent ones. There appear to be advantages to both types of schedules.

Consecutive schedules permit the student to focus intensively and specifically on one job, thus devoting all instructional time to the skills required by the specific experience. Such time intensive scheduling may allow for faster acquisition of skills and an opportunity to evaluate performance and productivity under the supervision of the site personnel rather than the service provider. A concurrent schedule of vocational instruction offers the opportunity for the student to

Table 2
Variables in Selecting Work Experiences and Job Placements

EARLY WORK EXPERIENCES

INITIAL CONSIDERATIONS

Distance from school; number of learners to be served; number of job types; valid future job opportunities

SAMPLING CONSIDERATIONS

Basic: job types; job tasks

Task: work position; mobility; physical demands; length of work task; variability; problem solving; production rate; work product quality

Social: co-worker (task related) contact; non-task related contact; social atmosphere; communication demands; supervisory contact; staff composition

Environmental: distraction level; comfort; equipment/tool use

INDIVIDUAL CONSIDERATIONS

Social behaviors; errors; hygiene or dress; accessibility; safety

PROGRAM CONSIDERATIONS

Age; number of hours; preferences of learner and family; unique site characteristics; learning needs; staffing; transportation; site availability (time and receptivity)

ADVANCED WORK EXPERIENCES

INITIAL CONSIDERATIONS

Job types experienced and represent job opportunities; interest in experiencing new job types

SAMPLING CONSIDERATIONS

Basic: job type preferences; job tasks preferences; performance proficiency

Task: work position; mobility; physical demands; length of work task; variability; problem solving; production rate; work product quality

Social: co-worker (task related) contact; non-task related contact; social atmosphere; communication demands; supervisory contact; staff composition

Environmental: distraction level; comfort; equipment/tool use

Other: employer paid; job placement potential

INDIVIDUAL CONSIDERATIONS

Social behaviors; errors; hygiene or dress; accessibility; safety

PROGRAM CONSIDERATIONS

Schedule; staffing or learner independence

JOB PLACEMENT

INITIAL CONSIDERATIONS

Job type preference; performance proficiency; employment is a possibility

SAMPLING CONSIDERATIONS

Basic: job type preferences; job tasks preferences; performance proficiency

Task: work position; mobility; physical demands; length of work task; variability; problem solving; production rate; work product quality

Social: co-worker (task related) contact; non-task related contact; social atmosphere; communication demands; supervisory contact; staff composition

INDIVIDUAL CONSIDERATIONS

Environmental: safety; accessibility; access to work materials

Work-related skills: personal needs; functional academics; communication

Other: transportation needs; job desirability (wages, benefits, work hours and schedule)

simultaneously experience two jobs (e.g., job one for three days a week, and job two for two days a week). This allows for a direct comparison of jobs, with the option of terminating either job at any time if it proves to be unproductive or a detriment to future employment opportunities. Another job can be added to replace the former without altering the current job schedule.

Evaluation

As with the previous phases, information must be recorded and summarized to reflect the student's performance and progress. The information collected at this point continues to provide a longitudinal perspective of the student's vocational experiences, job preferences, and skill acquisition. This chronological record adds a deeper level of understanding of the student's performance within specific job types or work sites and contributes to the decision-making process for a young adult seeking a long-term job placement.

Key Question #8: What does the selection of a long-term employment experience entail?

As stated previously, the targeted outcome of a longitudinal vocational training program for individuals with disabilities is post secondary employment in a job or career of their choice. Until an individual turns eighteen, such a model prescribes early work experiences, a wide variety of systematically sampled job types and work site characteristics, and a narrowing of work experiences for more focused and intensive instruction. In summary, the focus of the vocational program for a young adult is identification of the most appropriate "job match" and appropriate instruction in that job(s) to ensure long-term employment success. Consequently, considerable instructional time tailored to on-the-job training will be used to ensuring skill acquisition.

Considerations for Implementation

To systematically select an appropriate employment opportunity for a young adult, a number of variables must be reviewed with specific reference to the individual. No longer are general experiences the focus. Rather, the critical factors in determining a good "job match" are based upon qualities of the individual and characteristics of specific job types and employment settings.

Site Selection

Potential employment sites should include job positions consistent with an individual's job preference and proficiency from past work experiences. Sites must have the potential for real employment, not just another work experience. It is important that a business indicates a current or imminent job opening. Another criterion for job site selection is the acceptability of the site by relevant significant others. Family members or other significant persons may have opinions about the choices under consideration and may have information that affects the decision-making process. Therefore, in order to ensure support of the long-term outcomes and out of respect for the preferences of the family, their involvement in the decision-making process is crucial. Finally, there may be unique characteristics about a job or business that make it unsuitable. High productivity or autonomy demands may exceed the capabilities of some individuals, thereby precluding any possibility of a successful match.

Job Match

After the initial evaluation and identification of long-term employment opportunities and sites, additional variables should be reviewed and compared across sites on behalf of a specific individual. The process of matching persons with disabilities to jobs should parallel the same process that is valued by persons without disabilities. Employment options are defined by preferences and competencies. In addition, issues such as benefits and wages also will enter into the decision-making process. Renzaglia et al. (1995) have recommended that the variables for consideration should include job preferences, job proficiency, job responsibilities, preferences for social and work site characteristics, transportation needs and availability, job safety, work site accessibility and accommodations, and desirability of the job. (Refer to Table 2 for a list of variables to consider in selecting long-term placements.) A job preference ranking is then developed based upon input from the individual, relevant significant others, and service providers. At this point the "job match" is complete, and negotiations with individual businesses and employers can be initiated.

Evaluation

After a placement has been made, the manner in which an individual's performance is evaluated becomes critical, thereby demanding careful scrutiny of the evaluation methods. The information that has been collected serves as important documentation of an individual's proficiencies and deficiencies. This evaluative information can justify maintaining or terminating a placement, and is often the only objective view of the individual's performance, especially during "trying" times.

Performance data on specific instructional programs, including work task, work-related, and social skill objectives must be collected regularly and shared with the appropriate personnel at the employment site. The site supervisor of the business should conduct evaluations of the learner on the same schedule as the other employees. Integration into the work force routine may foster a commitment to the new employee and ensures increased site supervisor participation.

Key Question #9: What activities are critical in organizing effective vocational instruction in community-based sites?

Following the selection of a work experience or long-term job placement for an individual, the organization and implementation of the actual instruction must be considered. Further decisions related to establishing training sites, curriculum selection and sequencing, scheduling, and training time are necessary to maintain a longitudinal emphasis. Factors that may impact planning and implementation decisions include the age of the individual and the phase of the vocational program in which she or he is participating (i.e., early experience sampling, a more focused experience, and job placement).

Establishing Training Sites

Following the selection of experiences for the participants of the longitudinal vocational training program, instructional sites must be identified and established. In many cases, the work site itself is part of the chosen work experience. For other work experiences, sites may have to be negotiated in light of the availability of choices of appropriate experience. During the negotiation process, service providers may be required to address a variety of issues, such as the availability of learner orientation. Additional service providers may have to draft employer agreements and develop a site handbook.

Site Selection

Vocational instruction can occur in school or at community-based sites. For younger learners, experiences may be most appropriately conducted within the school building (if valid instructional opportunities exist) or within nearby businesses in the community. Furthermore, child labor laws regarding job training and employment must be carefully reviewed and followed for learners under the age of sixteen. As mentioned previously, it is important that the time spent in actual instruction be greater than the time spent commuting to the site. In addition, the selected site should offer opportunities for learning valid and critical work tasks, work-related skills, and social behaviors.

For the older participants in more focused work experiences, community sites are imperative for instruction. A critical factor in site selection is the availability of experiences that can be tailored to an individual's specific needs (e.g., tasks to learn, work environment, preferences). Other considerations in site selection include location and accessibility, available times for instruction, staffing demands, and the possibility for instructing more than one learner at the site.

Of course, for learners targeted for a long-term job placement, the site is selected based upon those variables mentioned previously for placement selection. However, it is advisable to develop a preference ranking of potential placements in the event the most preferred opportunities are not available.

Employer Agreements

Establishing employer agreements with individual sites provides a protocol that emphasizes communication from the start. It decreases the likelihood of a misunderstanding of the intent of the program and the mutual responsibilities of the service providers and the participating business. All agreements should result in a written document signed by the parties involved. Negotiate the agreement with a representative that holds a leadership role within the business and will serve as the liaison to the business during the work experience. Articulate the specific roles, responsibilities, and expectations of the service provider and the business and its employees during a work experience or job placement relationship. The agreement also should address other pertinent information such as:

1. a schedule for training
2. insurance and liability responsibilities
3. wages
4. tasks requiring instruction

Individual Orientation

As sites are selected and confirmed, participants of the vocational training program should be given an opportunity to view the business and meet the appropriate supervisors and co-workers prior to beginning work.

Site Handbook

A final suggestion for enhancing the successful implementation of a longitudinal vocational training program is the development of a "handbook" or set of guidelines for interacting with the business and the learner during instruction. Information useful for the service provider on site includes emergency information, the employer agreement, transportation schedules, instructional and behavior management plans, and an anecdotal journal documenting learner performance. The handbook assists in ensuring consistency across persons who may instruct and provide supervision at the site.

Curriculum Selection and Sequencing

As stated previously, one purpose of a longitudinal vocational training program is to systematically provide vocational instruction and a series of work experiences that contribute to a specific employment outcome. Therefore, the curriculum must be carefully developed to represent meaningful and socially valid skills and tasks that facilitate successful long-term employment. In addition, professionals must organize the targeted tasks for instruction to enhance job performance and independence. To ensure curriculum effectiveness, the following guidelines should be followed:

1. Vocational curricula targeted for instruction must reflect the actual tasks and responsibilities required by the specific business.

In order to identify relevant skills and tasks to target for instruction, conduct an analysis of the business and responsibilities of specific job positions. Typically, an initial job analysis would have been completed prior to evaluating the business for a work experience or job placement. Information concerning work task demands would have been a key factor in the selection of the business as a work experience or placement site. Professionals should not presume the availability of certain tasks or responsibilities. Rather, they should observe other employees as they perform the required job duties and negotiate with employers the specific job responsibilities desired for the individual's work experience.

2. Skills and tasks targeted for instruction should reflect the purpose of the experience or placement.

The curriculum should change focus as the individual matures. Younger participants who are sampling a variety of experiences will benefit from instruction on skills and tasks that are relevant not only to the specific work experience site, but also to similar job positions across other businesses. "Core skills" refer to those skills or work tasks common to the majority of similar job types. Providing early instruction on such skills promotes opportunities for specific skill generalization and success in future work experiences with similar job task demands. Individuals who are involved in more intensive and focused work experiences in high school should continue to expand their repertoire of core skills in the job types that they have targeted for themselves. Gaining increased proficiency in skills that are common to potential long-term job types enhances instruction and success in future job placements. Finally, participants in long-term job placements in which employment is the goal should receive instruction in the specific job tasks defined by the position in that business. If the position has been redefined or restructured to accommodate the individual, then careful negotiation with the employer is imperative to identify the scope of job responsibilities.

3. An individualized vocational curriculum should include instruction in work, work-related, and social skills.

Although a primary emphasis in a vocational training program is the acquisition of skills and tasks that define a specific experience or job position, instruction also must be provided on work-related skills (e.g., grooming, time, money) and social skills (e.g., initiating greetings and conversations) that are relevant to the job position or work site. Research into job termination has revealed that a lack of social skills and necessary work-related behaviors may be significant factors in an unsuccessful employment experience (Hanley-Maxwell, Rusch, Chadsey-Rusch, & Renzaglia, 1986). In addition, non-job-specific skills and behaviors that appear to influence job success (e.g., appropriate ways to ask for assistance, taking a timely break) may not be acquired without direct instruction. Therefore, experience or placement site must be analyzed carefully with respect to employer expectations of work-related and social competencies.

4. Instruction in targeted job tasks and work-related and social skills should be organized within naturally occurring routines.

A schedule and routine for presenting the tasks and work site demands must be designed for instructional purposes. In many instances, the duties of the position dictate the order in which each task is performed (e.g., maintenance persons dry mop or sweep a floor before wet mopping or buffing). Other positions may not have a preferred order of tasks (e.g., clerical persons may file, enter computer data, and sort mail). However, it is beneficial to consult site personnel regarding expectations for completing activities in a specific sequence and establishing a schedule of job task performance.

In addition to sequencing work tasks, an analysis can be made of other activities that naturally occur or could be scheduled to occur (e.g., breaks, hanging up coats, putting lunches in the office refrigerator). These tasks can be chronologically ordered to serve as a schedule for the time spent at the work site. Such an analysis also may identify additional instructional objectives that represent work-related and social skill needs. Many of the identified objectives can be integrated within the individual's vocational training schedule on site.

5. Consider organizing instructional objectives as a sequence of related tasks or a sequence of skills with similar demands or definition.

Within a selected schedule or routine, work tasks targeted for instruction can be sequenced using an organizational structure that promotes skill acquisition, generalization, and job independence. Skills can be sequenced for instruction based upon the natural order of task completion. This eliminates a need for verbal intervention by the instructor. For example, a housekeeper may clean the sink, the tub, the toilet, the mirror, and the floor to complete a bathroom sequence, or a clerical worker may enter new consumer data into the computer before filing the hard copies in the drawer.

Identifying common competencies across work tasks may offer another strategy for sequencing instructional work objectives that also facilitates skill generalization. For example, developing a sequence of wiping tasks (e.g., tables, chairs, condiment stations, utensil trays) for a dining hall attendant could promote efficient acquisition of a sequence of skills introduced for instruction. This is possible because many of the steps in the sequence are similar or identical (e.g., get a cloth/rag/sponge; dampen it; start in a corner of the surface; wipe back and forth to cover the surface; scrub any dirty spots). Sequencing target objectives based on their relationship or similar characteristics are strategies that can "ease" the need to teach everything at once when time does not permit.

Time

In addition to the selection and sequencing of target vocational objectives, the time spent engaged in vocational instruction also must be considered. The amount of time engaged in vocational instruction should increase with age. That is, as students near completion of their public school services, instructional time must focus on ensuring successful long-term employment. Specific periods for vocational instruction probably should not exist for elementary age learners. The suggested focus of their curricula targets competencies that may enhance successful work experiences later rather than teaching work skills directly. Therefore, "vocational skill instruction" is embedded within other instructional objectives that are a part of their educational program (e.g., toileting, communication).

Students at the middle school level, who are beginning to address the benefits of longitudinal vocational planning and instruction, may spend five to ten hours a week in a work experience. Students in this phase of work experience sampling will have many other educational objectives in other domains, and time spent in direct vocational skill instruction is just beginning. The hours spent should encompass the entire week (i.e., one to two hours per day for four to five days each week) in contrast to longer, intensive time periods for one or two days.

The amount of time devoted to vocational instruction should continue to increase as learners proceed into more focused work experiences and actual employment opportunities. For students in high school, approximately ten to twenty hours each week should be devoted to work opportunities. The increase in time permits further skill acquisition across work tasks. With increased opportunities for independent performance by the learner, evaluations can be conducted involving supervision and monitoring issues on the job. Finally, those individuals who are targeted for a long-term job placement may begin working shorter hours per week or on a part-time level and systematically increase the hours at work until working the number of hours expected by the employer.

Window to the World
Arthur

> Arthur was a learner with a combination of significant physical and developmental disabilities. He was able to communicate verbally with only a slight bit of articulation difficulty. Using a motorized wheelchair to move around school and the community, Arthur was quite social, enjoying the company of, and conversation with, friends and familiar persons in his environment. He was looking forward to having a job and living in a supervised community residential setting.

As a part of Arthur's career education program, he was able to sample several work experiences while he attended middle school. This marked the beginning of a process to identify and explore Arthur's preferences, proficiencies, and need for assistive technology in an employment setting.

Examples of some of his early work experiences included sorting mail into teacher's mailboxes in the school office and collecting daily attendance from each classroom and working at a local music printing company, where he used an adaptive device to stamp the company name and price on sheet music. In his early high school years, Arthur continued his work in the high school office, rewound videos and restocked shelves at a local video rental store, and completed simple data entry for the community fire station.

The work sampling experiences highlighted variables that deserved priority attention in targeting a long-term job match or placement. Arthur's wheelchair necessitated space in his work environment to maneuver around obstacles and furniture. The location of the business needed to be accessible by public transportation from his new living accommodations. He desired a social atmosphere where co-workers could chat freely about work and non-work related topics and offer assistance or support upon his request. Finally, the job needed to be defined by responsibilities or tasks that, with appropriate adaptations, Arthur could complete and monitor independently.

The long-term opportunity deemed suitable for Arthur was the video department of a state video and film center from which educators statewide could rent videos and films to supplement their teaching. Arthur worked twenty-five to thirty hours per week cleaning and rewinding all returned videos and making copies of videos from master tapes to increase the video inventory. The jobs were learned easily with systematic instruction from his public school job coach, and the equipment he operated required no adaptation. He worked in an area with the supervisor of the department. The work force itself was highly social, celebrating holidays and employee birthdays with fervor. He could use the bus without transferring between home and his single-level workplace. In addition, as a state employee, he was entitled to use all the facilities of the university campus where the office was located.

Window to the World
Jackie

Jackie received her public education with support from a special education resource teacher due to her mild cognitive disabilities. Her academic abilities were evaluated on an upper elementary grade level. Jackie was very outgoing and friendly, eager to please her teachers and family. As part of the career education plan, during middle school Jackie worked in the office photocopying for teachers and secretaries, greeted visitors, and entered attendance data into the school computer. In addition, during her middle school education, she participated with her peers in a variety of one- to two-day job shadowing experiences that occurred throughout each semester as a part of a school-wide career awareness effort. During high school, Jackie expanded her sampling of work experiences by becoming involved in vocational education and community-based learning opportunities. These experiences provided the contexts for her to explore careers in child care/day care, computer data entry, food service, and clerical tasks.

As Jackie added to her wealth of work experiences, her long-term employment goals became clearer. Her family felt strongly that they would prefer for Jackie to be in an environment in which she was using her academic abilities; they had strong preferences against food service. Jackie indicated that she had not enjoyed working with small children and seemed to increasingly favor clerical duties and an office atmosphere with frequent interactions among employees and the public. Her skills and proficiencies in clerical tasks such as copying, filing, and answering telephones supported her expressed interest. She was efficient, pleasant, and acquired independence on the targeted job skills without much difficulty. She preferred a Monday to Friday work week on a twelve-month calendar and hoped to find a job that offered a reasonable wage with eventual benefits.

Jackie was hired at a federal office in her community in which she worked among other clerical staff primarily to file, copy, and answer telephones. In fact, because of her strengths, the personnel director reallocated tasks to staff so that Jackie's job was "carved" for her from typical responsibilities of a clerical worker. Other employees were happy to let go of the tasks that were reassigned to Jackie, and the division of labor contributed to an effective team approach in the office.

Best Practice Recommendations

Effective vocational instruction requires careful planning and implementation to realize the outcomes sought by professionals, families, and individuals with disabilities. Although the vocational literature offers significant support for, and discussion of, implementation practices across many of the considerations shared in this chapter, it is imperative that these ideas and strategies be systematically integrated into an overall plan that focuses on a longitudinal approach. There is no indication that a "laissez-faire" strategy is successful, in which vocational instruction is provided in a splintered manner, with minimal regard for assessing community employment opportunities, evaluating the individual's strengths and preferences in work, assessing family concerns, and systematically teaching all relevant work and work-related skills necessary for successful employment. Most of the recommendations regarding best practices have been previously articulated in this chapter. However, several additional suggestions include:

1. Work as a team of professionals across all age levels. Do not expect the transition coordinator, vocational specialist, or job coach to be able to do it all alone. An entire team of educators within a system can share in initiating organized employer contacts or referrals, which are then pursued by specifically identified education personnel or students.

2. Do not expect to assess a community for all potential employment opportunities overnight. It takes years of continuous investigation. Identify a strategy for prioritizing contacts and follow-up calls and make a few introductions each week or month. Always finish out your follow-up calls and visits before initiating too many new contacts. It is a balancing act!

3. Maintain accurate records of employer contacts and create a file of information that you can access and update at any time. Include a telephone and personal contact log to note interactions over time, the employer

    interview, job analysis information, task analyses, instructional programs, and employer negotiation agreements.

4. Create resume portfolios for each learner to document the experiences in which they have participated and any evaluative information that is collected. Include interviews with family members or the learner regarding factors or considerations that may influence the selection of further experiences of long-term employment choices.

5. Maintain ongoing communication with family members and other education personnel concerning the integration of skills being instructed in vocational settings, and within other contexts at home or at school that might enhance independence and success on the job.

Vocational instruction and programming is complex. This chapter provided an overview of the considerations and recommended strategies that may be important to implement in order to achieve long-term integrated community employment outcomes for individuals with disabilities.

Future Research Issues

Although much effort has been directed toward realizing optimal employment outcomes for individuals with disabilities, success is not yet evident for all individuals with disabilities. As a result, practices have to be continually reassessed and reviewed with respect to effectiveness, and flexible means for achieving productive outcomes must be explored. Developing a longitudinal model for career development and employment outcomes makes intuitive sense. However, systematic implementation of such a model has not been common practice. Therefore, an evaluation of the long-term impact of participation in a longitudinal model should be conducted by closely following individuals with disabilities who have participated in such programs over time. Such a follow-up on program participants will assist educators in assessing the value of such a model. Additionally, validation or evaluation of the specific components of a longitudinal model is needed. For example, when considering work sampling, how many experiences are enough and for how long should individuals sample specific jobs? These questions have not been addressed with data to support recommendations. Educators and vocational instructors certainly would benefit from research that sorts out the critical components of a longitudinal model.

With the current emphasis on inclusive education, developing strategies for providing longitudinal vocational programs within inclusive educational models is a challenge to special educators and vocational educators. In fact, we must investigate strategies for integrating the components of a longitudinal model with models used in general education and vocational education. How can we bring the best of all "worlds" into one effective service delivery system that addresses the needs of a diverse group of learners? A part of such an effort must be the development of strategies that facilitate self-determination in career choice and employment outcomes. Although self-determination is a topic of discussion, we, as educators, need to constantly build in program components that directly teach and promote self-determination skills. Additional research is needed to help educators identify effective strategies.

Additionally, long-term support for individuals with disabilities in community jobs needs further investigation. Identifying creative ways of providing funding for long-term support might give service providers alternatives to the currently used supported employment models. Looking within the job site for ways to provide support might result in productive strategies that are more cost effective. Finally, further investigation of the use natural supports in employment sites also would be useful.

In summary, the development and implementation of a longitudinal career development and vocational training model is necessary to produce productive post-school employment outcomes. However, many aspects of a longitudinal model are in need of research. As the field of education for individuals with disabilities and the practices in general education evolve, we must constantly be open to new ideas and change, but at the same time we must be producing empirical evidence supporting that change.

Discussion Questions

1. How can a teacher promote and encourage self-determination skills in students who participate in a longitudinal vocational program?
2. How can school personnel address a lack of motivation by students (or their families) to obtain employment after finishing school or attitudes that the student's disability prevents viable employment?
3. Who is responsible for following up on graduates participating in vocational programs? What information should be collected? When should it be collected? How should the information be collected? How should the information be used?

Community-Based Activities

1. Identify a pool of different businesses within your local community (e.g., restaurant, government office, hospital, hotel, retail store, health club) and in teams explore the opportunities that exist for work experiences or long-term employment using the practices suggested in the chapter. Conduct an interview with the employer to find out more about the business, observe employees engaged in one or more job types, and evaluate the working environment. After the investigation is completed, compare and contrast your findings with the other teams to acknowledge differences in working climate, job skills, and attitudes.
2. Attend an IEP or ITP meeting for a student who is receiving vocational education services. Identify the preferences expressed by the family and the learner, the concerns and needs that may influence the identification of a work experience site, and the issues related to actual instruction (e.g., assistive technology, transportation, school schedule). Note the discussion, solutions, and persons responsible for implementation. If possible attend meetings of students representing two different ages or disability types and look for differences in how vocational outcomes were addressed.
3. Working collaboratively with local education personnel, create a "site handbook" for a specific work experience site being utilized by the school

program for a student or group of students. Identify what information would be helpful to include within the handbook. Gather the necessary information and materials. Finally, organize and present the information and materials in a user-friendly format that will serve as a helpful tool to the school program.

References

Agran, M., & Morgan, R. L. (1991). Current transition assessment practices. *Research in Developmental Disabilities, 12*, 113-126.

Banks, R., & Renzaglia, A. (1993). Longitudinal vocational programs: A review of current recommended practices for individuals with moderate and severe disabilities. *Journal of Vocational Rehabilitation, 3* (3), 5-16.

Bellamy, G. T., Rhodes, L. E., & Albin, J. M. (1986). Supported employment. In W. Kiernan & J. Stark (Eds.), *Pathways to employment for adults with developmental disabilities* (129-138). Baltimore: Paul H. Brookes.

Bellamy, G. T., Rhodes, L. E., Mank, D. M., & Albin, J. M. (1988). *Supported employment: A community implementation guide*. Baltimore: Paul H. Brookes.

Brolin, D. E. (1995). *Career education: A functional life skills approach*. (3rd ed.). Englewood Cliffs, NJ: Prentice Hall.

Callahan, M. (1991). Common sense and quality: Meaningful employment outcomes for persons with severe physical disabilities. *Journal of Vocational Rehabilitation, 1*(2), 21-28.

Callahan, M. (1992). Job site training and natural supports. In J. Nisbet (Ed.), *Natural supports at home, school, and in the workplace for people with severe disabilities* (257-276). Baltimore: Paul H. Brookes.

Clark, G. M., Carlson, B. C., Fisher, S., Cook, I. D., & D'Alonzo, B. J. (1991). Career development for students with disabilities in elementary schools: A position statement of the Division on Career Development. *Career Development for Exceptional Individuals, 14*, 109-120.

Clark, G. M., & Kolstoe, O. P. (1995). *Career development and transition education for adolescents with disabilities* (2nd ed.). Boston: Allyn & Bacon.

Council for Exceptional Children. (1978). *Position paper on career education*. Reston, VA: Author.

Ferguson, P. M., & Ferguson, D. L., Jeanchild, L., Olson, D., & Lucysyn, J. (1993). Angles of influence: Relationships among families, professionals, and adults with severe disabilities. *Journal of Vocational Rehabilitation, 13*(2), 14-22.

Gajar, A., Goodman, L., & McAfee, J. (1993). *Secondary schools and beyond: Transition of individuals with mild disabilities*. New York: MacMillan Publishing Company.

Hagner, D., & Vander Sande, J. (1998). School-sponsored work experience and vocational instruction. In F. R. Rusch & J. G. Chadsey (Eds.), *Beyond high school: Transition from school to work* (340-366). Belmont, CA: Wadsworth.

Hanley-Maxwell, C., Rusch, F. R., Chadsey-Rusch, J., & Renzaglia, A. (1986). Reported factors contributing to job terminations of individuals with severe disabilities. *Journal of the Association for Persons with Severe Handicaps, 11*, 45-52.

Hosack, K., & Malkmus, D. (1992). Vocational rehabilitation of persons with disabilities: Family inclusion. *Journal of Vocational Rehabilitation, 2*(3), 11-17.

Hutchins, M., & Renzaglia, A. (1990). Developing a longitudinal vocational training program. In F. R. Rusch, (Ed.), *Supported employment: Models, methods, and issues* (365-408). Sycamore, IL: Sycamore Press.

Hutchins, M., Renzaglia, A., Stahlman, J., & Cullen, M. E. (1986). *Project COOP: A cooperative model for the vocational placement of persons with severe handicaps in community industries and businesses*. Charlottesville, VA: University of Virginia.

McCarthy, P., Everson, J., Moon, M. S., & Barcus, J. M. (1985). School to work transition for youth with severe disabilities. In J. Everson, J. Kregel, M. S. Moon, and J. M. Barcus (Eds.), *Strategies for vocational preparation of learners with severe disabilities*. Richmond, VA: Virginia Commonwealth University.

Menchetti, B. M., & Flynn, C. C. (1990). Vocational evaluation. In F. Rusch (Ed.), *Supported employment: Models, methods, and issues* (111-130). Sycamore, IL: Sycamore Press.

Menchetti, B. M., & Piland, V. C. (1998). The personal career plan: A person-centered approach to vocational evaluation and career planning. In F. R. Rusch & J. G. Chadsey (Eds.), *Beyond high school: Transition from school to work* (319-339). Belmont, CA: Wadsworth.

Moon, S., Goodall, P., Barcus, M., & Brooke V. (1985). *The supported work model of competitive employment for citizens with severe handicaps: A guide for job trainers*. Richmond, VA: Virginia Commonwealth University.

Moon, M. S., Inge, K., Wehman, P., Brooke, V., & Barcus, J. M. (1990). *Helping persons with severe mental retardation get employed and stay employed.* Baltimore: Paul H. Brookes.

Moore, S., Agran, M., & McSweyn, C. (1990). Career education: Are we starting early enough? *Career Development for Exceptional Individuals, 13*, 124-134.

Nietupski, J., Verstegen, D., & Hamre-Nietupski, S. (1992). Incorporating sales and business principles into job development for supported employment. *Education and Training in Mental Retardation, 27*, 207-218.

Nisbet, J. (Ed.) (1992). *Natural supports at home, school and in the workplace for people with severe disabilities.* Baltimore: Paul H. Brookes.

Parent, W. S., Sherron, P., Stallard, D., & Booth, M. (1993). Job development and placement. *Journal of Vocational Rehabilitation, 3*(3), 17-26.

Parker, R. M., & Schaller, J. L. (1996). Issues in vocational assessment and disability. In E. M. Szymanski & R. M. Parker (Eds.), *Work and disability: Issues and strategies in career development and job placement* (127-164). Austin, TX: Pro-Ed.

Patterson, J. B. (1996). Occupational and labor market information and analysis. In E. M. Szymanski & R. M. Parker (Eds.), *Work and disability: Issues and strategies in career development and job placement* (209-254). Austin, TX: Pro-Ed.

Peterson, M. (1986). Work and performance samples for vocational assessment of special learners: A critical review. *Career Development for Exceptional Individuals, 9*, 69-76.

Renzaglia, A., Hutchins, M., & Banks, R. (1995). *A longitudinal model for facilitating transition from school to work for youth with moderate and severe disabilities,* unpublished manuscript.

Renzaglia, A., Hutchins, M., Koterba-Buss, L., & Strauss, M. (1994). *Acquiring meaningful employment for persons with severe multiple disabilities.* Unpublished manuscript, University of Illinois at Urbana-Champaign.

Rusch, F. R., & Chadsey, J. G. (1998). *Beyond high school: Transition from school to work.* Belmont, CA: Wadsworth.

Rusch, F. R., & Mithaug, D. (1980). *Vocational training for mentally retarded adults: A behavior analytic approach.* Champaign, IL: Research Press.

Sowers, J., & Powers, L. (1989). Preparing learners with cerebral palsy and mental retardation for the transition form school to community-based employment. *Career Development for Exceptional Individuals, 12*, 25-35.

Turnbull, A. P. (1988). The challenge of providing comprehensive supports to families. *Education and Training in Mental Retardation, 23*, 261-272.

Ward, M. (1993). Self-determination. In P. Wehman (Ed.), *ADA and the social mandate for change* (6-10). Baltimore: Paul H. Brookes.

Wehman, P. (1981). *Competitive employment: New horizons for severely disabled individuals.* Baltimore: Paul H. Brookes.

Wehman, P. (1993). From the editor. *Journal of Vocational Rehabilitation, 3*(2), 1-3.

Wehman, P., Wood, W., Everson, J., Goodwyn, R., & Conley, S. (1988). *Vocational education for multihandicapped youth with cerebral palsy.* Baltimore: Paul H. Brookes.

Wehmeyer, M., & Davis, S. (1995). Family and community resources. In D. E. Brolin (Ed.), *Career education: A functional life skills approach* (3rd ed.; 91-116). Englewood Cliffs, NJ: Prentice Hall.

Winking, D. L., O'Reilly, B., & Moon, M. S. (1993). Preference: The missing link n the job match process for individuals without functional communication skills. *Journal of Vocational Rehabilitation, 3*(3), 27-42.

Yancey, G. (1993). Importance of families in transition form school to adult life. *Journal of Vocational Rehabilitation, 3*(2), 5-8.

Sample Form: Work Performance Summary

Student Name:

Circle vocational phase student is in: Early Work Sampling   Focused Work Experience

1) Basic information:
Work Site: *Job Type(s) or Position(s):*

Dates of Experience: *Total Daily Work Time:*   *Number of Days /Week:*

Reinforcement Utilized and its Effectiveness:

2) Student preference information
Circle how much the student seemed to enjoy working at the site:
   strongly disliked   disliked   neutral   liked   strongly liked

Do you feel the student would be likely to choose employment at this site?
         yes   maybe   no

What is the student's family's acceptance of the job experience?
   strongly disliked   disliked   neutral   liked   strongly liked

Comments related to student and/or family preference for job type:

3) Job tasks experienced

Task   *Did student seem to like task?*   *Briefly describe adaptations needed (if any)*
a)
b)
c)
d)
e)
f)
g)

4) Community mobility training (pedestrian skills, bus skills, locating work site skills, etc.)
Skill Trained   *Description of Performance*
a)
b)
c)

5) Work position/general mobility
Work position was (circle one): mostly seated   mostly standing   combination of two

Did work position seem to effect performance?
yes   no
If so, briefly describe how:

How well did the student do in moving around the work site while working?
  very poorly   fair, occasional   not applicable   good   excellent,
  many problems   daily problems   few problems   no problems

Implications for training:

6) *Physical demands, gross and fine motor*
How well did the student handle the gross motor and stamina demands at the work site?
  very poorly   fair, occasional   not applicable   good   excellent
  many problems   daily problems   few problems   no problems

Implications for training:

How well did the student handle the fine motor demands at the work site?
  very poorly   fair, occasional   not applicable   good   excellent,
  many problems   daily problems   few problems   no problems

Implications for training:

7) *Functional academic demands*
How well did the student handle the functional academic demands that were involved in task completion at the placement site? Consider such functional academic skills as the reading or matching of words, simple adding or counting that was required, and so on. Circle the most appropriate rating, then briefly describe what the functional academic demands were, and the implications of student performance in relation to these demands for future training.
  very poorly   fair, occasional   not applicable   good   excellent
  many problems   daily problems   few problems   no problems

Description of functional academic demands and implications for training:

8) *Length of work tasks and daily routine variability*
Briefly describe the length of each work task in number of minutes to complete a unit of work.

Was there any variability to daily work routine?
yes   no

If so, how did the student handle changes?

9) <u>Work production rate</u>
Task   **Production rate (% of co-worker rates – estimate if necessary)**
a)
b)
c)
d)
e)
f)
g)

Did the student have difficulty working continuously (without pausing frequently for no reason)?
yes   no

If so, please describe.

Implications of student's work production rate for future training:

10) <u>Work skills acquisition</u> *(% of steps achieved independently)*
Work task   *Highest Performance*   *Average Performance*   *Range*
a)
b)
c)
d)
e)
f)
g)

Implications of work skill acquisition for future training:

If problem solving was involved in task performance, describe student's problem solving abilities demonstrated at this site:

11) <u>Social performance and communication</u>
List areas of strength and areas in need of improvement in social performance and communication at work. This can include any aspect of social behavior or communication (eye contact, asking for help when needed, understandability of speech, greeting staff and ability to "chat" with co-workers and site staff, and so on).

<u>Areas of strength</u>	<u>Priority areas in need of improvement</u>
a)	a)
b)	b)
c)	c)
d)	d)
e)	e)

Describe characteristics of site staff that the student seemed to prefer most (sex, age, education, ethnicity):

Implications of student's present social and communication skills for future training:

12) <u>Independence</u>
Did the student ever work without the immediate presence of a job coach (for any amount of time)?
yes   no

If so, rate the overall quality of work for the student when working independently (circle one):

poor, much worse than when supervised	fair, but always some daily problems	n/a	good, only occasional problems (not daily)	excellent, no problems

Implication for future training:

13) <u>Supervisory contact</u>
Rate how the student responded to supervision, job coach <u>or</u> site staff direction, and correction:

| poor, much worse than when supervised | fair, but always some daily problems | n/a | good, only occasional problems (not daily) | excellent, no problems |

Describe student's inappropriate reactions (if any):

Implications of student's ability to accept corrections/directions for instruction:

14) <u>Comfort factors</u>
Did the site have any problems related to lack of space, lighting, visual or noise distraction, temperature, or other sensory factor (odor, dust, etc.)?
yes   no

If so, what was the problem:

Describe how student handled these problems in terms of distractibility or other behaviors that interfered with their work in any way:

15) <u>Equipment/tool use</u>
Describe any equipment/tool used and relate how well student was able to learn to use them in the course of the work experience:

Description of competence achieved:

Implications for further training:

16) <u>Overall summary/additional comments related to work experience placement</u>

Chapter 5
Adult Employment

Teresa Grossi, Larry Schaaf,
Marcia Steigerwald, and David Mank
Indiana University, Indiana Institute on Disability and Community

Key Questions
1. What are the advantages for schools to collaborate with adult agencies during the transition process?
2. What do One-Stop Centers and vocational rehabilitation services offer for students transitioning to employment?
3. How do other adult agencies assist in the transition and employment process?
4. Regardless of the support need, what are the values for providing employment services to individuals with disabilities?
5. What activities are required to develop appropriate employment options?
6. Why is approaching each job site from a perspective of "typicalness" important?
7. How can employment specialists or job developers increase their success in finding sustainable jobs?
8. What is the role of the employment specialist during the job site training and support phase?
9. What must be considered during the follow-along phase?
10. What are the additional unique issues students with disabilities confront as they transition from school to adult life?

As a society we place a great deal of value on work. Work often generates the respect of others and provides self-respect and satisfaction for the individual worker. Work also provides access to social relationships, the power of purchasing goods and wares, and resources to participate in leisure and recreational activities. Where we live, how well we take advantage of leisure, and the level of our wages and benefits often determine our recreational activities. The process of transition from school to adult life should produce outcomes for the student that impact employment, community living, and community participation. Employment outcomes are one of the key components of transition planning.

The importance of transition planning and preparing students for the world of work becomes all too evident when comparing the employment gap between individuals with and without disabilities. In a 1998 survey of Americans with disabilities conducted by Louis Harris and Associates, the employment gap appeared to be widening. Among adults with disabilities of working age (eighteen to sixty-four), three out of ten (29%) work full or part-time, compared to eight out of ten (79%) of those without disabilities. Of those with disabilities age sixteen to sixty-four who are not employed, seven out of ten (72%) say they would prefer working. Over 80% of youths with disabilities required additional support, such as case management to achieve their employment, continuing education, and independent living goals (US Department of Education, 1999).

When youth with disabilities leave the public school system, their entitlement to special education and related services ends and they enter a world of services and supports based upon eligibility. Students and their families are faced with many questions to identify and obtain training and services needed for employment. All too often, however, they have no idea where to begin their search for postsecondary options and services. What type of employment training is available? What if additional supports are needed to secure a job? What job best fits my interests and capabilities? These and other questions need to be addressed throughout the transition process and prior to the student graduating.

It is true that as students transition from an entitlement program of public education to an eligibility requirement system of adult service programs, the issues become more complex and require a great deal of planning. To assist students and family members in the transition process, school personnel must be knowledgeable of the policies, procedures, services, and supports of community agencies available in their own local community and state. Although employment is only one component of transition planning—where students live, what they do for fun, who they socialize with, and what type of community connections they need are other important areas that must be addressed during the transition process. However, the focus of this chapter is on transitioning from school to work.

Key Question #1: What are the advantages for schools to collaborate with adult agencies during the transition process?

Numerous schools across the country have realized they cannot promote the transition of youth with disabilities to adulthood without the support of community agencies and organizations. The lack of personnel and fiscal resources necessitates collaborative efforts to achieve transition outcomes. Interagency collaborative efforts and, more formally, interagency agreements, are a characteristic of essential practices in transition programs (Certo, Pumpian, Fisher, Storey, & Smalley, 1997; Kohler, DeStefano, Wermuth, Grayson, & McGinity, 1994).

The importance of state and local collaborative and coordination efforts to support transition-age youth was recognized by the federal government in the parallel language and mandates of transition services in the Individuals with Disabilities Education Act (IDEA) amendments of 1990 and 1997 (PL 101-476), and the Rehabilitation Act Amendments of 1992 (PL 102-569). Both of these pieces of landmark legislation clearly establish the expectations that the delivery of transition services is a shared responsibility, with one of the primary partners being vocational rehabilitation programs.

IDEA states that by age fourteen for each student the IEP must include a statement of needed transition services, including, if appropriate, interagency responsibilities or needed linkages. [Section 300.347 (b)(2).] The law goes on to further emphasize shared responsibility for transition services by incorporating a provision: if a participating agency, other than the public agency, fails to provide the transition services described in the IEP in accordance with 301.347(b)(1), the public agency shall reconvene the IEP team to identify alternative strategies to meet the transition objective for the student set out in the IEP. The law goes on to state: Nothing in this part relieves any participating agency, including a state vocational rehabilitation agency, of the responsibility to provide or pay for transition services that the agency would otherwise provide to students with disabilities who meet the eligibility criteria of that agency. [Section 300.348 (a)(b).]

The Rehabilitation Act of 1992 and the 1998 Amendments mirror IDEA's definition of transition services, adding however that transition services must promote or facilitate the achievement of the employment outcomes identified in the student's individual plan for employment. [Section 7 (36 and 12) and 103 (a) (15).]

Sharing the responsibility requires an interdependent relationship in which all stakeholders acknowledge their contributions working together in the transition process to produce positive outcomes. Planning occurs at the state, local, and individual levels. At the state and local levels, a collaborative interagency team is defined as a group of individuals who represent multiple organizations and agencies who come together to address a common need and pursue a common goal (Everson & Guillory, 1998). Often at the state level, interagency agreements or "memoranda of understanding" are developed to focus on transition policies and procedures with the intention of assisting the local level planning team in implementing the provision of cooperative services. These partnerships are intended to enhance the quality of the transition planning process and the specific transition skills needed by students as they enter the adult world.

Students and Family Members as Partners

The principal partner in the transition and employment process is the student, along with family members. Like most other people, during this time families with young adults with disabilities often are absorbed with their daily household activities: working, running children to sporting and recreational activities, dealing with students' current school activities, and "just getting through the day."

Often schools and adult agencies struggle with a number of questions such as when to provide the adult agencies with information and how much information to share. Some families say the schools should begin repeatedly providing the information in elementary school through high school; other families say they will be able to understand the information only when it directly relates to them, so providing the information during high school is sufficient. Nevertheless, this is an overwhelming time for students and families. They are beginning to learn new and multiple systems (e.g., school, vocational rehabilitation, developmental disabilities, mental health, Social Security Administration), a new language (e.g., teacher, Individual Education Program (IEP), vocational rehabilitation counselor, employment specialist/job coach, Individual Plan for Employment (IPE), and new people. Schools have attempted a variety of information sharing methods to ensure that students and families understand the roles and responsibilities of community adult agencies, how the agency can support them in the employment process, the extent of the support, and the eligibility requirements for each agency.

Some examples of information sharing include:

- Career Days: students are provided a day to interact with employers and trade associations about occupations and careers.
- Transition "Fairs": many schools conduct a Transition "Fair" where school, agency, and higher education personnel come together to share their various programs, services, and supports for students and family members. This may take place during the school hours or in the evening.
- Written transition materials at the IEP conferences: many school districts distribute transition material during the IEP conferences prior to a child reaching the age of fourteen. It includes what to expect during the transition process and which adult agencies can support the students as they transition into adult life. School districts invite vocational rehabilitation counselors and other adult agency representatives to the IEP conferences within the last two years of school.
- Additional written materials: districts also may distribute a transition guide or handbook with local resource information and answers to frequently asked questions. This can help guide the student and families through the transition process.
- Local parent mentors: often there is a network of local parents familiar with the transition process that can support other families in their transition planning and maneuvering the adult systems. State parent training networks are often a good resource for such contacts.
- Websites: local, state, and national websites can assist students, family members, and school personnel in locating transition information. Some national websites that may be helpful include: National Transition Alliance: www. dssc.org/nta; transition services in the IEP: www.nichcy.org; Council for Exceptional Children: www.cec.sped.org; and supported employment: www.apse.org.

Key Question #2: What do One-Stop Centers and vocational rehabilitation services offer for students transitioning to employment?
Workforce Investment Act of 1998

One of the key elements of successful collaborative efforts is having a clear understanding of each of the agencies' roles and responsibilities. As stated previously, one of the primary partners in the transition from school to work is vocational rehabilitation. Vocational rehabilitation within each state has its own structure with support from the federal government. In 1998 the Rehabilitation Act was merged with other employment and training programs to create the Workforce Investment Act (WIA) of 1998 (PL 105-220) to consolidate employment and training services for all individuals. This single comprehensive initiative was designed to offer a single point of entry for all individuals who want to become employed.

One of main elements of the act was the expansion of One-Stop Centers, where all job seekers can come to one place to access the various employment and training services. For people with disabilities, this provides an opportunity to receive services alongside of people without disabilities. The WIA of 1998 developed several principles that affect services:

- Universal Access—any individual should be able to go into a One-Stop Center and receive core services to assist in job search and career exploration. Core services are available at no cost. Examples of core services include access to job banks, Internet access, job search skills training, interview techniques workshops, referral and determination of eligibility for additional services.

- Streamlining services—employment and training programs for all people should be brought together and easily accessible via One-Stop Centers.
- Increased accountability—the evaluation of the effectiveness of the One-Stop system is based on how many people get jobs and customer satisfaction.
- Empowering individuals—providing customers with information about services in order to make more of an informed choice and have more control of their services.
- State and local flexibility—each local One-Stop system is set up in ways to respond to the needs of their local communities.

The intention of WIA is based upon the premise of inclusion. This legislation has moved away from a disability-focused employment system or approach to a more generic approach.

Vocational Rehabilitation

Vocational rehabilitation programs assist people with disabilities to obtain essential services to pursue meaningful careers and secure gainful employment consistent with their abilities and capabilities. Most states have separate vocational rehabilitation services for individuals with visual impairments and those with other disabilities (physical, sensory, or mental impairments). Although each state will have specific procedures and eligibility processes to follow, services provided through vocational rehabilitation programs can include but are not limited to:

- an assessment to determine eligibility and vocational rehabilitation needs
- counseling and guidance, including information to assist in making an informed choice
- referral and other services to secure needed services from other agencies
- job-related services including job placement assistance and job retention services, on-the-job services, including personal assistance, supported employment services and rehabilitation technology
- vocational and other training services
- diagnosis and treatment of physical and mental impairments, including corrective surgery or therapeutic treatment necessary to correct or modify a condition that is considered an impediment to employment
- interpreter services for individuals who are deaf or hard of hearing and orientation and mobility services for individuals who are blind
- transition services for students with disabilities to help make the transition from school to work
- specific post-employment services necessary to assist an individual to retain, regain, or advance in employment

One-Stop Centers

Anyone who is searching for a job or needs to acquire skills to obtain a job can access One-Stop systems. They are designed to bring together employment and training services to meet the needs of all job seekers, including people with disabilities. Typically, three types or levels of services are available through the One-Stop systems—core services, intensive services, and training services. Access to each level depends on the needs of the individual.

Core services include work exploration, job search skills training, interviewing techniques workshops, resume development, and referral to an employer with a position available. Intensive services are for individuals who are unable to obtain employment through using the core services. These services require individuals to meet an income eligibility criteria to receive services for free; other individuals may be required to pay for the services.

Intensive services may target specific groups such as youth, people with disabilities, or people with limited income. They include such services as comprehensive assessments of skills, development of an individual employment or career plan, intensive career counseling, computer workshops, one-to-one assistance for resume development, and case management.

When individuals do not become successfully employed through the use of the core and intensive services, they may be referred for training services. Often the type of training varies based upon the local community and local economy. However most services include occupational skills training, on-the-job training, job readiness, adult education, and customized training for an employer.

Key Question #3: How do other adult agencies assist in the transition and employment process?

There are a number of additional service providers in states and local communities to assist transition-age youth in gaining access to employment. Some agencies provide direct employment services; others provide financial resources or indirect supports. Table 1 summarizes other key agencies involved in transition from school to employment.

Key Question #4: Regardless of the support need, what are the values for providing employment services to individuals with disabilities?

Many students with disabilities leave high school and directly enter the labor market or competitive employment. Competitive employment is defined as compensation at or above minimum wage for work performed on a full- or part-time basis. The level of support needed by students often determines their eligibility for services available by state and local agencies. For students with minimal support needs, family support or time-limited support by vocational rehabilitation or other community agencies often is provided in job seeking, job placement, and possibly job site training services and supports.

Students with more intensive support needs often require multiple services from community agencies to successfully access and participate in employment, community living, and other facets of adult life. Sheltered workshops are licensed by the US Department of Labor to pay less than minimum wage on a piece-rate basis for contractual work obtained from local businesses and industries. Sheltered workshops are facilities where a large number of people with disabilities, usually 30-200, perform vocational tasks in a setting where they typically do not interact with workers without disabilities other than their paid support. Adult day activities centers, day treatment centers, or work activities centers are terms used for programs classified as non-vocational that focus primarily on

Table I
Major Adult Service Programs and Services for Employment

EMPLOYMENT SERVICES
Vocational Rehabilitation
> Assists eligible people with disabilities to obtain services to help them to develop, restore, or preserve their ability to work. Competitive employment, including supported employment, in the community is considered the option of choice for all workers. Federally and state funded.

State Mental Health and Mental Retardation/Developmental Disabilities Agencies
> Assist individuals with long term funding of supported employment. Services such as case management, follow-along services, and community connections are provided.

Workforce Development Centers
> Assist people seeking to advance to higher paying positions within their current occupations, or helps those who must get additional training to keep pace with their current jobs. Also assist displaced workers whose former occupation has become obsolete and need to be retrained to enter a new field. Federally and state funded.

Work Opportunities Tax Credit
> Available on an elective basis for employers hiring individuals from one or more of several targeted groups, including vocational rehabilitation referrals, qualified summer youth employees, high-risk youth, and qualified food stamp recipients. Credit generally equal to 35% of qualified wages.

SOCIAL SECURITY AND HEALTH CARE SERVICES
Social Security Disability Insurance (SSDI)
> Provides disability insurance in the form of monthly payments to individuals with disabilities who have a work history and thus have paid into the Social Security system. Minors or children with disabilities are also eligible. Does not require a financial needs test.

Social Security Income (SSI)
> Provides monthly cash assistance to individuals who are needy, elderly, or have disabilities and who have little or no work history. Requires a financial needs test.

Medicaid
> Hospital and health care insurance for eligible elderly persons and persons with disabilities. Federally regulated and state administered by the Social Security Act, as amended. Typically accompanies SSI benefits.

Medicare
> Hospital and health care insurance for eligible elderly persons and persons with disabilities. Federally regulated and state administered. Typically accompanies SSDI benefits.

COMMUNITY LIVING AND SUPPORT SERVICES
Housing and Urban Development Programs
> Federally administered and state-authorized housing assistance programs that provide low cost loans (Section 202) to finance construction or rehabilitation of residential facilities for persons who are elderly or who have disabilities. Section 8 provides for rental aid to low-income families and individuals and to persons with disabilities.

Supported Living Providers
> Assist adults who have developmental disabilities who require a range of support needs in order to live in their own homes. Usually accommodate between one to three people per home setting.

Group Home Providers
> Provides services to persons of all ages with developmental disabilities or mental illness. Twenty-four hour supervision is provided by paid staff in a structured, homelike setting, which is often a single-family dwelling. Group homes generally house between five and eight individuals.

Independent Living Centers
> Independent living assistance for employment, housing, personal attendant registers, legal assistance, accessibility consultations, person counseling, and ADA consultations. State and local funded and locally administered.

Food Stamps
> Provides stamps that may be exchanged for food at grocery stores. Individuals and families are eligible depending on income and financial needs. Federally funded through the Department of Agriculture and state and locally administered by social service agencies.

Public Health Services
> Health care and treatment for persons not covered by health insurance. State funded and locally administered.

Adapted from Sitlington, P., Clark, G. M., & Kolstoe, O. P. (2000).
Transition education and services for adolescents with disabilities. Boston: Allyn & Bacon

daily living and adaptive skills training. Many individuals who are assigned to these facilities are viewed as "unemployable" for both sheltered and community work.

Facility-based proponents often operate on a "readiness principle." People with disabilities are viewed as "not ready" for community employment until they have learned sufficient work and social skills. Placing people in isolated, sheltered settings rarely prepares them for the ever-changing expectations and demands of the real work world. Sadly, facility-based services, including sheltered employment and non-work services, continue to be the largest services, representing 61% of the total of people with more intensive service needs (Butterworth, et al., 1999).

Supported employment is a service option that originated in the early 1980s because of the dissatisfaction with segregated vocational options available such as day activity services, work activity centers, and sheltered workshops. Supported employment is based upon the belief that all people, regardless of the severity of their disability, can perform meaningful work, if given the proper supports. People with disabilities who had not been successfully employed are now working and contributing to society. Since inception of supported employment, the number of individuals with disabilities participating the US is well over 140,000 (Wehman, Revell, & Kregel, 1997).

The 1992 and 1998 Rehabilitation Act Amendments (PL 102-569), defines supported employment as follows:

(i) competitive work in an integrated work setting, or employment in integrated work settings in which individuals are working toward competitive employment, consistent with the strengths, resources, priorities, concerns, abilities, capabilities, interests, and informed choice of the individuals with ongoing support services for individuals with the most significant disabilities

> *(A) for whom competitive employment has not traditionally occurred; or for whom competitive employment has been interrupted or intermittent as a result of a significant disability; and*

> *(B) who, because of the nature and severity of their disability, need intensive supported employment services ... and extended services ... to perform such work, and*

(ii) transitional employment with a series of temporary job placements in competitive work in integrated settings with ongoing support services for individuals with the most significant disabilities due to mental illness. (706[18][A & B]).

The key terms used in supported employment are real, meaningful work, in integrated settings with ongoing supports. In transitional employment, the provision of ongoing support services must include continuing sequential job placements until job permanency is achieved. Regardless of the support need, all individuals deserve the right to be treated with respect and dignity and as equal partners in the employment process. Table 2 lists the values that should guide the employment process.

Table 2
Employment Services Delivery Values

Values	Values Clarification
Careers	People have the opportunity and support to advance to other employment opportunities, which may provided new or greater responsibilities, compensation, and challenge.
Choice	There are sufficient options related to each individual's interest and desires in life in order to exercise control and autonomy over his or her life's direction. The choices made by an individual are the result of being fully informed through direct personal experience or considering information on potential alternatives.
Control	A concept used to refer to an individual's ability to access employment services and to freely act upon his or her choices and decision without fear of reprisal.
Competence	Individuals are provided opportunities to develop skills of interest and use in their lives by discovering and expressing gifts and capacities.
Community Presence	Individuals have the opportunity to actively participate in all their chosen pursuits of life.
Continuous Quality	Service providers must listen and respond to the wishes and desires of individuals with disabilities to determine the agency's mission, goals, and objectives. People with disabilities must participate in developing and evaluating services.
Person-Centered	Seeks to support the contributions of each person in his or her planning team from the local community by building a support group around the individual.
Social Inclusion	People have access to diverse individuals in social contexts in order to build friendships, working relationships, and networks of individuals who go to shared places, have similar interests, or experience other commonalties.

Adapted from: Brooke, Inge, Armstrong, and Wehman, 1997;
DiLeo, MacDonald and Killam, The Association for Persons in Supported Employment, 1998

The Role of the Employment Specialist

An employment specialist (also known as job coach, job developer, employment consultant, job trainer) is someone responsible for all or a part of the services and supports provided throughout the employment process. Adult service providers may use either a generalist approach or a specialist approach to providing employment services. Within the "specialist" approach, each of the job tasks, i.e., job development, job site training and supports, and follow-along, are separated and one person is responsible for each job task/duty. In the "generalist" approach, one person is responsible for job development, job site training and support, and follow-along. Each employment specialist within an agency has his or her own caseload, and provides all or most of the services for each individual they are assigned.

Regardless of the approach used, a major role of the employment specialist is to facilitate the collaborative consultation process where each party has knowledge and plays an active role in the planning, implementation, and evaluation of the employment process (Grossi, Regan, & Regan, 1998). The role of the employment specialist is often multifaceted and can include anything related to the individual employment situation and to ensure success. This role involves working collaboratively with all stakeholders—individuals with disabilities, family members, employers or co-workers, and funding agencies. An employment specialist can be a coordinator or facilitator of services and supports or directly provide the services or supports.

Key Question #5: What activities are required to develop appropriate employment options?

There are five major components to the employment process:
1. vocational or customer profile
2. developing natural supports
3. career or job development
4. employment match
5. job site training and supports
6. follow-along or long-term supports

The specific activities that need to be conducted within each of the components will vary depending on the support needs of the individual.

Window to the World
Dustin: From School to Work

Dustin is an eighteen-year-old senior who will be graduating in the next few months. During the last two years, Dustin has been attending vocational education classes in auto mechanics and has worked various part-time jobs through the work-study program. Dustin really enjoys auto mechanics class. However, his severe learning disability really comes through in reading and math. In developing a vocational profile, the transition coordinator gathered information from Dustin, his family, teachers, and current and past employers.

The vocational profile indicated a number of strengths and support needs for Dustin. Dustin is a pleasant young man who likes to work with his hands. His social interactions skills are very appropriate and he enjoys being around people. Dustin has had an interest in cars since a young age. He has struggled with the academic requirements of auto mechanics class, but did fairly well in the applied section of the course. One of Dustin's transition goals is to work with cars or trucks.

To support Dustin's goal, the transition coordinator referred him to vocational rehabilitation during his junior year. Vocational rehabilitation assisted Dustin in a number of ways, including further vocational assessment in his employment goal, which included situational assessments or "internships" at various employment settings that related to cars or trucks. Dustin applied for a position like most other people, and completed a job application

and an interview. Because of the relationships the transition coordinator and the vocational rehabilitation counselor had with numerous employers, Dustin obtained a part-time job during his final year of educational services at a local car dealership as an auto mechanic technician. Dustin changes oils, works on batteries, fixes tires, and assists the auto mechanic in repairing cars.

Support is provided to and his employer on an as-needed basis. When he graduates, Dustin will work full-time with company benefits. Vocational rehabilitation will continue to support Dustin for at least three to six months after graduation. Providing Dustin with numerous experiences, gathering good assessment data, and schools and agencies working collaboratively can result in good transition outcomes.

Vocational or Customer Profile

The term "customer" represents a change in our thinking about how professionals provide services and supports to people with disabilities. Employment services need to be developed, marketed, and delivered based upon the needs of the customer rather than professionals or the service system (Brooke, Inge, Armstrong, & Wehman, 1997). A customer or vocational profile (Brooke, et al., 1997, Mcloughlin, Garner, & Callahan, 1987) is a planning tool that provides a "snapshot" of the individual that includes his or her strengths, interests, needs, and expected employment outcomes.

The most effective means of gathering the profile information is by spending time with the person and those who know him or her best. Family members, relatives, neighbors, caregivers, teachers, friends, and previous employers all can provide valuable information to help the individual with a disability establish a vision for his or her employment outcome. Additionally, the profile includes identifying possible business and community supports, conducting situational assessments, identifying support needs, interpreting formal records, assessing technology needs, and overall directing the job development activities.

The information gathered during paid and nonpaid work experiences during high school will be beneficial during the profiling process. Information such as aspects of the experience that were favorable, types of environment that match the needs of the individual (e.g., noisy vs. quiet, small vs. large, busy vs. slow-paced), level of supervision, work performance (quality and quantity), appearance, social interactions, initiative, strength, endurance, communication, and attention to task.

Developing Natural Supports

One of the main roles of the employment specialist is to facilitate the natural or typical supports already existing in the workplace that are available to all employees. Natural supports or workplace supports refer to assistance, resources, interactions, and relationships that occur in the workplace without being artificially contrived or paying for the service or support. Natural supports in the workplace may include but are not limited to such things as co-workers teaching the new employee the job, co-workers redirecting the worker or reminding the employee of a task or to take a break, orientation training, employee assistance programs, or co-workers assisting the new employee to meet other co-workers.

Key Question #6: Why is approaching each job site from a perspective of "typicalness" important?

Mank and his colleagues conducted a series of studies investigating natural supports or "typicalness" and the features of employment and outcomes for employees with developmental disabilities (Mank, Cioffi, & Yovanoff, 1997a, 1997b, 1998, 1999), mental illness (Banks, Charleston, Grossi, & Mank, 2001; Banks, Grossi, & Mank, 2000), and brain injury (Grossi, Jenaro Rio, Banks, & Mank, 2000). The focus of these studies was to determine how "typical" the employee's work conditions and features of employment were when compared to other employees without disabilities in the same work setting.

Based on the results of these studies, there are a number of implications for employment specialists when providing employment services. Highlights from the studies suggest that employees with disabilities who are better integrated work more hours and have higher hourly and monthly wages. Additionally, employees with disabilities are more likely to be well integrated in the workplace and earn more if the job acquisition process (e.g., recruitment, application, and interviewing), compensation package (e.g., work schedule, hours of work, hourly pay, company benefits), work roles (e.g., similarity in work tasks), and initial orientation and training (e.g., initial job training activities) are more typical when compared to employees without disabilities in the same workplace. Therefore, the more typical the employment features of individuals in supported employment, the higher the wages and social outcomes that can be expected.

The concept of approaching each job site from a "typicalness" implies that the employment specialist must maximize the use of existing employer supports and conditions already present in the workplace to allow workers with disabilities to function in a manner typical to other employees in the company. The approach to using "typicalness" must begin at the onset of the employment process to enhance natural supports.

Job Development

The primary purpose of job development is to assist the job seeker with a disability to find a job that matches his or her preferences, interests, and abilities identified during the vocational profile or person-centered planning process. The job seeker, family members, friends, teachers, vocational rehabilitation counselor, adult agency representatives, and the employment specialist work collaboratively to conduct the job development activities. Job information is identified to focus the job development activities, such as the type of job to pursue, type of business, location, hours, transportation needs, and so forth. All stakeholders take responsibility for the job development activities using personal connections, cold calls, and various marketing approaches. For example, a family member may have a personal contact at a local office complex where the student is interested in pursuing a job as an office assistant doing filing, mailings, copying, sorting, and general office duties.

The job seeker must actively participate and direct the job development activities and process. The student can participate in a variety of ways in the job development process, including creating a resume, asking family and friends for job leads, calling and working with the employment specialist on job leads, completing job applications, and calling on employers.

Key Question #7: How can employment specialists or job developers increase their success for finding sustainable jobs?

In order to increase the business network and reach potential employers, with the ultimate goal of securing a job of choice for the job seeker, employment specialists market both their organization and assist the job seeker to market him- or herself. The employment specialist should have a thorough knowledge of the business community and establish a strong business network through labor market screening activities (Nietupski, Verstegen, & Petty, 1995). To better meet the needs of the job seeker and the employer, it is imperative that the employment specialist know the job seeker well before beginning the job development activities. The employment specialist can increase their success in finding jobs by:

- knowing the job seeker and their interests and needs
- knowing the needs of the employers
- understanding the labor market trends (growth and declines)
- understand business approaches
- understanding disability-related legislation such as the Americans with Disabilities Act (ADA), and community perception and experience with inclusion and supported employment
- networking with the job seeker's family, friends and their own connections
- conducting a thorough job analysis to understand the workplace culture and employment features
- understanding the use of assistive technology in the workplace
- developing business partnerships
- using promotional tools such as brochures, business cards, and advertisement.
- approaching job development in a businesslike manner

In a recent study to determine employer's preferences on job development strategies, Owen-Johnson & Hanley-Maxwell (1999) found employers prefer to receive marketing information on supported employment through professional associations (e.g., local/national human resource association). When employers had previous experience or knowledge of supported employment, the preferred job development method was governmental agencies such as local supported employment providers. (For more information on specific job development strategies see Brooke, et al., 1997; Mcloughlin, Garner, and Callahan, 1987; and Hagner & DiLeo, 1993).

Window to the World
Beth: Stressing Typicalness at a Worksite

Beth just secured a job at a local bookbindery. The job matches many of Beth's strengths and support needs:
- fairly structured work environment where the job duties must be followed as prescribed by the employer
- a steady work pace
- movement throughout the day
- co-workers in the same work area in case redirection is needed
- a moderate noise level

Because of Beth's autism, the employment specialist knows the co-workers will have to understand Beth's needs to better support her. Prior to Beth starting her job, the employment specialist, Mike, observed the job and co-workers at the work site. Mike interacted with the two co-workers in Beth's immediate work area asking questions about the job and sharing some of Beth's needs.

In a very positive and informal manner, Mike explained to the co-workers that Beth sometimes engages in stereotypic behaviors, such as finger flicking or hand biting when she is frustrated and can become aggressive if it is interrupted. He requested that if they saw Beth finger flicking or hand biting to ask her if she was frustrated and if they could help her. Mike also shared that Beth responds well with clear expectations and consequences and has some difficulty with social interactions. He also explained she has some difficulty with changes and that preparing her as far in advance as possible of co-worker or routine changes would be helpful.

Although Mike was present at the work site for Beth's first few weeks on the job, he stood back as the co-workers showed Beth around, introducing her to other co-workers and teaching her the job. Mike was ready to step-in when the co-workers requested assistance. Mike partnered with the co-workers throughout the training process, sometimes stepping in and directly teaching and supporting Beth, other times, showing the co-workers how to teach Beth. Mike often had to be a role model in interacting with Beth and showing the co-workers how to reword their questions for Beth to better respond.

Three months later, Mike checks in at the work site at least one a week at the employer's request. During this time, Mike assesses Beth's work performance, both quality and quantity, her social interactions with co-workers, hers and co-workes' satisfaction, and her behaviors. Both the employer and co-workers were surprised and satisfied at how well Beth adjusted in such a short time—an unanticipated accomplishment.

Key Question #8: What is the role of the employment specialist during the job site training and support phase?

The job coach enters the workplace setting with a number of goals:
1. to support the employee with a disability to ensure job success
2. to facilitate social integration
3. to provide the "tools" necessary for the co-workers to support the employee
4. to support co-workers in their efforts in supporting the employee (Grossi, Banks, & Pinniyei, 2001)

The employment specialist must be well prepared and competent to serve two primary roles: a consultant and a technician (Brooke, et al, 1997; Grossi, et al., 2001; Grossi et al, 1998). As a consultant, the employment specialist facilitates the typical supports available in the workplace and offers knowledge and assistance to the employer and co-workers who in turn will support the employee with a disability. For example, if co-workers typically train new employees, then the employment specialist might provide information or teach the co-workers how to support the employee with a disability. The employment specialist may problem-solve with the co-workers, offer suggestions, and demonstrate how to support and instruct the supported employee, and how to encourage social interactions.

The employment specialist will use a number of skills at varying times to facilitate the job site training and supports for supported employees. Critical facilitation skills include communication, listening, observation, negotiating, discovering, and exploring. In order to facilitate co-worker involvement, Mank et al., (1999) suggest the employment specialist should consider the following:

- Co-workers and supervisors who receive information on how to support the employee with a disability should be those in the immediate work area.
- Information should be provided individually or in small groups rather than in a formal, structured training session.
- Information should include specific support needs of the supported employee and the job. For example, how a person learns best or may need occasional redirecting or reminders to complete certain tasks.
- Information is best provided prior to the employee starting the job. This suggests the importance of developing co-worker involvement at the beginning of job placement rather than later.

As a technician, the employment specialist must be competent in the technical skills required to teach the co-workers and the employee with a disability. Situations will arise when the employment specialist will continue to partner with co-workers during the training process, but will directly teach the supported employee. Technical skills include: identifying and implementing appropriate instructional strategies to teach new skills, developing work routines, systematic instructional techniques, compensatory strategies, natural cues, reinforcement strategies, self-management strategies, and data collection procedures. Additionally, the employment specialist must be skillful in fading instructional cues and physically leaving the job site.

Components of the initial training and acquisition phase include:

1. establishing a training schedule and job duty analysis
2. providing a task analysis of the job duties to be instructed
3. establishing an instructional program to includes systematic instructional procedures, reinforcement procedures, and data collection procedures
4. developing a contingency plan, if appropriate

Facilitating job site training and supports requires employment specialists to address several areas to ensure success for the employee and the employer (co-workers). These areas include communicating their role on the job site, providing support unobtrusively, and involving the employee with a disability and co-workers throughout the employment process. Employment specialists also provide initial training and support in understanding the workplace culture, identifying job adaptations and modifications, fading from the worksite, and understanding off-site support needs (see Brooke, et al., 1997; Fussell & Petty, 1998; Grossi, et al., 1998; Mcloughlin, et al.,, 1987; Moon, et al., 1990).

Key Question #9: What must be considered during the follow-along phase?

A key factor that distinguishes supported employment services from other employment services is the provision of follow-along or ongoing supports. Once the employee is performing the work skills to the employer satisfaction, the employment specialist gradually reduces his or her level of support to the employee and co-workers and presence on the job site. For students working upon graduation where the primary supports came from school personnel, this phase may include the transfer of supports from the school to the adult agency. During the follow-along phase, a number of guidelines should be considered:

1. Establish a regular schedule of contact with the employee and employer.
   The employment specialist will establish a regular schedule of contact (e.g., in person, telephone) based on the needs of the employee and employer. Overall work performance, social interactions, and satisfaction should be assessed.
2. Assess the work performance.
   How well the employee is performing and keeping up with company standards is vital for job maintenance. A number of factors can impact the employee's performance, such as not performing all the steps in the task analysis as designed, inefficient use of workspace, distractions, and the speed of performance.
3. Assess job satisfaction from the employee and the employer.
   Regular contact with both the employee with a disability and the employer will determine satisfaction with the work and the performance.
4. Develop a long-term support plan.
   There are a number of factors that can influence the stability of a job. A long-term support plan should include strategies that ensure present and future supports to ensure job success. This comprehensive plan should address areas that may result in a job loss, such as behavior or health needs, preferences, retraining needs for changing job duties, co-workers changing, transportation, family change, or residence change.
5. Expand or monitor natural supports.
   Since the workplace is constantly changing, monitoring the naturally occurring workplace supports to assist the employee in developing social relationships and competency may increase job retention.
6. Facilitate job changes or career advancements.
   Adult employment is more than obtaining a job. It is about identifying and pursuing a career. Assess career interests and goals continuously.
7. Assess social interactions and integration.
   Social integration and interactions in the workplace are as critical to the employee's success as mastering the job duties. Social integration is more than just physical proximity. Employees must be able to "fit in" and participate within the workplace culture.

Customer Satisfaction

Agencies committed to providing quality employment services must continuously assess the satisfaction of their customers, i.e., employees with disabilities, employers, funding agencies, and family members. Information gathered should reflect upon quality and excellence in services and supports. A number of questions should guide services in assessing quality:

- Are the customers satisfied with the services?
- Is the employee with a disability empowered to direct his or her employment process (e.g., selecting service providers, directing and/or participating in decision-making such as the job selection)?

- Is the employee with a disability able to retain the job? For what period of time? Have there been any career advancements?
- Do the supported employment services result in meaningful employment outcomes (e.g., wages, work hours, fringe benefits, physical and social integration)?

Key Question #10: What are the additional unique issue students with disabilities confront as they transition from school to adult life?

As student's transition from school to adult employment, a number of issues can become obstacles to employment or need to be considered to enable a smooth transition. The following are some of the most important issues faced by students and their families leaving school.

Transportation

All communities, large and small, urban and rural, deal with the need to have reliable and dependable transportation to assist people with disabilities in entering the workf orce. Many individuals with disabilities must rely on family members, friends, public transportation or other modes of transportation. Prior to leaving school, students with disabilities depend on family members or schools to transport them to their employment during the school years. Upon graduation, schools are no longer responsible for supporting the transportation needs of the student. Family members often tire of the responsibility shortly thereafter. It is critical that reliable transportation is established prior to leaving school to avoid job loss.

Assistive Technology

Learning to use appropriate assistive technology increases a person's independence, employability, and ability to access community life—recreational, social, and home. The 1994 Reauthorization of the Technology-Related Assistance for Individuals Act (Tech Act) defined assistive technology as *"any item, piece of equipment, or product system, whether acquired commercially off the shelf, modified, or customized, that is used to increase, maintain, or improve functional capabilities of individuals with disabilities."* [20 USC 140(25)].

Whether a student needs low technology devices (i.e., reachers, keyguards) or high technology devices (i.e., power wheelchairs, augmentative communication devices), a number of questions arise for the student and family members as they transition to the world of work. Who will pay for these devices? If schools pay, does the equipment follow the student? If augmentative communication devices are used, has instruction been given to all involved parties on how to program the device and ensure it enhances the user's social interactions? Are the devices functional for the employment setting? It is essential that these and other questions be addressed prior to transitioning to work.

Friendships and Social Relationships

Like most adolescents, students with disabilities are mostly concerned about their friends, dating, and engaging in the same type of activities as most other teenagers. One of the most challenging issues students and family members face as they transition from school to the adult world is the lack of daily contact with their school peers.

According to Asher and Gottman (1981) three conditions exist when friendships are developed. First, two people must have something in common and a shared interest for the friendship to flourish. Second, there must be opportunities for interactions. Most friendships are developed gradually over time with opportunities for spending time together and interacting. Third, the individual must be competent in social skills in order to maintain relationships. To facilitate social interactions and integration in the workplace, the employment specialist should identify potential co-workers who have interest similar to the employee's. The ultimate goal would be for friendships with co-workers to extend outside of the workplace.

Meaningful Day

School consumes most of a student's day. When students graduate, a job should consume most of the day. When students leave school without plans for full-time employment, a number of concerns arise for family members. What will the student do when he or she is not working? If supervision is needed, who will provide the it if the parents work? What activities can a student engage in if part-time employment is the most viable option due to health or other support needs? When questions similar to these are not addressed, families often are forced to pay for assistance or choose less attractive segregated options.

Summary

Adult employment is a critical component of the transition process. Obtaining meaningful employment outcomes will require all partners to share in the responsibility of the transition process. As students leave an entitlement program and enter into an adult system based upon eligibility requirements, students, family members, and adult agencies need to understand each other's roles and responsibilities to obtain positive employment outcomes.

Best Practice Recommendations

1. The individual with a disability drives the employment process and is an active participant throughout the process. The individual's choice, preferences, and desires permeate throughout the process.
2. The employment specialist serves both as a facilitator and a technician to the employee with a disability and the employer.
3. The employment specialist approaches each job site from a "typicalness" standpoint, that is, how co-workers without disabilities in that job setting acquire jobs and participate in orientation and training.
4. The employment specialist must understand the workplace culture to make a good job match and to increase adult agencies' share in the responsibility for obtaining meaningful employment outcomes for employees with disabilities.

Future Research Issues

1. What are the barriers to increasing the number of people in integrated community employment vs. segregated settings? What are strategies to eliminating those barriers?

2. Does teaching self-advocacy and self-determination skills to students with disabilities in high school make a difference during post-school activities?
3. What specific strategies can be developed to eliminate the issues such as transportation, meaningful day, etc., that students face as they leave school?

Discussion Questions

1. Compare and contrast the values of inclusion in schools to inclusion in employment? How can schools better prepare students to be included in the workplace?
2. What information should students and family members have and plan for when searching for employment during their last year of school or as they leave school?
3. Identify the factors that impact quality employment service delivery. Identify indicators to determine a quality service delivery.

Community-Based Activities

1. Ask a vocational rehabilitation counselor to come in and speak to your class or conduct an interview to understand their roles and responsibilities during the transition process to promote employment outcomes.
2. Visit a sheltered workshop. Compare and contrast sheltered employment to competitive employment (including supported employment) quality issues such as wages, hours worked, social integration, variety of tasks, choice, and community access.
3. Visit a job site. Identify the academic and social skills required of the position. How can you begin to integrate the skills in your curriculum? How can the skills begin to be taught at the elementary school level and be built upon through high school?
4. Interview an employment provider to determine his or her value base and customer-driven process for providing services.
5. Visit a One-Stop Center to learn more about the services it offers to individuals with and without disabilities.

References

Banks, B. Charleston, S., Grossi, T, & Mank, D. (2001). Workplace supports, functioning, and integration outcomes for people with psychiatric disabilities. *Psychiatric Rehabilitation Journal, 24,* 389-396.

Banks, B, Grossi, T, & Mank, D. (2000). *Analysis of typical employment process and outcomes for people with psychiatric disabilities.* Unpublished manuscript.

Brooke, V., Inge, K. J., Armstrong, A., & Wehman, P. (1997). *Supported employment handbook: A customer-driven approach for persons with significant disabilities.* Virginia Commonwealth University: Rehabilitation Research and Training Center.

Brooke, V., Wehman, P., Inge, K., & Parent. W. (1995). Toward a customer-driven approach of supported employment. E*ducation and Training in Mental Retardation and Developmental Disabilities, 4,* 308-320.

Certo, N. J., Pumpian, I., Fisher, D., Storey, K., & Smalley, K. (1997). Focusing on the point of transition: A service integration model. *Education and Treatment of Children, 20,* 68-84.

DiLeo, D., MacDonald, R., & Killam, S. (1998). *Ethical Guidelines in Supported Employment.* Richmond, VA: The Association for Persons in Supported Employment.

Everson, J. M., & Guillory, J. D. (1998). Building statewide transition services through collaborative interagency teamwork. In F. R. Rusch and J. G. Chadsey, *Beyond high school: Transition from school to work.* Belmont, CA: Wadsworth.

Fussell, E., & Petty, D. (1998). *UT-TIE: Supported employment technology training resource manual.* Knoxville, TN: University of Tennessee

Grossi, T., Banks, B., & Pinniyei, D. (2001). Facilitating job site training and supports. In P. Wehman (Ed.) *Supported employment in business.* St. Augustine, FL: Training Resource Network.

Grossi, T., Jenaro Rio, C., Banks, B., & Mank, D. (2000). *Integration, typicalness, and employment outcomes for people with brain injury.* Unpublished manuscript.

Grossi, T., Regan, J., & Regan, B. (1998). Consumer-driven training techniques. In P. Wehman & J. Kregel, (Eds.), *More than a job* (119-148). Baltimore: Paul H. Brookes.

Hagner, D., & DiLeo, D. (1993). *Working together: Workplace culture, supported employment, and persons with disabilities.* Cambridge, MA: Brookline Books.

Kohler, P. D., DeStefano, L., Wermuth, T. R., Grayson, T. E. & McGinity. S. (1994). An analysis of exemplary transition programs: How and why are they selected. *Career Development for Exceptional Individuals. 17,* 187-202.

Mank, D. M., Cioffi, & A., Yovanoff, P. (1997a). Analysis of the typicalness of supported employment jobs, natural supports, and wage and integration outcomes. *Mental Retardation, 35,* 185-197.

Mank, D. M., Cioffi, & A., Yovanoff, P. (1997b). Patterns of support for employees with severe disabilities. *Mental Retardation, 35,* 433-447.

Mank, D. M., Cioffi, & A., Yovanoff, P. (1998). Employment outcomes for people with severe disabilities: Opportunities for Improvement. *Mental Retardation, 36,* 205-216.

Mank, D. M., Cioffi, & A., Yovanoff, P. (1999). The impact of coworker's involvement with supported employees on wage and integration outcomes. *Mental Retardation, 37*(5), 383-394.

Mcloughlin, C. S., Garner, J. B., & Callahan, M. (1987). *Getting employed, staying employed: Job development and training for persons with severe handicaps.* Baltimore: Paul H. Brookes.

Moon, M. S., Inge, K. J., Wehman, P., Brooke, V., & Barcus, J. M. (1990). Helping persons with severe mental retardation get and keep employment: *Supported employment issues and strategies.* Baltimore: Paul H. Brookes.

National Organization on Disability/Louis Harris and Associates (1998). *Survey programs on participants and attitudes.* www.nod.org/presssurvey.html.

Nietupski, J., Verstegen, D., & Petty, D. M. (1995). *The job development handbook: A guide for facilitating employer decisions to hire people with disabilities.* Knoxville, TN: University of Tennessee.

Owens-Johnson, L., & Hanley-Maxwell, C. (1999). Employer views on job development strategies for marketing supported employment. *Journal of Vocational Rehabilitation, 12,* 113-123.

Sitlington, P. L., Clark, G. M., & Kolstoe, O. P. (2000). *Transition education and services for adolescents with disabilities.* Needham Heights, MA: Allyn & Bacon.

US Department of Education (1999). *To assure a free and appropriate education for all children: The twenty-first annual report to congress on the implementation of the individuals with disabilities act.* Washington, DC: Office of Special Education and Rehabilitative Services.

Wehman, P., Revell, W. G., & Kregel, J. (1997). Supported employment: A decade of rapid growth. In P. Wehman, J. Kregel, & M. West (Eds.), *Promises fulfilled: Assessing the effectiveness of natural supports efforts to improve supported employment outcomes.* Richmond, VA: Virginia Commonwealth University, Rehabilitation Research and Training Center on Supported Employment.

Chapter 6
Modifying and Managing Employment Practices:
An Inclusive Model for Job Placement and Support

Michael P. Brady and Howard Rosenberg
*Florida Atlantic University College of Education, Boca Raton, FL
and Florida International University College of Education, Miami, FL*

Key Questions
1. How does the "goodness of fit" model relate to job placement and support?
2. What characteristics of the worker enhance success in a job?
3. What characteristics of the work setting and the job tasks enhance success in a job?
4. How can traditional vocational assessment practices be complemented by evaluations that include on-the-job work performance and employment support?
5. What modifications can be made to the way a job is performed that would enhance success in that job?
6. What teaching or performance strategies provided by a job coach, supervisor, co-worker, or the employee would enhance success in a job?

Beyond Job Slotting: It's All About "Fit"

In our culture, work is the one activity in which adults are expected to engage to achieve full membership in the mainstream. Hence, work occupies a central position in society and takes on a high priority. Unfortunately, many people with disabilities have not had opportunities to pursue meaningful work. To close this gap, there is a clear need for improving employability by teaching job skills, making workplace modifications, and providing appropriate supports.

Unfortunately for many professionals, promoting a person's employability just means that the habits of a worker must be changed. This practice ignores the developmental and educational nature of employability. The values, habits, skills, and interests in work are developed and shaped during childhood and throughout adulthood. Schools socialize children toward their future work roles. Early work experiences continue to mold young adults' orientation to work. Thus, employability is more than changing a square peg by smoothing the edges so that it fits into a round slot. Yet, the philosophy of many employment specialists is based on the concept of making people with disabilities "change their shape" to fit into available jobs. While there are other significant factors that affect employability, perhaps the most intriguing factor involves "goodness of fit."

Key Question #1: How does the "goodness of fit" model relate to job placement and support?

Making a person do work that isn't a good match for him or her is like crunching your toes into a tight pair of shoes. Selecting a job is a sensitive and multidimensional process. After all, most individuals spend a third of each day for two-thirds of their lives engaged in work. Given the amount of time that a person spends working, the job should reside within a comfort level for a person. When assisting people with disabilities to find that comfort level on a job, professionals should consider two variables: the characteristics of the worker (aptitude, behaviors, interests, and skills); and the requirements of the job tasks and employment settings.

Successful job placement requires that employment specialists integrate these variables to match a particular employee to a job. This is the essence of the goodness of fit construct applied to employability. Goodness of fit increases comfort and effectiveness, and thus increases job satisfaction among workers and their employers.

Key Question #2: What characteristics of the worker enhance success in a job? Critical Vocational Behaviors

Critical vocational behaviors have been linked to job success for entry-level positions during the past four decades. Warren (1961) identified characteristics that included self confidence, cooperation, cheerfulness, ability to accept criticism, ability to concentrate on one's work assignment, respect for one's immediate supervisor, initiative, and promptness. A decade later, Ehrle (1970) recommended that vocational development programs teach positive work habits and attitudes. Krantz (1971) categorized these attitudes and behaviors under the concept of "critical vocational behaviors"—specific behaviors that all employees must demonstrate to obtain and maintain employment. Murphy (1972) elaborated upon these specific work behaviors and attitudes associated with job maintenance by adding responsibility, pride in one's work, being well groomed, honesty, and quality of one's work. In a further study conducted during the 1970s, Prep Research Reports (1976) identified job seeking and job keeping behaviors including courtesy, persistence, integrity, reaction to mistakes, dependability, reaction to supervision, reactions to co-workers, initiative, and social judgment.

Ultimately, the work characteristics of every employee will be evaluated by supervisors responsible for employment decisions such as promotions, job retention, salary increases, probationary-period outcomes, and job termination. These supervisors typically may be employers or immediate supervisors. For employees with disabilities, these supervisors often are referred to as job coaches, work adjustment specialists, vocational educators, special educators, rehabilitation counselors, support coordinators, and others. These work supervisors typically base employee evaluations on their performance in three areas (Rosenberg & Brady, 2000):

- Work-Required Daily Living Activities
- Work-Required Behavior
- Work-Required Job Duties

Work-Required Daily Living Activities

Some people have difficulties obtaining and maintaining employment due to patterns of behavior involving personal hygiene, grooming, punctuality, work attendance, and other activities of daily living. While these do not directly affect the skills needed to perform a job task, they affect the social fit of the worker and one's co-workers at a work setting. As early as 1971, Krantz recognized these patterns as "critical vocational coupled behaviors."

In our own review of four decades of work adjustment literature in special education, counseling, and rehabilitation, we culled multiple daily living requirements and grouped them into thirteen clusters (Rosenberg & Brady, 2000). These clusters are:

1. Attendance
2. Punctuality
3. Personal Hygiene and Grooming
4. Travel
5. Verbal Communication
6. Non-Verbal Communication
7. Money Use
8. Employment Related Reading
9. Employment Related Math
10. Self-Identification
11. Following a Work Schedule
12. Following a Personal Schedule
13. Using Work Facilities

Work-Required Behavior

This represents the interpersonal and social skills that are required in job settings. Social factors are a critical aspect of how employees fit in a job role. Successful employees must juxtapose the etiquette, skill, and judgment to interact with supervisors, co-workers, and the public. Unfortunately, many people with disabilities may have poor social etiquette, skill, and judgment. As early as 1968 Neff described these social factors as a "work personality." Since then, the work adjustment literature has consistently identified work-required behavior as a critical component of successful job placement and maintenance (Neff , 1968). Rosenberg and Brady (2000) identified eight clusters of work-required behavior:

1. Stress Tolerance
2. Interpersonal Work Interactions
3. Interpersonal Social Interactions
4. Reactions to Changes in Routines
5. Honesty
6. Reaction to Criticism
7. Work Initiative
8. Work Endurance

Family Variables

Within each family structure there is a set of circumstances, history, and work values that influences each family member's work orientation and future employment choices. Messages based on this work orientation are delivered to family members from a very young age. Family variables influence future work orientation in any number of ways. Some families pass along expectations for very specific job roles. In other families, the orientation is less specific, and is more of an orientation to work classification or social values.

What impact does this make on a goodness of fit model of job placement? First, the job has to be compatible with the family's work value system. This principle is critical when considering work placement and support for people with disabilities. Traditionally, job placement has been made based on job availability. Second, if a worker had the skill and temperament to do the job, so much the better. Clearly, job availability, skill, and temperament are important, but a family's work orientation also plays a major role in successful job placement.

The Complexities of a Person

Who we are is a complex mix of variables including our histories, aptitudes, interests, and the presence of limiting factors, including medical issues, physical prowess, and disability. A goodness of fit model takes into account that you can have appropriate work required behavior, sufficient daily living skills, and a strong interest—but you might not meet the requirements of a job. Said broadly, the job just isn't you.

This could be due to a special employment need. Take for example a person being considered for a job as a trucker's helper. Even though the person has a sincere interest in the position, this job might not fit an individual who has a history of recurring back injuries, prefers to move about continuously, and who lacks physical stamina. This job could exacerbate the person's back injuries and requires more physical prowess and a more sedentary temperament. Ultimately this lack of fit could result in job termination.

It is important to recognize that disability is not always a limitation in job placement and support. The impact of any disability is relative to the context of the work. For example, a person with a hearing impairment might work well (and safely) in an environment where loud environmental noise would be a health hazard for other workers. In this instance, the presence of a hearing impairment is not a disability for the worker. Thus, using an employment model based on goodness of fit requires that professionals and employers rethink a perceived disability as just one of many characteristics of workers.

Key Question #3: What characteristics of the work setting and the job tasks enhance success in a job?

Any model of employability using goodness of fit must consider the culture and colleagueship of work (Hagner & DiLeo, 1993). Work culture involves the mores, values, and shared belief systems regarding "acceptable" behavior in a work environment. Work culture varies across different occupations. Occupational colleagueship represents the shared demeanor of workers within an occupation. People within particular occupations tend to think, look, and speak in similar ways. Goodness of fit requires that professionals responsible for preparing individuals for work, placement on the job, and evaluating their performance attend to the culture and colleagueship of work.

Many self-directed professionals consider work culture and occupational colleagueship as inherent criteria in their own careers. For example, a university professor considered somewhat eccentric self-selects a field of study and research that permits independent thinking and minimal social interaction.

This same approach is needed for employees with disabilities. For example, suppose a man in his fifties with mental retardation lives at home with his mother and father. He has minimal contact with peers; he has not previously been employed and has not participated in any educational or recreational programs since he left school at age eighteen. During his job interview, he enters a work setting with his mother who is in her eighties. When he enters, he is dressed in a suit and carries his lunch in an attache case. Other workers wear casual clothes to work and bring bagged lunches and lunch boxes.

It is obvious that the new employee likely will not fit into the culture of the worksite given his present demeanor, nor will he share the occupational colleagueship of his co-workers. Even though this man might perform the tasks of the various jobs quite well, the likelihood of his job success and social integration is reduced due to his inability to "fit." With minimal preparation prior to job placement, his transition to this work setting could become successful.

Culture and colleagueship are concepts that drive the employability model far beyond initial job placement. To maintain employment, and for businesses to remain solvent, employees must continue to fit in and to grow and develop in a manner congruent with the work culture. This growth is a developmental process. A current example of the developmental nature of work cultures involves the use of technology. In many job settings, e-mail memoranda have replaced paper memos. Other basic job functions such as maintaining product inventories or submitting order forms require applications of technology once considered specialized and restricted to highly skilled employees. Employees must keep up with these developments or they are considered outsiders in the jobs they may have worked at for years.

Traditionally, job preparation for people with disabilities has targeted skill training for new employees. The employability model described here obviously incorporates other factors, including concepts of culture and colleagueship. However, any examination of work requirements also must consider the actual tasks required in a particular job. Rosenberg and Brady (2000) identified nine work task requirements that facilitate employees' abilities to perform those tasks:

1. Work Quality
2. Work Quantity
3. Speed of Learning New Tasks
4. Performance of Previously Learned Tasks
5. Ability to Perform Multiple Tasks
6. Ability to Organize Work Tasks
7. Safety Procedures
8. Cleanliness of Work Environment
9. Employee Motivation

Successful job placement requires attention to the sociocultural milieu of the work environment. While employment professionals and work supervisors readily recognize the skill requirements of job tasks and work settings, work culture and occupational colleagueship are important components of the overall goodness of fit job placement equation.

Matching Workers and Job Requirements

Traditional vocational and career assessment reflects a model in which assessment results affect two outcomes: employment placement, and employee productivity. Initially, assessments are conducted for the purpose of gaining valid information regarding job placement options, and the assessment results are used to make career and job placement decisions. These decisions might result in a person enrolling in a vocational class, selecting a career path, entering into a work experience program, or obtaining a supported or competitive job.

The goal of this initial assessment typically is to ascertain each person's aptitudes and interests. What many educators, rehabilitation specialists, and vocational specialists often overlook is the limited world view of the potential employee. For example, vocational assessment with high school students faces inherent limitations due to the ages of these students and, subsequently, their limited exposure to real work. Since aptitudes and interests are a function of work exposure and experience, it is clear that secondary students are prone to express interest in careers that are commonly portrayed in an enticing way in the popular media (e.g., professional athletics), or that they have personally experienced (e.g., jobs held by family members).

Another factor influences the assessment results of people with disabilities. Just as one's chronological age limits exposure to knowledge of careers, the presence of a disability often is a limiting factor. In many ways, the presence of a disability can be considered a risk factor for limited exposure to work experience. People with disabilities who have been restricted from accessing typical community living and working environments, often have restricted interest preferences and aptitudes (Brady & Cunningham, 1985). Growing up in segregated school environments may predispose graduates of those programs toward non-work and sheltered activities rather than supported and community jobs (Brown et al., 1983).

Once a person is hired, the assessment model shifts to a focus on worker productivity. Traditional measures of worker productivity involve quality and quantity targets. Obviously, these targets are important and are used for employment decisions including raises, promotions, and job maintenance. To increase the relevance of this assessment tradition for people with disabilities, however, it is necessary to consider the supports that are used by employees as part of their productivity evaluations.

The traditional vocational assessment model has served many people well over the years and continues to do so. However, many employees discover their true interests and preferences, as well as develop their patterns and habits of work, only after structured and successful work experiences. Furthermore, career development is a continuous process; people continue to grow and change their work and personal interests throughout their working years. Knowing this, its incumbent upon professionals to promote a model of assessment that is more dynamic than static, and that is responsive to individuals' career growth and development *after* initial job placement. Further, any model of vocational assessment that is sensitive to issues facing people with disabilities also should attend to employee productivity within a context of support provided to that employee.

Key Question #4: How can traditional vocational assessment practices be complemented by evaluations that include on-the-job work performance and employment support?

There is an enormous body of evidence that shows that people with disabilities can succeed in competitive and supported employment if they can access appropriate supports (Conley et al., 1989; Storey & Certo, 1996; Wehman & Kregel, 1995). A now classic paper by Baumgart et al. (1982) suggested that people with disabilities could participate in most school and work routines by arranging three types of adaptations. These are changes in:

1. the routine, sequence, or rules of an activity
2. the materials used during the activity
3. social or instructional interactions

These adaptations, when applied to the employment world, can be considered as either natural or arranged supports (Nisbet, 1992). For employees who rely on these supports, assessment should consider at least three vocational variables beyond the traditional interest and aptitude measures:

1. level and quality of work productivity.
2. type and level of support used to achieve this productivity.
3. implications of the assessment for improvements in work productivity, job satisfaction, and quality of life.

One assessment tool that takes these three factors into consideration is the Job Observation and Behavior Scale or JOBS (Rosenberg & Brady, 2000). JOBS is an employee performance evaluation that was developed for businesses and organizations that hire workers with supported employment needs, such as students enrolled in vocational education, special education, ESOL, and alternative education, as well as for adults enrolled in rehabilitation programs, vocational technical schools, sheltered workshops, and community welfare-to-work programs.

JOBS' standardization permits employers and human service professionals to evaluate the quality of workers' job performance, assess their need for appropriate supports, and compare the quality of their performance to workers not receiving supports who perform the same competitive jobs. JOBS can help to identify areas in which employees could become more productive if adaptations were made in the type or level of support. For example, an employee's evaluation showed that she was performing a job task adequately (such as replenishing empty food bowls at a salad bar), but was unable to complete tasks that required remembering the order of the vegetables. Using JOBS, a pictorial sequence might be identified as an appropriate support to maintain or even increase her productivity. Thus JOBS assesses employee performance and the support provided to obtain this performance and suggests changes in supports that would enhance productivity.

Key Question #5: What modifications can be made in the way a job is performed that would enhance success in that job?
Key Question #6: What teaching or performance strategies provided by a job coach, supervisor, co-worker, or the employee would enhance success in a job?

The special education literature is replete with strategies, adaptations, and modifications that can be made so that a person with a disability can perform or learn a new task. The adaptation strategies described by Baumgart et al. (1982)

provide a convenient synthesis and can be used as a conceptual framework for many of these modifications. Success on the job will require some level of support or modification for many employees. Five specific modifications and supports presented here are:

- change the task or use adaptive materials to perform the task
- restructure "complex" jobs into "single task" jobs
- use direct instruction
- use self management
- add natural supports

Change the Task or Use Adaptive Materials to Perform the Task

A tried and true strategy used by rehabilitation professionals for the last half century involves changing or modifying the task or materials so that an employee's particular disability does not handicap his or her performance. Examples of task modification are found throughout the professional literature (Woolcock, 1995; Murphy & Rogan, 1994).

Consider the following example of task modification for a person with a limited range of motion. In a position as a "bagger" at a grocery store, the person might be required to retrieve paper bags stored in slots below the counter where groceries are placed once their prices have been scanned. The location of these bags represents an unnecessary barrier for this person. If the location of the storage bin is changed so that the bags are positioned adjacent to the counter, this person can perform the required motion and bag the groceries. A modification to this task was a minor change in placement of materials.

For some employees, materials can be modified to compensate for limitations in strength, dexterity, or coordination. For example, an employee in a landscaping service might have difficulty pushing a lawnmower due to limited strength and endurance. A lawnmower can be modified for this employee by adding larger wheels that make it easier to push and balance. The handgrip might be enlarged or padded to make the mower easier to maneuver while reducing stress to an employee's hand, wrists, and fingers.

Task modification is well integrated into the fabric of society. For example, many people without disabilities now use voice activated computer software to compensate for their limited typing skills. While this modification is an option for many, it might become a required modification for some people with disabilities if they are to be successful in a work routine.

Restructure Complex Jobs into Single Task Jobs

Many jobs performed by employees are quite complex, and require a degree of academic and intellectual skill. For example, being an auto mechanic requires computer skills, mathematics, and technical reading. While the "complex job" of being an auto mechanic might be beyond the reach of some people, an analysis of the job will identify several "single task" job roles in which people with disabilities could be completely successful. An employee who is unsuccessful learning to read technical English or make computer diagnoses could learn to change oil and obtain gainful employment in a business that specializes in oil changes.

A similar example exists in cosmetology. This is a highly regulated industry, and cosmetologists must pass a range of licensing exams that include academics. A person with a disability who does not possess this academic proficiency but has an interest and aptitude in cosmetology could become successful and derive satisfaction in a "single task" job by shampooing hair.

Use Direct Instruction

Many vocational experiences operate on the assumption that students in the programs will learn the skills and routines of a job incidentally, simply by experiencing them. Many people do learn skills and routines without being taught, but often not with the specificity and accuracy needed to work competitively. Other employees simply do not learn by such subtle means, as sensory and cognitive disabilities often interfere with the ability to learn incidentally. For these employees, specificity, rehearsal, and instructional feedback are needed.

Consider the skill of distinguishing among various sizes of nails, a skill needed by a person working as a carpenter's assistant. This skill is often difficult for employees with significant mental retardation, since relative size is rather abstract and nail size has minimal functionality outside of the workplace. To work successfully, this employee must reliably select and deliver these nails to a carpenter. This employee might need direct instruction to learn to distinguish nail size. At least two approaches exist to performing this task:

1. Teach the employee to compare the size of the nail to a model.
2. Teach the employee to find the measurement code on the box label.

Obviously alternate instructional strategies exist to teach an employee to distinguish the size of nails. Strategies most effective, however, will have the employee actively engaged, the task expectation clear, a specific outcome identified, the employee obtaining specific performance feedback, the employee's progress evaluated, and the instruction altered as the employee progresses or fails to progress.

Use Self-Management

Often, employees benefit from a self management system that encourages them to maintain their productivity while engaging in positive and cooperative behavior. Such a system can be used to strengthen their skills, then faded as an employee becomes more independent. For others, a self-management system can become a long term "prosthetic," or a permanent prompt.

Freagon et al. (1985) described a low-tech permanent prompting system in which employees used laminated picture lists to help "remember" all the tasks to perform when cleaning hotel rooms. Audiotape systems also have been used for this purpose. Tapes with directions or prompts are prerecorded, and employees listen to these tapes using personal tape recorders and headphones. Such systems can help employees learn new skills (Alberto, Sharpton, Briggs, & Stright, 1986) , become more fluent in their current work skills (Davis, Brady, Williams & Burta, 1992), or work cooperatively without interfering social behavior (Davis et al., 1992).

Add Natural Supports

Traditionally, supports needed by an employee with a disability have been provided by human service professionals (e.g., job coaches, special education teachers) external to the work environment. With the advent of supported employment models, a shift toward more naturally occurring supports has taken place (Wehman & Kregel, 1995). Natural supports are used to overcome barriers so that an employee with a disability is able to maintain the quality and quantity of work commensurate with nondisabled workers who perform the same tasks. These supports can be delivered to the employee with a disability, or to others who might interact with that employee.

Storey and Certo (1996) provided a working definition of natural supports as people who are not disability service providers but who provide assistance to people with disabilities that enables them to function as independently as possible in integrated employment or other community settings. Furthermore, Storey and Certo made the point that support from people found in the work environment (e.g., co-workers, supervisors) enhances integration more effectively than relying on specialized service providers. For example, one type of natural support strategy might involve arranging for a co-worker to provide occasional feedback to a worker with a disability who needs intermittent reinforcement on the quality of his or her performance. A second type of natural support strategy might involve a brief intervention to co-workers to teach them to communicate more effectively with an employee with a hearing impairment or other communication disorder.

Window to the World
The case studies that follow provide examples of how two employees with disabilities can perform their work at comparable levels of quantity and quality when provided specific employment supports.

Susan
> **Age: 32**
> **Employment Barriers: Mental retardation resulting in significant need for support**
> **Job Type: Busses tables**
> **Work Status: She is a full-time hourly supported employee, who has been working for eight months with frequent monitoring by a job coach**

Maria
> **Age: 26**
> **Employment Barriers: No work experience; health concerns resulting in minimal support needs**
> **Job Type: Busses tables**
> **Work Status: This is her first paid job as a full-time hourly employee. She has been working for fourteen months, and received temporary support from a job coach during her first two months.**

Analysis of Susan and Maria's Work Performance
To evaluate their performance on-the-job, Susan and Maria were administered the Job Observation and Behavior Scale (JOBS). By comparing Susan and Maria's work performance scores to JOBS' normative data, three trends became evident. First both Susan and Maria's Quality of Performance scores were well within the range of employees without disabilities. Second, there was no difference in the Quality of Performance scores between Susan and Maria. Third, there were substantial differences in Susan and Maria's scores representing the Level and Types of Support needed to maintain their work performance. Specifically, Susan's "support score" was nearly half that of Maria's score, indicating substantially greater need for support.

These profiles point out fundamental assumptions of supported employment. That is, employees with disabilities can perform work routines at the same level of productivity and quality as employees without disabilities, when provided with an appropriate level of employment support. The type and level of that support will differ across employees. Some employees may have significant support needs if they are to work productively, while others' support needs will be minimal or even transitory.

While the results of the assessment indicate that the quality of performance of both Susan and Maria's work matches overall employee expectation, their performance surpassed the normative scores of other adults in supported and sheltered work programs. The reason this occurred involved the types and levels of employment supports provided to Susan and Maria. The level of assistance, supervision and support differed dramatically for the two.

For example, to obtain above average work quality ratings, it was necessary for Susan to obtain support levels in excess of other supported workers. An adaptive materials support used to help Susan remember how to bus tables was a pictorial representation of tables with and without dishes, silverware, and napkins. The pictures also were arranged in a sequence that prompted her to remove and place used dishes in the bus tray. This tray was then returned to the kitchen for cleaning. For Susan it was not necessary to break the complex task into parts, so she performed the entire sequence of bussing tables. It was necessary, however, to use direct instruction for one part of the task. Susan needed to be taught how to scrape remaining food from plates before stacking them into the bus tray. This instruction was provided initially by a job coach; after she achieved mastery of this, two co-workers (i.e., a natural support) were asked to "keep an eye out" to make sure that she continued to do this carefully during the next three months.

Maria, on the other hand maintained high job quality ratings with far less assistance, supervision, and support. Like Susan, Maria had a job coach at the beginning of her employment. The similarities, however, stopped there. Maria did not require adaptive materials or alterations to the job routine. With only a few days of orientation and instruction on how to bus tables, Maria learned the task. Then the job coach helped Maria develop a self-management task checklist.

Using this checklist, Maria remembered to complete each task needed to work in the restaurant. After teaching her to use it, the job coach reduced her involvement with Maria so that Maria simply showed the coach the completed checklist at the end of the work shift. This was faded until Maria showed the coach the checklist once per week. Over two months, Maria learned to complete all the requirements of her job, and the job coach was able to discontinue her supervision.

What do these assessment results mean qualitatively? For both Susan and Maria, the quality of their work was adequate to maintain their employment. Depending on the policies of their respective businesses (e.g., longevity, collective bargaining procedures, merit criteria), Susan and Maria might be positioned for salary increases or promotions. However, the quality of their performance would likely be compared to other employees who do not receive supports in these restaurants. After two months, Maria's job coach determined that a decrease in support for Maria would not hinder her work performance. For Susan, however, any decrease in supports could place her work quality at risk. This is particularly evident given (a) the high degree of supports currently received, and (b) the short duration of her employment at this job (eight months).

What do these two analyses mean for employers who might ask, "How can these two employees produce similar quality of work performance when they receive very different levels of support?" To address this, an employer would consider various contextual variables that affect the current and future job performance of Susan and Maria.

First, consider that Susan spent many of her school years in separate special education programs for students with moderate to severe disabilities. Susan had minimal opportunities to interact with students without disabilities, and seldom, if ever, competed with them on tasks and routines. In school, Susan was successful in learning to perform daily living and vocational tasks, and as a result, she is currently performing as well as other employees in her job. To perform at this level, however, she currently requires considerably more supervision and assistance than most other workers, including Maria. While a significant level of support is necessary now for Susan, she can be expected to perform her job with lowered levels of support as she gains experience and success in her job duties and routines. Appropriate future work performance for Susan would involve continuing her current level of productivity as the intensity of her supports is faded out over the next twelve to eighteen months. The addition of adaptive or prosthetic materials (such as personal schedules, laminated task lists, permanent prompting tapes) might be used to enhance Susan's independence.

Maria's employment history is quite different from Susan's. Maria was a high school graduate who seldom needed supports or remediation beyond that available to most students in general education classes. However, Maria was frequently absent from school due to health problems. As a result, she never participated in any career awareness activities, and consequently never entered the workplace. She registered with the local vocational rehabilitation program and is now in her first paid position. Maria also is participating in a part-time program where she is learning desktop publishing skills; her employer has offered to promote Maria from bussing tables to an office position if she does well. She is performing well in her current job, even while taking classes and maintaining a household. Maria is well positioned for promotion with this company should her current performance continue.

Best Practice Recommendations

Obviously, there have been tremendous strides for students with disabilities to help them become fully included into the workplace. Many promising practices of the past two decades have become best practices today, including preparation for work and job placement and employment support.

Best practices involving preparation for work has long been a focus of special and vocational educators. For example, Kohler (1996, 1998) identified five clusters of work preparation activities needed to make smooth transitions from secondary special education into the adult work force. These practices have recently been adopted by the Council for Exceptional Children Division on Career Development and Transition (DCDT, 2000) as best practices for secondary student preparation. Highlights of these activities include:

1. Student-focused planning: Students guide the identification of their career goals, vocational experiences, personal learning patterns, and need for support.
2. Student development: Secondary educators work to ensure that the focus of learning includes "real life" academics, self-determination, career awareness, independent and family living, and social and community skills.
3. Interagency collaboration: Educators and community service providers collaborate to plan and implement services and supports so that school-to-work transitions are planned and successful.
4. Family involvement: Family members are actively involved in identifying future career goals, planning activities that assist the student to achieve these goals, and relevant decision-making.
5. Program structures and policies: Educators develop integrated educational options and curricula that match the intended outcomes of community-based, competitive or supported employment.

There are a number of sources for identifying best practices for job placement and employment support (Rosenberg & Brady, 2000; Nisbet, 1992). Cumulatively, these practices include:

1. Monitoring employment trends: Educators and community employment specialists should keep abreast of developments in the local economy so that schools prepare graduates for jobs that are plentiful and in high demand in their local economies. Vocational classes should correspond to these employment trends.
2. Developing partnerships with industry: Educators and community employment specialists should use these partnerships to establish an infrastructure where schools' graduates move to local business and industry with minimal disruption.
3. Developing job specialization opportunities: Job designers should examine the tasks required in various jobs and establish partial-task routines that can be performed more efficiently by employees. For example, a job designer might task analyze a job (e.g., automotive repair) and discover partial routines (e.g., oil changing) that can be mastered easily by an employee with support.
4. Using natural supports: Job coaches and placement specialists should strive to link each supported employee to naturally occurring supports that exist or can be easily arranged on a job. The systematic (and opportunistic) replacement of external supports with natural supports should be a goal for most employees.

Future Research Issues

This chapter presented an inclusive model of supported employment. Research findings and best practices involving job placement, employment modifications, and preparation models for transition were presented. Clearly the state of the practice is sound, and has an empirical and experiential database. In spite of the solid history of supported employment in more inclusive communities, numerous empirical questions remain (Butterworth, Hagner, Kiernan, & Schalock, 1996).

1. Cost studies: Several research issues have evolved in the past decade involving the costs of supports. For example, a line of longitudinal cost research is needed to establish the extent to which costs per employee increase or decrease over time. Variables included are initial training costs, employee turnover, the availability of support, and the relative costs of on-the-job (co-worker, supervisor) support vs. job coaches and trainers provided by human service agencies.

2. Curriculum and learning studies: There continues to be a need for research on effective models of job preparation. This research includes psychological bases of learning (e.g., applications of research on self-efficacy and motivation), as well as investigations of training techniques (e.g., uses of technology for task simulations or job-specific prompting systems). More research on natural supports, self-control, and naturally occurring prompts also is needed, as well as curriculum research and development aimed to reduce the gap between school and community work also is needed.

3. Impact studies: The impact of supported employment on workers, their families, co-workers, and society-at-large needs to be investigated in a much more serious manner than we've seen in past decades. For example, while the psychosocial impact of having (or losing) one's job has been studied extensively among professionals, little research has occurred on this among entry level workers, including those with significant disabilities. Similarly, the impact of moving from more sheltered employment to supported or competitive employment has received scant attention (Griffin, Rosenberg, Cheyney, & Greenberg, 1996).

Discussion Questions

1. Employment for adults with disabilities has changed throughout history as people with disabilities have become progressively included into society. Describe how changes in societal values, the state of the economy, technical knowhow, and pedagogical and vocational training methods have influenced employment practices.

2. How does the goodness of fit job placement model apply to other community inclusion issues faced by people with disabilities, including schooling, recreation, health services, and residential life?

3. Employees without disabilities obtain a wide range of supports (e.g., on-site child care, flex-time) designed to help them remain productive and satisfied at work. First, identify some of the supports available to you or others you know. Next, discuss the availability, appropriateness, and utility of these supports for persons with significant and relatively mild employment support needs.

Community-Based Activities

1. Interagency planning: Supported employment requires organized planning across agencies that serve adolescents and adults with disabilities. Participate in these planning sessions with educators, rehabilitation professionals, and employers. Attend and participate in an interagency council meeting. Look, listen, and observe what happens during these meetings. Consider the following questions each time you visit.
   - What is the topic of the meeting?
   - Which agencies are involved?
   - Is the planning agency-focused or person-centered?
   - To what extent does the planning involve:
     a. personal planning?
     b. legislative initiatives?
     c. agency business?
     d. family participation?
     e. other topics?

2. Shadowing a job coach: Go to a work environment in which an employee is receiving the support of a job coach. Observe when the job coach is and is not present. Look for differences in the nature of the activity and productivity of the employee and others. List any physical, social, or other factors that interfere with the employee's productivity and satisfaction. Write down any recommendations you have for removing these interfering factors. Determine whether these interfering factors can be ameliorated with natural supports (such as co-workers). Identify other external supports that might need to be provided.

3. Creating job descriptions using task analysis: Visit two different job sites where employers have agreed to hire a new employee with a disability. Observe different job routines performed by the current employees. Task analyze three of these jobs by listing the way those tasks were conducted; include the materials and tools used, the sequence of steps, etc. Next, meet with a job coach and prospective employee who are involved in developing a support plan in anticipation of job placement. Provide the recommendations for the plan based on your job analysis.

References

Alberto, P., Sharpton, W., Briggs, A., & Stright, M. (1986). Facilitating task acquisition through the use of a self-operated auditory prompting system. *Journal of the Association for Persons with Severe Handicaps, 11,* 85-91.

Baumgart, D. Brown, L., Pumpian, I., Nisbet, J., Ford, A., Sweet, M., Messina, R., & Schroeder, J. (1982). Principle of partial participation and individualized adaptation in educational programs for severely handicapped students. *Journal of the Association for the Severely Handicapped, 7*(2), 17-27.

Brady, M. P., & Cunningham, J. (1985). Living and learning in segregated environments: An ethnography of normalization outcomes. *Education and Training of the Mentally Retarded, 20*(4), 241-252.

Brown, L., Nisbet, J., Ford, A., Sweet, M., Shiraga,. B., York., J., & Loomis, R. (1983). The critical need for nonschool instruction in educational programs for severely handicapped students. *Journal of the Association for the Severely Handicapped, 8*(3), 71-77.

Butterworth, J., Hagner, D., Kiernan, W. E., & Schalock, R. L. (1996). Natural supports in the workplace: Defining an agenda for research and practice. *Journal of the Association for Persons with Severe Handicaps, 21,* 103-113.

Conley, R., Rusch, F., McCaughrin, W., & Tines, J. (1989). Benefits and costs of supported employment: An analysis of the Illinois Supported Employment Project. *Journal of Applied Behavior Analysis, 22,* 441-447.

Davis, C., Brady, M. P., Williams, R., Burta, M. (1992). The effects of self-operated auditory prompting tapes on the performance fluency of persons with severe mental retardation. *Education & Training in Mental Retardation, 27,* 39-50.

Division on Career Development and Transition (2000). *Transition related planning, instruction, and service responsibilities for secondary special educators* (Fact Sheet). Reston, VA: Council for Exceptional Children.

Ehrle, R. A. (1970). The criterion of success problem in providing employability services. *Vocational Guidance Quarterly, 18,* 306-310.

Freagon, S. Wheeler, J., Brankin, G., McDonnel, K., Stern, M., Usilton, R., & Keiser, N. (1985). Increasing personal competence in the community. In M.P. Brady & P. Gunter (Eds.), *Integrating moderately & severely handicapped learners: Strategies that work* (283- 263). Springfield, IL: Charles C Thomas.

Griffin, D., Rosenberg, H., Cheyney, W., & Greenberg, B. (1996). A comparison of self esteem and job satisfaction of adults with mild mental retardation in sheltered workshops and supported employment. *Education and Training in Mental Retardation and Developmental Disabilities, 31,* 142-151.

Hagner, D., & DiLeo, D. (1993). *Working together: Workplace culture, supported employment, and persons with disabilities.* Cambridge, MA: Brookline.

Kohler, P. (1996). *A taxonomy for transition programming: Linking research and practice.* Champaign, Transition Research Institute, University of Illinois.

Kohler, P. (1998). Implementing a transition perspective of education: A comprehensive approach to planning and delivering secondary education and transition services. In F. R. Rusch & J. G. Chadsey (Eds.), *Beyond high school: Transition from school to work* (179- 205). Belmont, CA: Wadsworth.

Krantz, G. (1971). Critical vocational behaviors. *Journal of Rehabilitation, 37*(4), 32-34.

Murphy, P. D. (1972). *Teaching for employability.* Bismarck, ND: North Dakota Research Coordinating Unit State Board for Vocational Education.

Murphy, S. T., & Rogan, P. M. (1994). *Developing natural supports in the workplace: A practitioner's guide.* St. Augustine, FL: Training Resource Network.

Neff, W. S. (1968). *Work and human behavior.* New York: Atherton Press.

Nisbet, J. (1992). *Natural supports in school, at work, and in the community for people with severe disabilities.* Baltimore: Paul H. Brookes.

Prep Research Reports (1976). *The determination of behavior attitude categories which define the concept of employability* (Vol. 1, No. 8). Trenton: Prep Research.

Rosenberg, H., & Brady, M.P. (2000). *JOBS: Job Observation and Behavior Scale: A work performance evaluation for supported and entry level employees.* Wood Dale, IL: Stoelting Co.

Storey, K., & Certo, N.J. (1996). Natural supports for increasing integration in the workplace for people with disabilities: A review of literature and guidelines for implementation. *Rehabilitation Counseling Bulletin, 40*(1), 62-76.

Warren, F. G. (1961). Ratings of employed and unemployed mentally handicapped males on personality and work factors. *American Journal of Mental Deficiency, 65,* 629-633.

Wehman, P., & Kregel, J. (1995). At the crossroads: Supported employment a decade later. *Journal of the Association for Persons with Severe Handicaps, 20,* 286-299.

Woolcock, W. (1995). Natural supports in the community. In W. Woolcock, & J. Domracki (Eds.), *Instructional strategies in the community: A resource guide for community instruction for people with disabilities* (199-220). Austin, TX: Pro-Ed.

Chapter 7
Social Life

Janis Chadsey and Debra Shelden
University of Illinois at Urbana-Champaign

Key Questions
1. What are the types of social relationships?
2. What are the skills associated with self-advocacy?
3. What are the types of strategies that can be used in employment settings to impact social integration?
4. What are strategies that can be used to meet new people in community settings?
5. What are the strategies that could be used across postsecondary, work, and community settings to create a satisfactory social life?

What does it mean to have a "social life?" In general terms, having a social life means that one has interactions and relationships with others in society. Clearly, this broad description does little to help us understand when a social life has been achieved or how a social life could or should be facilitated. This description also does not tell us how persons with disabilities can achieve a satisfying social life as they make their transition from high school to adult life.

This chapter is based on the premise that all humans desire some sort of social life. One only has to look past research to see that relationships with others are associated with less stress (House, 1981), better health (House, 1981), and a higher quality of life (Hughes, Hwang, Kim, Eisenman, & Killian, 1995; Schalock, 2000). In addition, the establishment of social relationships is often cited as an important outcome of transition planning (e.g., Halpern, 1993).

How does one know when a satisfactory social life has been achieved? This is a difficult question to answer because it is individually determined. For some people, a satisfactory social life might consist of one best friend and several acquaintances. Further, a satisfactory social life might include seeing the best friend several times a month for lunch, dinner, or a movie and having pleasant interactions with acquaintances (in this case co-workers) on a daily basis. Additionally, the satisfactory social life also may consist of taking a cooking class at the local community college once a week and going to church every Sunday.

For other people, a satisfactory social life might occupy more time in their lives. For example, the social life might include having four best friends and seeing them several times a week. One best friend might be from work and interactions with the person might occur daily over coffee and sometimes lunch. Two best friends might be seen outside of work for movies, exercising at the gym, and lunches. And the fourth best friend might be a spouse where daily interactions occur in the mornings, evenings and during gardening and hiking on the weekends. In addition, the social life might include a close knit family that is seen every Sunday for dinner, and several pals who are seen several times a month for dinner parties and birthday celebrations. Finally, the social life might include a number of acquaintances who are seen on a daily basis at the gas station, bakery, and grocery and drug stores.

These two examples illustrate how different social lives can be for people. Yet, each social life could be judged as being satisfactory from the perspective of the people who experience them. This is an important issue. Similar to questions about what constitutes a quality life (Hughes et al., 1995), questions could be raised about what constitutes a satisfactory social life. Only individuals can answer the question about whether or not they are satisfied with their social life. Yet, it is quite possible that some answers or judgments from people with disabilities may make some uncomfortable and may go against the prevailing philosophy of integration and inclusion. For example, what if an individual with a disability has several best friends who also have disabilities? What if an individual with a disability likes to participate in a segregated group activity of others with disabilities? What if an individual with a disability likes to spend the majority of his free time with his family?

In order for people to have a satisfactory social life, it is critical that they have opportunities to explore and experience all aspects of society without any artificial constraints. If, in the above example, an individual with a disability liked the segregated activity only because she had never participated in any other community leisure pursuits, then her choice of the segregated activity would be artificially constrained because she had not experienced other leisure activities. Similarly, if the individual with the disability had friends only with disabilities because he did not have an opportunity to meet people without disabilities, then his choice would be made under artificial constraints. The critical variable in making a valid judgment about one's social life is having choice, and choices can best be made by having opportunities to engage in more than one experience.

As we think about what constitutes a quality social life for persons with disabilities when they make the transition from high school to adulthood, it is important to realize that all sorts of activities and interactions and relationships with others can constitute reasonable outcomes. One's social life can be influenced by the different environments one experiences (e.g., at home, work, community) and by the different types of relationships one engages in. In this chapter, we will discuss literature related to the types of social life experienced in three environments: postsecondary educational settings, work contexts, and community settings. These three settings were chosen because they constitute three environments that generally are experienced by adults when they leave high school. In addition, all three environments offer rich opportunities for a social life to occur. We also will discuss different types of relationships that can contribute to a satisfactory social life. Literature that highlights relationships involving individuals with disabilities from each setting (e.g., work) will be reviewed. At the end of the chapter, we will offer recommendations for practice, and we will also highlight future research areas. We begin by describing different kinds of relationships that could contribute to a satisfactory social life.

Relationships

Generally, when we think about relationships, we think about friendships or romantic relationships as being the "ultimate" social life outcomes. Yet, there are many other types of relationships that can contribute to a rich social life. In this chapter, we will describe Pogrebin's (1987) categorization of different types of relationships that could evolve into friendships. Space precludes a discussion of romantic relationships, although dating is a typical social behavior displayed by young adults and is an activity that should be encouraged for individuals with disabilities if it is of interest to them.

Key Question #1: What are the types of social relationships?

Pogrebin (1987) describes seven different types of relationships that vary in their degree of exchange and communal qualities. **Acquaintances,** the first type of relationship, are individuals who we know by name or face because we see them periodically. As Pogrebin points out, everyone we know (except for family members) always starts out as an acquaintances. Acquaintances may be people like our grocery store clerk, mail carrier, or a bus passenger that we see regularly on our commute to work. Acquaintances are not chosen by us, but occur in our lives because of what we do or where we live.

Neighbors are a type of acquaintance often used for mutual help or protection; with neighbors, there is often a mutually agreed upon exchange relationship that exists. With some neighbors, we may exchange greetings only on weekends during yard work. With other neighbors, we may have extended conversations over coffee. But generally, we feel comfortable asking neighbors to watch our homes or offer us a form of protection, if needed.

A **confederate** relationship exists between two people who may not be equal in terms of their social, economic, or educational background, yet they have formed an alliance and they need each other for a particular reason. Pogrebin cites examples of confederate relationships as being the popular teenager who needs a sidekick, or the lesbian and the gay man who need a "socially acceptable" social escort on occasion, or a businessperson who needs several people for business contacts. Confederate relationships are often temporary, but for the time period that they last, they seem like a "pseudo friendship."

Pals are defined by two people who are of equal ability and who "play" together because they have common interests, such as watching old movies, participating on the same sports team, or attending concerts. With pals, the activity is the essential element that ties the two people together. Pogrebin has noted that the intimacy level of pals is generally shallow and engaging in the activity supersedes conversation or the disclosure of emotional feelings.

Close kin (e.g., siblings, parents, spouses, children) constitute a fifth kind of relationship. As with all of the above relationships, close kin also can turn into best friends. Interestingly, Pogrebin stated that friends who are close kin often occur in social groups who may need some sort of economic assistance, and occur less regularly in groups who are affluent and well educated.

Co-workers are listed as a special category because work occupies so much of our time and gives us ample opportunities to form a relationship with one another. As Stewart (1985) noted, one's work setting is probably the most important social context we have after one's immediate family context. Considering that most employees work between twenty and forty hours a week, there is plenty of time and opportunity to develop relationships with co-workers.

The last category described by Pogrebin is that of **friends**. A friend is typically described as someone with the following qualities: honest, trustworthy, respectful, committed, supportive, loyal, understanding, and generous (Rubin, 1985). Friends often have common interests and are intimate with one another. Mannarino (1980) has noted that the concept of reciprocity is an essential component of friendship; reciprocity implies that each persons contributes something similar in kind or quantity to the relationship.

These seven categories of relationships suggested by Pogrebin indicate that our social life can be quite varied. Within each category, it is important to note that friendship can emerge from any one of them. For example, pals can be people who are fun to shop with, and they can also turn into friends. As we consider the list of relationships, it is quite likely that the most rewarding social life is one where all, or nearly all, types of relationships are present. If we only had close kin or confederate relationships, we may not judge our social life as being very meaningful or rewarding.

How do we form relationships with others? How can we make certain that individuals with disabilities achieve this very important outcome? These are not easy questions to answer because interpersonal relationships are extremely complex and involve intricate processes that exist at many different levels (Hinde, 1995). For example, the individuals involved in a relationship affect that relationship because each brings a particular social orientation, temperament, and repertoire of social skills that influence one another. Also, relationships exist over time and are influenced by past and current interactions that create expectations for future interactions. Hinde also notes that every relationship is unique in some way and that we need to be careful about interpreting group data that is used by most social psychologists to describe relationships. Additionally, all relationships exist in social contexts; "no relationship can be considered independently from the social, cultural, and temporal situation in which it is embedded" (Hinde, 1995, p. 3).

This complexity of relationships could make the task of trying to achieve this outcome for persons with disabilities a daunting one. And, certainly, the literature is sparse in suggesting strategies. Most strategies that have been suggested have focused on a narrow component of relationships, such as the teaching of social skills and interactions with others (Meyer, Park, Grenot-Scheyer, Schwartz, & Harry, 1998). Nonetheless, some literature has suggested ways to promote relationships for people with disabilities. While these suggestions may not be empirically proven, they are offered here for discussion.

Settings Where Relationships Can Develop

Relationships can develop in many different types of settings and social contexts. This chapter discusses the kinds of strategies used to facilitate relationships and social integration in postsecondary educational settings, work contexts, and various community settings. These settings were chosen because they are ones often frequented by youth with disabilities when they make their transition to adulthood. They all offer many opportunities for relationships and a social life to occur.

Postsecondary Educational Settings

College life is so full of social opportunities that some students view the social life of college as being more important than the academic part! When students enter college, many of them are on their own for the first time. They enter an environment where they may not know many people and may even live among strangers. The transition from high school to college is difficult for quite a few students because they leave behind the familiar relationships they were used to. Not only do students lack the day-to-day interactions with their family, but they also may lack the social support they had from friends, pals, and others.

The literature that has looked at the social life of students with disabilities in postsecondary educational settings has focused primarily on students with learning, physical, and sensory disabilities. Although the literature is sparse, it does suggest that many students with disabilities experience social problems when they enter postsecondary educational settings (cf., Chadsey & Shelden, 1998). In their review of the literature, Chadsey and Shelden reported that some students were lonely and had feelings of poor self-esteem and personal social adjustment, and difficulties with conversational skills. Some students did not participate in extracurricular activities, but this was not true for all students. Unfortunately, the literature to date reveals little about the type of relationships experienced by these students. Instead, the literature has focused on different emotions (e.g., loneliness) and social skills deficits (e.g., trouble with conversational skills) experienced by these students. Because problems do seem to exist, the critical issue for those who care about these students, or are providing services to them, is to find out which students are having problems and then try to help them.

Strategies for Achieving a Social Life

When students with disabilities enter postsecondary settings, their chances of achieving both academic and social success hinge on the supports they receive and their ability to advocate for themselves (Gajar, 1998). These two areas, self-advocacy and support, are discussed in more depth below.

Self-Advocacy

Self-advocacy requires individuals to effectively communicate or negotiate their own interests, needs, and rights; it also requires that individuals make informed decisions and take responsibility for those decisions and actions. Self-advocacy skills, which are closely related to self-determination skills, have been identified as being critical to making a successful transition from secondary to postsecondary education (Merchant & Gajar, 1997).

Key Question #2: What are the skills associated with self-advocacy?

In a review of the literature, Merchant and Gajar (1997) identified several skills associated with self-advocacy. These skills include being able to:
1. understand one's own disability (strengths and weaknesses)
2. know one's rights under the law
3. understand and be able to express accommodations needed
4. be able to communicate effectively

Gartin, Rumrill, and Serebreni (1996) also stressed the importance of teaching students assertiveness training. Gartin et al., believed that assertiveness training, in addition to directly teaching self-advocacy skills, would help students to handle frustration and turn aggression into assertive action.

Self-advocacy skills primarily have been taught through direct instruction and role-play. As described by Durlak, Rose, and Bursuck (1994), students are:

1. given descriptions of the specific skills by the trainer
2. asked to watch the trainer and an assistant role-play the self-advocacy skills
3. given opportunities to ask questions
4. provided opportunities to rehearse self-advocacy skills
5. given feedback on their performance
6. asked to practice the skills until mastery is demonstrated
7. asked to use the skills in the natural environment

In their review of seven programs that had taught self-advocacy skills, Merchant and Gajar (1997) reported that four of the programs reported outcomes that were empirically based. The majority of the outcomes were positive (i.e., students learned the skills, were able to apply them with other students and professors, and achieved positive results). However, there were some negative results reported; some students were embarrassed to discuss their disability with others and ask for accommodations.

Support

Support to students can come from many sources. Most postsecondary education settings have disability support services available to students. In addition, students can get support from adults (e.g., individuals working in disability support services, professors who might serve as mentors), friends, and social groups (e.g., groups involving only students with disabilities and groups involving students with and without disabilities.)

Gartin et al. (1996) discussed how important it was for students to receive support in getting to know college campuses and communities. For example, students need to be encouraged to participate fully in campus life. Support services can encourage participation in college activities (e.g., sporting events, dances, clubs) and community events (e.g., church activities, concerts, movies). Individuals also can support students by facilitating friendships through formal introductions and informal activities that include all students with similar interests.

Offices on campuses that provide support to students with disabilities (e.g., Disability Support Offices) are critical. For example, Dale (1990) reported that students who participated in a support program on Purdue's campus were significantly more likely to stay in school than those who did not participate in the program. Interestingly, students reported that just knowing that help was available when they needed it was the most helpful service. Similarly, a recent research brief from the National Center for the Study of Postsecondary Educational Supports (April, 2000), revealed that individuals associated with support services were especially helpful in giving advice and "just being there" for students to voice their experiences, concerns, and dreams.

Peers, both with and without disabilities, also can offer support that can enhance the social life of students. In another research brief from the National Center for the Study of Postsecondary Educational Supports (Anderson & Heyer, 2000), interviews with students with disabilities revealed that peers were especially helpful in acting as resources and providing guidance about campus activities, services, and accommodations. In fact, students thought that peers were more patient and helpful than faculty in this regard. Peers were viewed as being critical to integrating students into the campus community. Also, interactions with nondisabled peers were very important to the socialization process because it taught students "how to deal with others." Providing opportunities for students with and without disabilities to participate in activities together and live in the same residential unit would be beneficial. For some students with particular disabilities (e.g., deafness), this may require explanations of disability culture (Longmore, 1995).

Although interactions with peers without disabilities are thought to be important, there is an empowerment movement on some campuses that is making a contribution to some students' social lives. For example, Campbell and Morris (1994) reported the experience of forming a student organization on campus that consisted only of students with disabilities. The goals of the organization were to establish a way for students with disabilities to make their voices hard on issues related to disability, create a social system of support, and provide leadership experiences.

Although faculty associated with the disability support office initially assumed leadership for the group (Campbell and Morris, 1994), they also provided leadership training to the students and gradually the students took more of the initiative for planning and implementing activities. Campbell and Morris (1994) reported that a number of benefits occurred as a result of students forming their own group. First, students increased their self-confidence and self esteem. Additionally, their social and leadership skills improved. As a group, they spoke out on issues related to disability across campus and were able to get priority registration for students with disabilities and fee money allocated for tutoring and other services.

Part of the success of "disability only groups" on campus may be due to identity development (Gill, 1997). As Gill notes, individuals with disabilities need to work out a comfortable identity and social role for themselves even though they are part of a socially marginalized group. Part of this process is feeling comfortable associating with peers who also have disabilities. For some individuals, interacting with others who have disabilities may be associated with unpleasant memories, such as special schools, stereotypes, and stigma contagion. Gill (1997) stated that when individuals with disabilities finally affiliate with others who also have disabilities, they describe it in positive terms of finally "coming home." Additionally, through affiliating with others, individuals with disabilities celebrate their culture and affirm their worth with their disabilities.

Summary

There is little research that talks about specific strategies that will help individuals achieve a satisfactory social life in postsecondary settings. And, very little research has discussed specific strategies that can be used to establish the different types of social relationships that were discussed at the beginning of the chapter. However, it is clear that students need two things in college to help them with their social lives. They need to understand their disability so they can advocate for themselves, and they need the social support of others.

Self-advocacy is very important. For example, if a student has a physical disability and cannot enter a particular building where the student council is meeting, the student needs to know how to advocate for accessibility. Social support is also very important. If accessibility issues are widespread on campus, making it difficult to participate in social activities, then students may need the help and support of disability services on campus. In addition, students with disabilities likely will flourish when they have the support of students with and without disabilities to help them connect to social activities and events. Attending social activities with other students helps to form "pal" relationships that may ultimately lead to friendships.

Employment Settings

While most of us work so that we have money to meet our basic needs of shelter, food, and clothing, we also work to fulfill other needs, including the formation of social relationships. Certainly the nature and quality of social relationships in the workplace will vary by individuals and work cultures. Yet, because social interactions play a critical role in all employment settings, it is essential that individuals with disabilities have these skills when they make the transition from school to work.

Two general types of social behaviors occur in work settings: work-related and non-work-related interactions (Kirmeyer, 1988). Work-related interactions relate to tasks and include following directions, requesting assistance, sharing work information, and accepting criticism (Chadsey-Rusch, Gonzalez, Tines, & Johnson, 1989). Nonwork-related interactions are not related to job tasks and include teasing or joking, sharing information about sports, or asking questions about a co-worker's family (Chadsey-Rusch & Gonzales, 1988). The nature of the interactions in a particular work setting will vary depending on the culture of that workplace, and the individuals who work there.

Several studies have examined employers' perceptions on which social skills are important to employment success. Typically, employers have indicated that work-related social skills are more important than non-work-related social skills (e.g., Salzberg, Agran, & Lignugaris/Kraft, 1986). Employers also have indicated that the importance of a social skill to employment success varies by context (Salzberg et al., 1986). For example, social behaviors might be more important for a salesperson whose job depends on positive social interactions than for a custodian who typically works by herself. And while work-related behaviors are consistently rated as more important than nonwork-related behaviors, the latter still may impact the overall perception of an employee and may be important for developing relationships. Therefore, students making the transition from school to the work force will be served best by having a broad array of positive social skills.

Key Question #3: What are the three types of strategies that can be used in employment settings to impact social integration?

Chadsey and Shelden (1998) described three general types of strategies or interventions that could improve workplace social integration and make an impact on one's social life:

1. individual interventions designed to change the social skills of the targeted employee
2. co-worker interventions designed to change people other than the targeted employee in the work setting

3. contextual interventions designed to change the work environment or social context

Individual Interventions

Individual interventions are those designed to change the social skills (e.g., greetings, initiating conversations) of the targeted individual. Chadsey-Rusch (1986) identified common components of social skills training programs, including:

1. a rationale explaining why the targeted behavior is desirable
2. an opportunity to observe examples of the behavior (i.e., modeling)
3. an opportunity to practice the behavior, usually in role play situations
4. feedback regarding performance

Other strategies for individual interventions have included problem-solving techniques and self-monitoring techniques (Collet-Klingenberg & Chadsey-Rusch, 1991; Misra, 1992; Park &Gaylord-Ross, 1989). More recently, studies have examined the effectiveness of combining traditional social skills training programs with audiotape and video-assisted instruction and feedback (e.g., Grossi, Kimball, & Heward, 1994).

A number of studies have demonstrated the effectiveness of social skills training in teaching new social skills to individuals with disabilities. (See Chadsey & Shelden, 1998 for a review.) Yet, many of these studies also have demonstrated limited maintenance and generalization of the learned social skills. Also, few of these studies assessed whether or not the intervention had an impact on a person's social life. Still, individual interventions may be an effective tool in a multifaceted approach to improving social integration.

Co-Worker Interventions

Chadsey-Rusch and Heal (1995) identified several possible co-worker or employer interventions related to social integration. Examples included teaching them to implement a social skill training program, requesting that they develop a social integration plan, and asking that they participate in mutually enjoyed activities outside of work. Co-worker interventions may be developed either formally or informally. Several examples are presented below.

For instance, young adults who were deaf reported utilizing co-workers as social integration supports (Steinberg, Sullivan, & Montoya, 1999). They described developing a close relationship with a hearing informant who would provide information, answer questions, and explain social expectations and dynamics.

A more formal co-worker intervention strategy might involve formally teaching co-workers new skills. Storey and Garff (1999) taught instructional skills to co-workers who then trained employees with disabilities on new job tasks. All four employees with disabilities demonstrated increased social interactions and integration.

In contrast, Chadsey, Linneman, Rusch, and Cimera (1997) held a series of meetings with co-workers and a supported employee to discuss possible strategies to increase social interactions. Though participants did not see an increase in their total number of interactions, there were increases in non-work interactions.

The success of a social integration intervention involving co-workers may depend somewhat on characteristics beyond the intervention itself, such as the presence of paid staff and the culture of the workplace. Chadsey, Shelden, Horn, and Cimera (1998) compared socially successful and unsuccessful pairs of supported employees who had been involved in co-worker interventions. Socially successful supported employees seemed to work in businesses where most employees worked the same shift, had more non-work-related interactions with supervisors, got together outside of work for informal social activities more frequently, and had more relaxed settings. Supported employees who were unsuccessful were involved in a greater number of interventions in addition to the co-worker interventions, were more often "matched" with a co-worker who was popular, and more often had co-workers asked to be advocates.

Linneman and Horn (1998) provide guidelines for enlisting co-workers to assist with social integration interventions, including

1. get approval for approaching co-workers from the targeted employee
2. identify a co-worker who has similar interests, already interacts with the targeted employee, works directly with the targeted employee, is well-liked by other co-workers, or is suggested by a supervisor or the targeted employee
3. encourage the co-worker to offer suggestions on ways to increase the targeted employee's inclusion in the workplace

Contextual Interventions

Contextual interventions are those strategies that involve manipulating or accessing additional opportunities to interact. Contextual interventions can be used during job development or after a person finds a job. During job development, one can help a job seeker target jobs at workplaces that are friendlier and more relaxed, where co-workers socialize together both at work and off the job, and where there are co-workers with similar interests. Once a job is found, one can create opportunities for interactions by adjusting a transportation schedule so that the employee with a disability arrives in time for morning coffee talk, suggesting a rearrangement of work stations so that the employee with a disability is situated around co-workers with similar interests, or arranging for job sharing between the employee with a disability and her co-workers.

Hagner (2000) suggests assessing thirty-one workplace characteristics and using that information to develop support strategies. These types of interventions are strongly suggested in recent literature on natural supports and workplace cultures (Hagner 2000; Nisbet, 1992). Research demonstrating the effectiveness of such procedures is lacking but suggests that integration (or interaction) opportunities do differ in differing contexts.

For instance, the presence of a job coach may hinder social integration by dampening the number of interaction opportunities for the employee with a disability (Chadsey et al, 1997; Storey & Garff, 1999). Kregel et al. (1996) reported that various job types are more prone to have interactive work cultures. Mank, Cioffo, & Yavanoff (1997) reported that employees with disabilities who are better integrated are those who work more hours and have work roles and initial orientation and training the same as co-workers without disabilities. Chadsey, Shelden, Cimera and Horn (1998) found that workplace characteristics were significant predictors for social integration outcomes. Successful workers were more likely to work in places where there were non-work-related interactions with supervisors, and where there was potential for career advancement. All of these findings suggest that contextual interventions may be useful tools for promoting social integration through increased opportunities.

Summary

The research reported above suggests that successful interventions are complex. Also, it is clear that little research has discussed the impact of these interventions on the formation of relationships, such as pals or friends. Additionally, while all three areas of interventions have demonstrated some promise, most often they will not be used in isolation.

Chadsey and Shelden (1998) suggest an ecological process to identifying social integration interventions. No intervention will work consistently in all workplaces for all employees. Instead, you should consider the individual social skills and intensity of support needs of the employee with a disability; the willingness, ability, and availability of co-workers to implement formal or informal interventions; the characteristics of the workplace; and the desired social outcomes for the particular employee. All of these factors examined together will assist in appropriately matching the needs of the employee to an intervention, or package of interventions, that will assist her in achieving desired social life at work.

Community Settings

Key Question #4: What are strategies that can be used to meet new people in community settings?

While workplaces and family might be our most important contexts for forming social relationships, most of us also look beyond them for some relationships. Whether with neighbors, teammates, fellow civic group members, or just individuals we met and with whom we "clicked," we look to our general community to make new friends and acquaintances. Unfortunately, for individuals with disabilities, particularly those with more intense support needs, there are many barriers to forming social relationships with other community members. While many people with disabilities have increased opportunities for physical integration in their communities (e.g., living in a home in a typical neighborhood), this physical integration does not often lead to meaningful community relationships. Transition services should address supports for both forming and sustaining community relationships.

Creating Opportunities

In order to meet pals and develop friendships, people must have an opportunity to meet new people. Amado (1993) identified several strategies for supporting individuals with disabilities in meeting new people. First, identify the interests, gifts, and contributions of the individual. Second, explore possible connections for the individual based on his or her interests, gifts, and contributions. Where can this interest be expressed? What are the welcoming places in the community? Are there people in the community who have expressed an interest in forming a relationship with a person with a disability?

Newton, Olson, and Horner (1995) interviewed fourteen community members (ten ex-staff, three volunteers, and one friend of staff), each of whom had a social relationship with a person with a disability. Relationships formed from different origins. Some ex-staff reported that they just "clicked" with the individual when they were on staff. Others reported that the relationship began when they assisted the individual through difficult times or that they had filled the role of a "missing" family person. Based on interviews, the authors suggest that, rather than attempting to match individuals with disabilities and other community members, staff would be more helpful in assisting the person to meet as many new people as possible and eventually a relationship will "click."

Transition-related professionals can assist young adults with disabilities by supporting multiple and diverse opportunities to meet people. Assist the individual in exploring the community and identifying places and opportunities of interest. Amado (1993) suggests looking for places where there are opportunities for relationships to develop. Potential arises from opportunities to see the same people over time, or being a "regular," and having a basis for exchange. She also suggests accessing environments where other community members engage in

1. personal business
2. leisure and recreation
3. hobbies
4. continuing education and personal development
5. clubs and organizations
6. volunteer opportunities

Of course, many of these strategies could be addressed concurrently with other transition services and activities.

Supporting Relationships

Once initiated, relationships take work and time to develop and sustain. For individuals with disabilities, there may be unique barriers to sustaining relationships, brought on by a lack of accessibility, inadequate transportation, or rigid program rules. Newton et al. (1995) found that logistical characteristics were viewed as annoyances rather than serious barriers. Community members reported that they often took the initiative for getting together and sometimes had scheduling difficulty with residential staff. They also at times provided transportation and often paid for their friends' costs. In an evaluation of relationships formed through a volunteer matching program, Jameson (1998) found the most commonly encountered logistical barriers to relationships between individuals with mental retardation and their matched friends were:

1. too many other responsibilities preventing more frequent contact
2. difficulty in scheduling
3. life transitions
4. too much geographic distance
5. difficulty with transportation

Newton et al. (1995) discussed the importance of reciprocity to sustaining social relationships. They found that community members often found tangible reciprocity (e.g., exchanging cards and gifts) to be missing from their relationships, while interpreted reciprocity (e.g., complete acceptance, the meaning of an exchange) was present and appreciated. Mutual effort and need also were identified as important to sustaining these relationships.

Logistical barriers and reciprocity issues both point to strategies for transition-related staff to support ongoing relationships. Staff may remind and assist an individual to send a birthday card or call to say hello, or assist a person in identifying activities that would be of common interest and initiating the planning for that activity. Of course, the level of support needed to sustain a relationship depends on the individuals involved. One person may need assistance in selecting a birthday card, signing it, and mailing it. Another person might need a prompt to write "send card to..." reminders in an organizer. As with all other transition services, the nature and intensity of support depends on the individual's needs and preferences.

Summary

Amado (1993) describes three framing contexts to consider when examining your own efforts to build community connections. First, what are your personal values toward and appreciation of individuals with disabilities? Are you willing to form relationships with them? Second, do you have faith and trust that community members will be open to forming relationships with people who are different? Are you willing to ask people you know personally to connect with the individuals you support? Finally, do you believe in the importance of assisting individuals with disabilities in forming relationships in the community?

Amado warns us not to assume that a person who is physically integrated into a community or neighborhood is automatically socially integrated into that community. Even the act of participating in an activity does not indicate that someone is a *member* of that community. If social integration and social relationships are to be attainable transition outcomes for youth with disabilities, transition-related staff must look not only at relationships within work and educational settings, but also to the diverse relationships possible within one's broader community. By supporting a young person's exploration of her interests through community connections, we can support her opportunities to create a wider array of relationships.

Key Question #5: What are the strategies that could be used across postsecondary, work, and community settings to create a satisfactory social life.

As discussed in the beginning of this chapter, there is no one ideal social life; it needs to be individually determined. However, it is quite likely that diverse relationships lead to a more satisfying social life. It may not be necessary for everyone to have all seven of the relationships described by Pogrebin (1987), but interacting only with close kin or acquaintances might not be very satisfying.

Before any strategies are used to create opportunities for relationships, it is essential that individuals with disabilities be asked two important questions. Do you want to have more relationships with people? What kind of relationships do you want? Unless individuals can indicate in some way that they want more friends or closer co-workers, for example, they will not be motivated to work on the strategies that might be recommended.

Best Practice Recommendations

A list of ten recommended practices that cross postsecondary, work, and community settings are listed in Table 1. While these general practices could be used in all three settings, it is important to remember that each particular work, college, and community setting will have a specific culture. The culture of each setting will need to be studied before an intervention strategy is tried. Make notes about what people talk about, what they wear, and how they act. For example, if you are teaching an individual to start conversations with students at a university football game, it would be important to know what the students at the particular university were likely to talk about. Without knowing about the culture of the

Table I
Recommended Practices for Achieving a Social Life across
Postsecondary, Work, and Community Settings

If individuals want to establish new relationships, and also want to learn new social skills, they should have a voice in choosing the skills they want to learn.

Individuals need to know how to communicate effectively. For example, teach individuals to initiate and respond to others and engage in conversations.

It is important that individuals know how to discuss their disability with others. For example, if individuals in a work setting use an augmentative communication system, it is important that co-workers know how to alter their own communication behaviors (e.g., by waiting longer for a conversational turn). In this example, the worker with the disability or a service provider will need to explain the augmentative system to the co-workers.

Individuals should be taught to accept and celebrate their disability and the disabilities of others.

Teach individuals to discuss their rights, desires, and accommodations with others.

Persons without disabilities need to be taught about disability culture and the need to focus on the abilities of a person rather than the disabilities.

Provide opportunities for individuals with disabilities to interact with others. The primary focus should be placed on enjoying the activity (e.g., church, baseball game, birthday party at work) rather than forcing the interactions.

Make certain that all activities on campus, in the community, and at work are accessible and available to everyone.

If appropriate, ask others (e.g., students, co-workers) about strategies they know that could be used to socially involve an individual with disabilities.

Always evaluate the strategy picked and see if social relationships are forming. If they aren't, try a new strategy.

specific football context, you could make and initiate inappropriate conversations. As noted by Hinde (1995), all relationships need to be considered within the social, cultural, and temporal situation in which they occur. For more information about understanding the culture of work settings, see Hagner (2000) and Hagner and DiLeo (1993).

Future Research Issues

The most pressing research issue is which strategies will lead to increased social relationships with others. We cannot say at this time that the implementation of particular set of strategies will result in a particular social relationship. And, we don't know if some strategies, for example, are better suited for forming pal relationships rather than friendships. Of course, there is also the possibility that we will never be able to say with certainty that any strategy will result in the development of relationships. It may be that certain relationships (e.g., friendships), cannot be "programmed" but just naturally occur. Nonetheless, research that helps to predict the types of strategies that lead to specific relationships would be very helpful.

Another issue of concern is the need for researchers to use different types of relationships as outcome measures. Most of the research in this area has primarily assessed a narrow set of social behaviors as the primary outcome. While these measures are important, it would also be important for future research efforts to include different types of relationships as outcome measures.

Research also is needed to better understand the types of relationships that individuals with disabilities desire. How can we assess this if we are working with an individual who has little conventional communication? Also, what kinds of relationships do people with disabilities have with one another? Are their pal and friendship relationships, for example, similar in intent and structure to relationships between people without disabilities? And, there is a need to better describe the types of relationships that exist between people with and without disabilities.

Actually, the field of social relationships is so complex that an entire chapter on future research issues could probably be written just on this topic. Until research is conducted, it is best to try various strategies suggested in this chapter to see what works. If a strategy is not helpful, try another. Social relationships are so important that it is critical we do all that we can to assist individuals with disabilities in achieving this outcome as they make their transition from school to adulthood.

Window to the World
Jamie

At twenty-two, Jamie completed her high school experience. She had spent most of her school years in a self-contained classroom for students with severe cognitive disabilities, but had some previous community-based vocational experiences. In addition to having a cognitive disability, Jamie has cerebral palsy, a hearing impairment, and a speech impairment. She communicates primarily with gestures.

Jamie's first job after high school was as an aide at a daycare center. Her duties included washing toys, assisting with laundry, preparing snacks, and playing with the children. Both her job developer and her supervisor considered Jamie's inclusion in the workplace to be important to her success, and they used several strategies to promote that.

Prior to Jamie starting her position, her job developer met with co-workers to teach them the meanings of the gestures that Jamie used. She also gave them suggestions for communicating with Jamie (e.g., give simple one or two-step directions). These strategies gave co-workers tools to feel more comfortable and be more effective when communicating with Jamie.

The job developer also worked with the supervisor to develop an intense, systematic training program for Jamie so that she could learn her job duties. Prior to Jamie's first day on the job, the job developer taught two co-workers how to implement the training program so that they could be the primary trainers. The job developer provided ongoing consultation to the co-workers as they implemented the program. This allowed Jamie immedi-

ate and typical opportunities to interact with her co-workers. In all of her duties, Jamie was paired with a co-worker doing similar tasks or working in the same area so she could have ongoing interaction with co-workers.

Jamie's transportation to and from work was going to be provided by the agency from which she received services. The agency transportation schedule demanded that Jamie arrive at work later than most co-workers and leave earlier. Her job developer arranged for one of Jamie's neighbors to pick her up from work once a week. This allowed Jamie to participate in some casual non-work-related interactions at the end of the day, as well as to spend regular time with one of her neighbors. After a few weeks on the job, Jamie and her neighbor started going to a neighborhood coffee shop on the way home to relax. Not only did this give Jamie even more opportunity to get acquainted with her neighbor, but also gave her an opportunity to meet other neighborhood residents.

The combination of contextual and co-worker strategies designed by Jamie's job developer and supervisor facilitated Jamie's membership in the workplace and assisted her in exploring her interests in the neighborhood. After several months on the job, Jamie had greatly expanded her communication skills, developing new gestures and using meaningful vocalizations. Her co-workers, as well as children in the daycare center, communicated effectively with her. Jamie was included in all workplace social activities, was a valued employee of the daycare center, and started forming close relationships with some co-workers. She also developed a friendship with her car pool neighbor and met several new acquaintances in the neighborhood.

Window to the World
Geraldo

At eighteen years of age, Geraldo was starting his freshman year in college. He had been a good student in high school, but was somewhat concerned about succeeding in college. Like many first year college students, he was both concerned and excited about a chance to meet new people and develop new friendships. He had selected his school based on the strength of its history program (his desired major) but also on its level of accessibility. Geraldo uses a motorized wheelchair and has a speech impairment.

Geraldo decided to be proactive in developing new relationships. His first week on campus, he went to the disability services office to discuss its support services. He also asked for information on the most accessible "hang outs" on and around campus so that he could have more opportunities to meet people. The staff of the disability services office provided him with accessibility maps, but also introduced him to a junior who also used a motorized wheelchair and had more knowledge of accessibility beyond campus. This junior became something of a mentor for Geraldo, particularly in terms of requesting accommodations from professors.

Geraldo knew that many people had difficulty understanding his speech, particularly when they first met him. As he did in high school, he assured people that it was okay to ask him to repeat himself if they did not understand him, and assured them that he would prefer that over having his words misunderstood. While he sometimes made these assurances through speaking, he also had them written on a card that he could show people. As he developed relationships, some of the individuals who had become more accustomed to his speech were able to serve as interpreters when necessary.

Geraldo was not a particularly outgoing person by nature, but he decided to take early steps in meeting people. He quickly identified a likeable, outgoing person on his dormitory floor and got to know him. Through this dorm pal, Geraldo felt more comfortable meeting other people in his dormitory. He joined student organizations that reflected his interests and began introducing himself to people in classes. He initiated social gatherings and study groups, always being sure to suggest accessible meeting places. Geraldo's proactive approach, his strategy for putting people at ease with his speech, and the social mentors he identified assisted him in developing acquaintances and friendships during his first year of college.

Discussion Questions

1. Much discussion on inclusion and integration highlights the importance of people with disabilities having relationships with individuals who do not have disabilities. How important is having an integrated social network to achieving positive social outcomes? Are there concerns about using integration as a benchmark for the quality of a social network?
2. Many people with disabilities who receive daily support from professionals will identify those professionals as their best friends. Is that a desired social outcome? What are the pros and cons?
3. Currently, many organizations that support individuals with disabilities have programs through which they try to arrange social relationships by matching individuals with disabilities with community members who have volunteered for the program. What are the pros and cons of such a program? Can arranged friendships be a reality?

Community-Based Activities

1. New Relationships through Community Connections
   Identify an individual with a disability who would like to form new relationships. Interview that individual about his or her likes and dislikes, hobbies, and values. Then, identify five to ten community connections the individual could make related to likes, dislikes, hobbies, and values. Considering the person's strengths and support needs, develop a support plan to assist the person in making those community connections.
2. Social Skills at Work
   Select an employment site. Schedule a face-to-face interview with a supervisor or manager at that site. Ask the employer to identify (a) social skills he or she considers to be necessary for maintaining employment and (b) social skills he or she considers to be important for career advancement within the agency. Also, ask the employer to identify one of his or her best employees and describe the characteristics that make that person a top employee.

References

Amado, A. N. (Ed.). (1993). *Friendships and community connections between people with and without developmental disabilities.* Baltimore: Paul H. Brookes.

Anderson, J., & Heyer, K. (2000, April). *Third general methodology: Special supports and viewpoints of students and graduates. Focus groups: Procedural description.* www.rrtc.Hawaii.edu/products.

Campbell, K., & Morris, J. (1994). *Empowering students with disabilities through organization and involvement in student government: A step-by-step approach to creating a student organization.* Paper presented at the meeting of the AHEAD Conference, Columbus, OH.

Chadsey, J. G., Linneman, D., Rusch, F. R., & Cimera, R. E. (1997). The impact of social integration interventions and job coaches in work setting. *Education and Training in Mental Retardation and Developmental Disabilities, 32,* 281-292.

Chadsey, J. G., & Shelden, D. (1998). Moving toward social inclusion in employment and postsecondary school settings. In Rusch, F. R., & Chadsey, J. G. (Eds.), *Beyond high school: Transition from school to work* (406-437). Belmont, CA: Wadsworth.

Chadsey, J. G., Shelden, D. L., Cimera, R. E., & Horn, J. R. (1998). Personal and environmental variables that predict successful social integration. In J. G. Chadsey & D. L. Shelden (Eds.), *Promoting social relationships and integration for supported employees in work settings.* Champaign, IL: University of Illinois.

Chadsey, J. G., Shelden, D. L., Horn, J. R., & Cimera, R. E. (1998). Descriptions of variables impacting successful and unsuccessful cases of social integration involving co-workers. In J. G. Chadsey & D. L. Shelden (Eds.), *Promoting social relationships and integration for supported employees in work settings.* Champaign, IL: University of Illinois.

Chadsey-Rusch, J. (1986). Identifying and teaching valued social behaviors in competitive employment settings. In F. R. Rusch (Ed.), *Competitive employment: Issues and strategies* (273-287). Baltimore: Paul H. Brookes.

Chadsey-Rusch, J., & Gonzalez, P., (1988). Social ecology of the workplace: Employer's perceptions versus direct observation. *Research in Developmental Disabilities, 9,* 229-245.

Chadsey-Rusch, J. & Heal, L. (1995). Building consensus from transition experts on social integration outcomes and interventions. *Exceptional Children,* 165-187.

Chadsey-Rusch, J., Gonzalez, P., Tines, J., & Johnson, J. (1989). Social ecology of the workplace: Contextual variables affecting social interactions of employees with and without mental retardation. *American Journal on Mental Retardation, 94,* 141-151.

Collet-Klingenberg, L. & Chadsey-Rusch, J. (1991). Using a cognitive-process approach to teach social skills. *Education and Training in Mental Retardation, 26,* 258-270.

Dale, P.M. (1990). *A successful college retention program.* Unpublished manuscript. Purdue University, West Lafayette, Indiana.

Durlak, C. M., Rose, E., & Bursuck, W. D. (1994). Preparing high school students with learning disabilities for the transition to postsecondary education: Teaching the skills of self-determination. *Journal of Learning Disability, 27,* 51-59.

Gajar, A. (1998). Postsecondary education. In F. R. Rusch, & J. G. Chadsey (Eds.), *Beyond high school: Transition from school to work* (383-405). Belmont, CA: Wadsworth.

Gartin, B., Rumrill, P., & Serebreno, R. (1996). The higher education transition model: Guidelines for facilitating college transition among college-bound students with disabilities. *Teaching Exceptional Children, 29,* 30-33.

Gill, C. J. Four types of integration in disability identity development. *Journal of Vocational Rehabilitation, 9,* 39-46.

Grossi, T. A., Kimball, J. W., & Heward, W. L. (1994). "What did you say?" Using review of tape-recorded interactions to increase social acknowledgments by trainees in a community-based vocational program. *Research in Developmental Disabilities, 15,* 457-472.

Hagner, D. C. (2000). *Coffee breaks and birthday cakes: Evaluating workplace cultures to develop natural supports for employees with disabilities.* St. Augustine, FL: Training Resource Network, Inc.

Hagner, D., & DiLeo, D. (1993). *Working together; workplace culture, supported employment, and persons with disabilities.* Cambridge, MA: Brookline Books.

Halpern, A. S. (1993). Quality of life as a conceptual framework for evaluating transition outcomes. *Exceptional Children, 59,* 486-498.

Hinde, R. A. (1995). A suggested structure for a science of relationships. *Personal Relationships, 2,* 1-15.

House, J. S. (1981). *Work stress and social support.* Redding, MA: Addison-Wesley.

Hughes, C., Hwang, B., Kim, J., Eisenman, L. T., & Killian, D. J. (1995). Quality of life in applied research: A review and analysis of empirical measures. *American Journal on Mental Retardation, 99,* 623-641.

Jameson, C. (1998). Promoting long-term relationships between individuals with mental retardation and people in their community: An agency self-evaluation. *Mental Retardation, 36 (2),* 116-127.

Kirmeyer, S. L. (1988). Observed communication in the workplace: Content, source, and direction. *Journal of Community Psychology, 16,* 175-187.

Linneman, D., & Horn, J. R. (1998). Enlisting co-workers to help plan interventions. In J. G. Chadsey & D. L. Shelden (Eds.), *Promoting social relationships and integration for supported employees in work settings.* Champaign, IL: University of Illinois.

Longmore, P. K. (1995). The second phase: From disability rights to disability culture. *The Disability Rag & ReSource, 16*(5), 4-11.

Mank, D., Cioffi, A., & Yovanoff, P. (1997). Analysis of typicalness of supported employment jobs, natural supports, and wage and integration outcomes. *Mental Retardation, 35,* 185-197.

Mannarino, A. P. (1980). The development of children's friendships. In H. C. Foot, A. J. Chapman, & J. R. Smith (Eds.), *Friendships and social relationships and children* (45-63). New York: John Wiley & Sons.

Merchant, D. J., & Gajar, A. (1997). A review of the literature on self-advocacy components in transition programs for students with learning disabilities. *Journal of Vocational Rehabilitation, 8,* 223-231.

Meyer, L. H., Park, H. S., Grenot-Scheyer, M., Schwartz, I. S., & Hamy, B. (1998). Participatory research approaches for the study of social relationships of children and youth. In L. H. Meyer, H. S. Park, M. Grenot-Scheyer, I. S. Schwartz, & B. Hamy (Eds.), *Making friends: The influences of culture and development* (3-29). Baltimore: Paul H. Brookes.

Misra, A. (1992). Generalization of social skills through self-monitoring by adults with mental retardation. *Exceptional Children, 58,* 495-507.

Morgan, R. L., & Salzberg, C. L. (1992). Effects of video-assisted training on employment-related social skills of adults with severe mental retardation. *Journal of Applied Behavior Analysis, 25,* 365-383.

Newton, J. S., Olson, D., & Horner, R. H. (1995). Factors contributing to the stability of social relationships between individuals with mental retardation and other community members. *Mental Retardation, 33,* 383–393.

National Center for the Study of Postsecondary Educational Supports: Research Brief (2000, April). *Focus groups: Faculty mentors and peer role models.* www.rrtc.Hawaii.edu/products.

Nisbet, J. (1992). *Natural supports in school, at work, and in the community for people with severe disabilities.* Baltimore: Paul H. Brookes.

Park, H. S., & Gaylord-Ross, R. (1989). A problem-solving approach to social skill straining in employment settings with mentally retarded youth. *Journal of Applied Behavior Analysis, 23,* 373-380.

Pogrebin, L. C. (1987). *Among friends.* New York: McGraw-Hill.

Rubin, L. B. (1985). *Just friends: The roles of friendship in our lives.* New York: Harper & Rowe.

Salzberg, C. L., Agran, M., & Lignugaris-Kraft, B. (1986). Behaviors that contribute to entry-level employment: A profile of five jobs. *Applied Research in Mental Retardation, 7,* 299-314.

Schalock, R. L. (2000). Three decades of quality of life. *Focus on Autism and Other Developmental Disabilities, 15,* 116-127.

Steinberg, A. S., Sullivan, V. J., Montoya, L. A. (1999). Loneliness and social isolation in the work place for deaf individuals during the transition years: A preliminary investigation. *Journal of Applied Rehabilitation Counseling, 30,* 22-30.

Stewart, N. (1985). *Winning friends at work.* New York: Ballantine Books.

Storey, K., & Garff, J. T. (1999). The effect of co-worker instruction on the integration of youth in transition in competitive employment. *Career Development for Exceptional Individuals, 22*(1), 69-84.

Chapter 8
Quality of Life

Carolyn Hughes and Susan Copeland
University of New Mexico
Stephanie Fowler and Penny Church-Pupke
Vanderbilt University

Key Questions
1. How do the 1997 IDEA Amendments address quality of life?
2. What are the major dimensions of a conceptual model of quality of life?
3. What are the major implementation issues when addressing quality of life in secondary transition programs?

Key Question #1: How do the 1997 IDEA Amendments address quality of life?

The Individuals with Disabilities Education Act (IDEA) Amendments of 1997 embody a coordinated set of activities and outcomes that comprise the secondary transition process. For example, IDEA-mandated transition activities include instruction, related services, community experiences, and functional assessments that address student outcomes such as employment, postsecondary education, independent living, and community participation. The amendments also propose educational goals that address the adult lives of students:

Disability is a natural part of the human experience and in no way diminishes the right of individuals to participate in or contribute to society. Improving educational results for children with disabilities is an essential element of our national policy of ensuring equality of opportunity, full participation, independent living, and economic self-sufficiency for individuals with disabilities. (Individuals with Disabilities Education Act Amendments of 1997, Section 601)

In addition, the IDEA legislation requires that educational personnel ensure that students *"have the skills and knowledge...to be prepared to lead productive, independent, adult lives, to the maximum extent possible"* (Section 601).

Clearly, an intent of the IDEA Amendments of 1997 is to maximize the quality of students' lives as they transition from high school to post-school experiences. Secondary educators are expected to provide transition services that are designed to promote the participation of all students in worthwhile and satisfying adult life experiences. These experiences may include having a promising career, engaging in personal relationships, living in a comfortable home, and enjoying leisure-time activities, expectations many of us hold for adulthood. Post-school outcomes targeted in the IDEA Amendments—equal opportunity, full participation in community life, independent living, and economic self-sufficiency—are goals that many would agree are essential components of what we call "quality of life." Indeed, researchers have argued that the effectiveness of educational programs should be judged by the quality of life outcomes experienced by program participants (Campo, Sharpton, Thompson, & Sexton, 1997; Hatton, 1998).

But to what extent is transition programming helping high school students experience quality in their adult lives? Stark and Goldsbury (1990) observed that:

...despite the billions of dollars that have been allocated in implementing policies such as deinstitutionalization, mainstreaming, early intervention, and community integration, we have not yet answered the critical question: "Has it really made a difference in improving the quality of life for persons with [disabilities]?" (p. 71)

Recent findings indicate that today, ten years later, the answer to Stark and Goldsbury's incisive question remains an emphatic "No!" Despite growing attention in federal policy, research, and the media, studies show that secondary educational efforts have not improved the quality of life experienced by large numbers of students (e.g., Blackorby & Wagner, 1996). Unemployment, financial dependence, and lack of social relationships are the outcomes faced by many students when they leave high school. Three to five years after leaving school, fewer than 8% of young adults with disabilities are reported to be fully employed or enrolled in postsecondary education, active socially, and living independently in the community (Wagner, 1995). In addition, students with disabilities who are from high poverty backgrounds and those who are nonwhite are more likely to drop out of or be expelled from school and be economically unengaged as adults (Lewit, Terman, & Behrman, 1997). These findings paint a dismal picture of the quality of life of many students leaving high school.

The 1997 IDEA Amendments require that transition programming takes into account students' preferences and interests, factors most would agree are critical to quality of life. But recent studies show that transition-age students have little opportunity to make choices and decisions. For example, teachers report little involvement by students nationally in developing their own educational goals and programs or in participation in their own individualized education program (IEP) meetings (Wehmeyer, Agran, & Hughes, 2000). Limited opportunities to choose, unfortunately, may persist into adulthood. Too often, choices about everyday living, such as what to wear or eat, how to spend free time, or where to live or work, are made by parents, teachers, or service providers, even after students leave high school (Stancliffe & Abery, 1997; Wehmeyer & Bolding, 1999).

What Is "Quality of Life?"

Although there is considerable discussion in the field of secondary transition addressing quality of life, there is little consensus regarding critical factors that comprise this construct (Brown, 1998). Researchers have argued that people's unique perceptions influence their conceptions of the quality of their lives, making it difficult to establish a universally accepted conceptual model of quality of life (Heal, Khoju, & Rusch, 1997). A consensus definition or conceptual framework is important, however, to allow transition specialists and other service providers to assess the degree transition programming efforts influence the quality of life that students experience during and after high school (Schalock, 1996).

Agreement on a conceptual model of the construct "quality of life" would help to provide a measure to determine if participation in transition programs has had a positive impact on students' everyday lives. Although specific events that influence the quality of people's lives may vary across individuals and their life spans, agreement may be reached regarding fundamental dimensions (Hughes, Hwang, Kim, Eisenman, & Killian, 1995). The remainder of this chapter:

1. describes a conceptual model and consensus list of dimensions of quality as derived from the literature
2. discusses implementation issues for addressing quality of life in transition programs
3. presents best practice recommendations
4. suggests future research issues related to quality of life and secondary transition

Key Question #2: What are the major dimensions of a conceptual model of quality of life?

After identifying definitions of "quality of life" in the empirical and conceptual literature, we then identified eighty-seven empirical studies investigating quality of life dimensions that conformed to the conceptual framework. Fifteen dimensions of quality of life consistent with the conceptual framework, and their representative indicators, became the conceptual model of quality of life. (See Hughes et al. [1995] for a more complete description of the process used to develop a conceptual model of quality of life and corresponding quality of life dimensions.)

Table 1 shows the fifteen dimensions and sub-dimensions along with representative examples of indicators of quality of life derived from the reviewed studies. The number of indicators identified across studies is listed after each dimension. Sub-dimensions are listed in decreasing order of frequency of indicators.

In total, 1,243 indicators of quality of life that were consistent with the model were identified. As shown in Table 1, the dimension with the greatest number of indicators ($\underline{n}$ = 198) was social relationships, suggesting strong support that social relationships has been identified in the literature as an important factor in the quality of people's lives. Other dimensions that were supported by one hundred or more indicators were psychological well-being ($\underline{n}$ = 183), employment ($\underline{n}$ = 150), self-determination ($\underline{n}$ = 128), and recreation and leisure ($\underline{n}$ = 100). Six dimensions were supported by sixty or more indicators (i.e., independent living skills, residential environment, community participation, lifestyle patterns, support received, individual and family resources). The final four dimensions were supported by fifteen or less indicators (i.e., personal development, social acceptance, physical and material well-being, civil rights, and responsibilities).

Implications of the Conceptual Model of Quality of Life

The fundamental dimensions of a model of quality of life may have relevance for many people, including secondary transition-age students. However, the means for addressing these dimensions may be specific to each person (Hughes et al., 1995). For example, this model strongly supports social relationships as a dimension of quality of life. However, satisfying relationships may be experienced by a variety of means, such as being married and spending time at home with family,

Table 1
Dimensions, Subdimensions, and Representative
Indicators of a Model of Quality of Life

Social Relationships (198)[a]

Friendship
   Number of friends with and without disabilities, variety of friends, having a best friend
Interpersonal relationships
   Number of relationships, having a girlfriend or boyfriend, relationships with neighbors
Social interaction
   Frequency of interacting with friends, interaction with family, group size during social interaction
Interpersonal and social activities
   Type of activities engaged in, eating out with family or friends, visiting with others

Social support networks
   Extent of involvement of family members, sources of social support, number of people in social support network
Social skills
   Getting along with others, making friends, initiating social interaction
Type of social support received
   Personal and emotional support, being helped to maintain level of self-care, reliance on benefactor or advocate
Affection
   Smiling when interacting; touching a person in a friendly, appropriate manner
Social responsibility
   Having social responsibility

Psychological Well-Being (183)

Life satisfaction
   Satisfaction with residential situation, satisfaction with friendships, and satisfaction with leisure and free time activities
Feelings
   Feeling lonely, feeling depressed, feeling "on top of the world"
Perception of one's life situation
   Perceived level of independence, perceived well-being, perceived level of feeling "normal"
Personal values
   Perceived importance of getting recognition on the job, aspirations for independence, perceived importance of interpersonal relationships

Self-concept
   Self-confidence, self-esteem, body image
Mental health
   Emotional stability, coping with anger, verbalizing feelings
Sense of general well-being
   Zest for life, enjoyment of life, qualitative dimension of life
Happiness and contentment
   Maintaining personal happiness, general feeling of happiness
Personal dignity
   Feeling of personal dignity

Employment (150)

Job satisfaction
   Satisfaction with wages, satisfaction with opportunities for promotion, responding positively toward going to work
Vocational skills
   Job initiative, attendance, job skills
Support at the worksite
   Social support network at work, family support at work, employer support

Social interaction at worksite
   Frequency of social interaction at work, having friends at work, interacting with co-workers and supervisor during work
Employment-related interpersonal skills
   Getting along with others at work, physical appearance at work, communication skills
Working environment and conditions
   Wages, number of co-workers, type of supervision

Employment, continued

Employee history and characteristics
Length of employment, employee health, promotions received

Work performance
Productivity, quality of work, consistency of work performance

Job characteristics and requirements
Job type, task demands, worker's description of job tasks

Positive effects of job on employee
Increased self-worth of employee, improved worker attitudes, increased employee independence

Opportunity for advancement
Upward mobility, opportunity for advancement on the job

Worksite integration
Level of integration at the worksite, involvement of co-workers without disabilities

Job match
Match between worker's preference and job held

Job prestige and status
Employment status

Perceived role in work environment
Employee's perceived importance of work to employer

Self-Determination (128)

Personal control and autonomy
Having control of when to go to bed and when to get up, being able to refuse entry into one's room, being allowed to go alone to places in the community

Preference and choice
Preference for spending time alone, choosing with whom to live, choosing own menu

Independence
Level of independence when choosing home, level of independence when banking, self-sufficiency

Opportunity to live independently
Opportunity to live alone

Personal decision-making and problem solving
Decision-making skills, personal problem solving, deciding how to handle one's money

Self-direction
Goal setting, self-control, self-management

Opportunity for expressing preference
Opportunity to attend IPP meeting, opportunity to voice selection of television shows, opportunity to individualize routine

Personal freedom
Freedom to choose to go or not go on group outings, freedom to take risks, freedom from restrictiveness and routines

Recreation and Leisure (100)

Type of activity
Watching television, visiting friends, going to a movie

Opportunity for recreation and leisure
Availability of leisure activities, opportunity to participate in leisure activities, availability of a partner for activities

Recreation and leisure skills
Leisure time skills, degree of supervision needed

Quality of activities
Frequency of participation, active participation versus "being kept busy"

Independent Living Skills (92)

Domestic skills
Preparing meals, doing laundry, cleaning house

Self-care skills
Eating, grooming, selecting clothes

Communication and language skills
Receptive language skills, mode of communication, written language skills

Personal finance skills
Money management, having a credit card, making purchases

Responsibility
Personal responsibility

Independent living skills
Shopping for groceries, able to work, frequency of performing daily living skills

Survival skills
Time management, using telephone, taking safety precautions

Adaptive functioning
Ambulatory skills, continence, adaptability

Personal competence
Coping skills, managing day-to-day needs

Cognitive skills
General cognition

Table 1, continued

Residential Environment (92)

Living conditions
Number of co-residents, sense of unity and cohesion in a home, living in a healthy, safe place

Residential environment
Proximity of services to residence, urban versus rural environment, physical integration of home into neighborhood setting

Living arrangement
Supervised apartment, living independently, living with parents

Community Participation (72)

Community integration and participation
Frequency of visiting church or synagogue, frequency of visiting friends and relatives, use of resources/facilities in the community

Mobility
Frequency of using public transportation, moving around community safely and independently, ability to leave a building independently or with assistance

Community living skills
Using telephone, frequency of performing community living skills, adapting to community life

Opportunity for participation in community activities
Isolated settings in which public interaction not possible, opportunity to engage in community

Lifestyle Patterns (65)

Activity patterns
Age appropriateness of activities, routines, and rhythms, variety of activities, purpose of activities (functional, social, isolated)

Daily lifestyle
Variation in times getting up and going to bed throughout the week; privacy; attending leisure activities alone, with support person, with another resident, or with all residents

Service models
Staff attitudes toward activities promoting independence and normalization, use of socially appropriate terms to refer to individuals, application of normalization principles by residence

Support Received (61)

Services received/needed
Income support (SSI) received per month, home assistance, health services received

Support staff characteristics
Staff support for facilitating positive relationships at home, staff turnover, home care providers' expectations of resident

Quality of care (services)
Respect for individual's personal dignity, residents' perception of staff support, individualization of services

Individual and Family Resources (60)

Individual demographics
Age, gender, income earned

Environmental demographics
Community characteristics, access to community facilities/activities, cost of public transportation

Individual characteristics
Initiative at work or home, individual's persistence, degree to which behavior problems are manageable

Family characteristics
Family income

Personal Development (15)

Instructional opportunity
Independent living skills training, employment skills training, access to classes
Academic skills
Reading and writing skills, improving academic skills
Educational attainment
Attending school, frequency of attending educational classes, educational program enrolled in

Spiritual and personal fulfillment
Engaged in self-improvement, maintaining personal interests
Access to a stimulating environment
Degree of stimulation of community living
Opportunity for personal development and fulfillment
Freedom to try new tasks and develop new skills

Social Acceptance (12)

Social acceptance
Social acceptance on the job, people's response to resident in public, neighbors' responding to resident in a friendly, accepting manner

Social role functions
Contributing to the community, producing work that contributes to a household or community
Respect
Mutual respect among staff and residents

Physical and Material Well-Being (9)

Physical health
Weight, blood pressure, physical development

Personal safety
Safety from abuse, freedom from exploitation

Civic Rights and Responsibility (6)

Asserting and performing civic rights and responsibilities
Rate of court appearances, history of arrests, voting

Opportunity for civic activities
Not assessed

Total (1243)
ªNumber of indicators.

Adapted from Hughes C., Hwang, B., Kim, J., Eisenman L.T., and Killian, D. J. (1995) "A quality of life in applied research: conceptual model and analysis of measures," American Journal of Mental Retardation. Reprinted with permission.

or living alone or with a roommate and spending time with friends or co-workers at work or sporting events.

The broad array of indicators of quality of life supports the interrelationship among multiple environmental and personal factors as diverse as working in quiet or noisy environments, having a best friend, and budgeting one's money. For example, environmental indicators include working environment and conditions, living situation, residential environment, and proximity of services and community resources. Personal characteristics identified as indicators of quality of life included personal competence, community participation, independent living skills, and financial resources. Corroborating these findings, a statistical relationship has been reported among multidimensional measures of personal competence (e.g., personal living skills, community living skills, social skills), environmental factors (e.g., support services, living arrangements, work environment), and indicators of quality of life (McGrew, Bruininks, & Thurlow, 1992).

Key Question #3: What are the major implementation issues when addressing quality of life in secondary transition programs?

Issues related to implementation of transition programming designed to address quality of life include providing (a) multidimensional efforts, (b) early intervention, and (c) ongoing evaluation. These issues are addressed below.

Multi-Dimensional Efforts

Efforts to impact students' quality of life must address multiple aspects of students' lives while they are still in school. For example, if transition teachers expect to improve the quality of students' lives during and after high school, transition programming should be expanded beyond the coordinated set of activities required by the 1997 IDEA Amendments. IDEA-mandated activities address student outcomes such as employment, independent living, postsecondary education, and community participation.

But, in order to address all dimensions of the quality of students' lives, teachers should incorporate additional activities that address students' social relationships and social acceptance, psychological and physical well being, personal development, self-determination, recreation and leisure activities, lifestyle patterns, residential and family situation, support received, and civic rights and responsibilities. Unless transition programming is a multifaceted effort that addresses all aspects of students' lives, youths leaving high school may continue to face grim post-school outcomes of dependence, social isolation, and lack of engagement in worthwhile activities.

Early Intervention

Efforts to affect secondary students' quality of life must begin early. The 1997 IDEA Amendments require that beginning at age fourteen or earlier students' transition service needs must be included in their individualized education programs (IEPs). These services include activities such as instruction, related services, employment training, and community experiences. Thus, the amendments acknowledge the necessity for addressing students' post-school outcomes well before students are expected to graduate or otherwise exit from high school. For many students, major life goals such as employment, economic independence, and community participation must be addressed over a long period of time if successful outcomes are expected.

Quality of life outcomes for students also must be addressed early in students' lives. Intervention goals, efforts, and services that are expected to improve the quality of students' lives must be developed for students by age fourteen and, to ensure their implementation, must be incorporated into IEPs.

For example, some students have not had ample opportunities to interact with their peers in order to develop the social skills required to develop friendships and close interpersonal relationships. IEP goals for these students should include early and ongoing opportunities to participate in general education classes and activities, as well as outside-school and community events, and to receive services such as peer mentoring to support this participation. Other students may have low self-esteem or inaccurate perceptions of their own competence. These students' needs could be addressed by IEP goals and services introduced well before students are planning to leave high school. For example, this could include participation in adolescent counseling or peer support groups or instruction designed to increase assertiveness or self-management skills. Addressing quality of life outcomes early in students' lives and incorporating quality of life goals and programming into their IEPs may promote desirable, long-term adult experiences for students participating in secondary transition programs.

Ongoing Evaluation

To ensure that quality of life outcomes are being addressed and achieved within a student's transition program, ongoing evaluation must be incorporated into program implementation. The success of a transition program in impacting a student's quality of life should be measured at an individual level. The quality of life model in Table 1 could be adapted for use as a checklist to determine the effectiveness of a transition program for individual students. Areas in which a student is not experiencing quality of life could become targets of transition programming. The following case study illustrates how the checklist could be used.

Window to the World
Warren

Warren had a smile as "wide as a barn door." As a freshman at Capri Beach High School, he was already well-known around campus. Warren's classes included English, culinary arts, business math, physical education, and world history. To get around school, Warren used a wheelchair. Because he had difficulty following a schedule and finding his classrooms, a classmate accompanied him in the hall from class to class. Warren considered this enjoyable because he got to say hello and hang out with his classmates.

Classmates also helped Warren complete his assignments because he did not read or write and used just a few short phrases when speaking. When class assignments were finished, Warren usually had time to have some fun with his classmates before going to his next class. Mr. Reynolds, Warren's transition teacher, stopped in often to visit with Warren and his teachers to check on how Warren was doing and to see if there were any problems. Mr. Reynolds used the Quality of Life Checklist when he stopped in each classroom to evaluate how Warren's life appeared to be doing in relation to the major quality of life dimensions. In general, Warren seemed to be accepted, happy, and healthy; involved in friendships and peer support groups; engaged in learning new skills that he could apply to a job or post-school training; and enjoying "hanging out" and engaging in other leisure activities with his friends.

Mr. Reynolds was surprised, then, when he made a visit to observe Warren at home. Again using the Quality of Life Checklist, Mr. Reynolds felt he was observing a completely different person! He saw a young man who rarely had friends visit him and who rarely left the house to participate in community activities. In fact, Warren's parents remarked to Mr. Reynolds that Warren spent practically every evening "zoned out and sitting in front of the television." Whereas at school Warren was sociable with his friends, at home he rarely even interacted with his parents.

The reasons for Warren's behavior soon became clear, however. The checklist evaluation revealed that Warren had no access to transportation, few friends whom he knew in his neighborhood, and little knowledge of resources available in the community. As a result, rather than spending time with peers and engaging in worthwhile activities as he did at school, Warren was living a life of almost complete inactivity and social isolation.

Mr. Reynolds responded first by determining Warren's preferences for community involvement. He taught him how to ride the city bus and found a peer in the neighborhood who could accompany Warren to community activities. Because Warren was interested in sports and social activities, Mr. Reynolds initially targeted recreational opportunities available at the neighborhood YMCA. Mr. Reynolds helped Warren's parents develop a simple communication booklet to encourage Warren to interact with them at home. With Warren's input, his parents also purchased some computer and board games that they could all enjoy together. Soon, through his activities at the local YMCA, Warren began to make other friends in his neighborhood who sometimes came over to his home.

Mr. Reynolds ongoing assessments of Warren's quality of life continued to show social participation and engagement in worthwhile activities at home, school, and in the community throughout the school year. He was glad he had learned to look at each student's total life, not just what he saw at school!

Best Practice Recommendations

Teachers want to use instructional strategies that they know are both empirically sound and that have worked for other teachers, whether they are targeting quality of life or other educational outcomes. Consequently, the secondary transition strategies discussed here both were derived from the empirical literature and were field tested by over one hundred secondary transition teachers (Hughes & Carter, 2000). In this section, we present best practice recommendations provided by these teachers, which specifically target enhancing quality of life of students in secondary transition programs. Recommendations are provided for each of the fifteen quality of life dimensions in Table 1.

1. Social relationships: A job is not just a place to work. Observe how employees at a worksite interact with each other, such as participating in a walking club at noon, chatting as they deliver mail to different offices, or celebrating a co-worker's birthday at break. Support students in getting involved in these activities and becoming a part of the social life of a workplace.
2. Psychological well-being: The best source regarding a student's psychological well-being may be the student. Take time to interview your students regularly to gain their insight into their own strengths, feelings, and psychological needs. Use alternative modes of communication with students who are nonverbal, such as pictures or objects, to find out what they have to say.
3. Employment: Provide frequent opportunities for community-based employment training. Student often learn expected skills easier by observing others perform them in the actual environment. For example, by observing a co-worker taking orders from customers at a restaurant or a supervisor doing the billing at a bank, a student can see expected behaviors in

action. Then, he or she can try performing the behaviors and get corrective feedback, if needed.

4. Self-determination: Self-determination means knowing how to make choices and prioritize activities in your life. Help students learn to prioritize their choices by making lists. For instance, list those things that must be done to achieve a goal such as passing a driver's test. Or develop a list of steps for preparing for a job interview. Picture lists can be used with students who do not read or write.

5. Recreation and leisure: Some of the best opportunities for leisure and recreation occur when we throw away our planning schedules and just take time to enjoy the moment! Although it's important to involve students in scheduled recreation activities that reflect their preferences, it is also important to give students the chance just to relax and spend time in a leisurely way with their peers.

6. Independent living skills: A home-living apartment affiliated with a high school transition program can be an ideal way for students to try out newly acquired independent living skills in a safe environment. Students can spend several nights per week at the apartment with supervision as part of their high school curriculum before graduating and living more on their own.

7. Residential environment: What are the living conditions like in your students' homes, with whom do they live, and what resources are available in their communities? Ask family members to help students complete home inventories that provide information about their homes and communities, and students' likes, dislikes, and concerns in relation to their residential environments. Teachers can use this information to develop transition programs and opportunities that address each student's preferences, strengths, and needs at home.

8. Community participation: Getting involved in helping others is a great way for students to interact with others in the community. Serving a meal at a homeless shelter, fixing up a halfway house, and building a wheelchair ramp are opportunities for students to contribute to and participate in the community.

9. Lifestyle patterns: How much are students participating in activities throughout the day that are similar to those in which their peers are involved? You can find out by observing a student's opportunity for and participation in community activities during a one-month period using a simple tally sheet that includes each day of the month. Keep track of all activities in which the student was involved during the month and compare this activity patterns to those of his or her classmates.

10. Support Received: How do you find out what sort of support is available in an environment? Begin by visiting and observing each environment in which the student will participate to uncover all signs of support, such as friendly co-workers at work or pictures of salad choices or desserts on a menu at a restaurant. Also, look for possible barriers to students' success in certain environments.

11. Individual and family resources: Students are an interactive part of their family, home, and community environments. In identifying a student's strengths and resources, it's important to pinpoint unique strengths of the

student's family and home environment. For example, a student may have an extended family that is particularly supportive or live in a community that offers a range of employment, transportation, and recreational opportunities.

12. Personal development: Help students enroll in courses that address their interests and preferences. Vocational courses in high school or at a community college can teach students employment skills they need for a desired promotion at work. Community education courses that teach recreation and leisure skills can help students pursue hobbies and develop new interests, such as photography or international cooking.

13. Social acceptance: Model an attitude of acceptance in the workplace, and build rapport with personnel at the worksite. Employers, co-workers, and customers will follow your lead. For example, you can show people at a bank how easy it is to talk with a worker who uses a communication board. When you discuss sports events at a hardware shop with a worker who is blind, just like you would with anyone else, others will be more comfortable to do it, too.

14. Physical and material well-being: There is a saying that you never think about good health until you don't have it! Help students develop and practice healthy lifestyles, such as getting proper daily nutrition and exercise. Inform them of how to reduce risks in their lives by wearing seat belts, avoiding substance abuse, and practicing home and work safety. Be a model for healthy living, as students will pattern their own behavior after yours.

15. Civic rights and responsibility: It is impossible to exercise your basic civic rights and responsibilities if you don't know what they are. Be sure students are informed of things such as voting, signing checks, or receiving counsel in court. Also, remind students that they are responsible, like everyone else, to follow laws such as obeying traffic signals, filing income tax returns, and respecting personal property.

In incorporating best practices for enhancing quality of life outcomes in secondary transition programming, it is important to conduct ongoing evaluation to determine if the desired effect is being achieved. Also, it is not necessary to intervene across all fifteen quality of life dimensions, just those that are relevant to an individual student's needs, strengths, preferences, and interests. Here's how one teacher addressed quality of life in a student's transition program.

Window to the World
Angelica

Angelica was getting frantic! It was the last semester of her senior year and she was really in trouble. During her first three years at Whitman High School, she always had worked hard. Schoolwork didn't come easily to Angelica, but she had made passing grades in her resource room and general education classes. She had good attendance at school. She also had made friends, got along well with her teachers, and had a supportive family. And, Angelica was even managing to hold down a part-time job. If this kept up, her dream to graduate from high school and attend the local community college would come true.

Everything changed, however, during Angelica's senior year, and she wasn't even sure how. Somehow, she just started to lose her ambition. Maybe it began when she started hanging out with Randall and some other students who had dropped out of Whitman last year and who weren't working or doing much of anything. When she had started partying with them, staying up late, she began missing her morning classes. She also had quit doing her homework and couldn't even find some of her schoolbooks. It had been fun for awhile. But now, she was in a mess. She had lent Randall her last pay-check when she really needed it for clothes and, even though he promised to, he still hadn't paid her back. She was flunking US history and if she missed anymore English classes, she wouldn't get credit for the semester. That meant she wouldn't graduate in June and then, what would she do? Angelica had to admit it was getting harder and harder to make decisions about her life. Maybe dropping out of school just like Randall was the best idea...

Ms. Blackstone, the senior class counselor at Whitman High, had other ideas, however. She had an eye for students who were headed for trouble, and when she looked at Angelica's grades and attendance report, she knew Angelica was in difficulty. Unless something changed now, Angelica would not make it to graduation. That's why Ms. Blackstone had made an appointment to have Angelica come to her office.

Ms. Blackstone smiled and asked Angelica how it was going when Angelica walked in the office door. Surprising herself, Angelica honestly admitted that it wasn't going too great. Because Ms. Blackstone seemed so friendly, Angelica soon started talking about how late she'd been staying out, how badly she felt about missing her classes, how confused she was about what to do about trying to graduate, and how she was afraid that she'd never get the money back she had lent Randall because he was using it to buy drugs.

Instead of getting angry like Angelica was afraid she would, Ms. Blackstone simply said, "Angelica, you have some important decisions to make and I'm going to help you do it." Ms. Blackstone then explained that making good decisions in her life was really Angelica's choice. She had the skills she needed, she just had to start using those skills.

Next, Ms. Blackstone said that it was important for Angelica to identify her goals for graduation and to start taking action to achieve these goals. Otherwise, she might find herself out of high school with nothing to do—just like Randall and his friends. Angelica, even though she liked hanging out with Randall, really didn't want to end up like him with nothing to do day after day. Angelica admitted that she really did want to go to the local community college. She wanted to become a secretary and work in an office. But how could she do it? She was in trouble in English and US history and even though she really wanted to, she didn't know how she could ever graduate.

Ms. Blackstone congratulated Angelica on choosing some important goals. She then suggested that it was a good idea to write down her goals and what steps she planned to take to achieve them. Angelica was beginning to feel better already, just saying what her goals were. Together with Ms. Blackstone, she listed out the actions she could take immediately in order to graduate. First, she would have to quit hanging out with Randall and spend more time with her friends at school who also were trying to graduate.

Second, she would start going to bed early and set her alarm clock in order to get to class on time. Third, she would get a planner and write down all her class assignments and work on them as soon as she got home from school or work. Fourth, she would ask Ms. Berry if she could do some extra credit work to bring her history grade up. If she took all these steps, there still was a chance that Angelica could graduate in June. Then, during the fall, she could enroll in the secretarial course at the community college.

Talking about her goals and her future was hard, but Angelica was glad she had done it. As she left the office, Angelica thanked Ms. Blackstone. They agreed to meet every week for the rest of the semester so that Ms. Blackstone could see how Angelica was coming on taking steps toward her goals. As Angelica met each step, they agreed to cross it off the list. Ms. Blackstone told Angelica that just doing so would give her a sense of satisfaction, and would remind her how proud she would feel when she walked across the stage at graduation with her high school diploma. Angelica agreed, but she knew, however, that the biggest satisfaction of all would be that she was learning to set goals, take control of her life, and make good decisions.

Future Research Issues

One major issue for future researchers is to investigate the extent to which secondary transition teachers are addressing quality of life outcomes and what practices they are using to incorporate quality of life concerns into secondary transition programming. The Quality of Life Indicators can be adapted for use as an instrument to guide program development as well as to evaluate how teachers are addressing each of the fifteen dimensions in students' IEPs.

Ultimately, the usefulness of the conceptual model of quality of life proposed in this chapter will be its effectiveness in addressing Stark and Goldsbury's (1990) question cited earlier: Has secondary transition programming really made a difference in improving the quality of students' lives? If programmatic efforts can be shown to positively impact post-school outcomes for students with disabilities and improve their quality of life, we will be able to answer affirmatively that, "Yes, we have really made a difference in high school students' lives."

Discussion Questions

1. Why should efforts to impact students quality of life be multidimensional?
2. Why should evaluation of quality of life be ongoing?
3. What "best practices" should be best at influencing quality of life?
4. How do we know when an acceptable quality of life has been achieved?

Community-Based Activities

1. Using the Quality of Life Indicators, develop a checklist to evaluate a student's quality of life, just as Mr. Reynolds did in Case Study 1. Then use the checklist to evaluate a student in your class across the fifteen quality of life dimensions. Write up your findings as a report and make programmatic recommendations for the student's IEP. Discuss your findings and recommendations in class.
2. Next, implement as many of your programmatic recommendations as

you can with the student. Use your checklist to evaluate the effects of your program. Present your findings as a written report and share them in class discussion.

3. Finally, interview the student and, if possible, his or her family members or important others. What effect did they believe your program had on the student's quality of life? What would you have done differently and what additional efforts would you make? Discuss your ideas in class.

References

Blackorby, J., & Wagner, M. (1996). Longitudinal postschool outcomes of youth with disabilities: Findings from the National Longitudinal Transition Study. *Exceptional Children, 62,* 399-413.

Brown, R. I. (1998). Personal reflections: Quality of life research and Down syndrome. *International Journal of Disability, Development, and Education, 45,* 323-329.

Campo, S. F., Sharpton, W. R., Thompson, B., & Sexton, D. (1997). Correlates of the quality of life of adults with severe or profound mental retardation. *Mental Retardation, 35,* 329-337.

Hatton, C. (1998). Whose quality of life is it anyway? Some problems with the emerging quality of life consensus. *Mental Retardation, 36,* 104-115.

Heal, L. W., Khoju, M., & Rusch, F. R. (1997). Predicting quality of life of youths after they leave special education high school programs. *Journal of Special Education, 31,* 279-299.

Hughes, C., & Carter, E. W. (2000). *The transition handbook: Strategies high school teachers use that work!* Baltimore: Paul H. Brooks.

Hughes, C., Hwang, B., Kim, J., Eisenman, L. T., & Killian, D. J. (1995). Quality of life in applied research: A review and analysis of empirical measures. *American Journal on Mental Retardation, 99,* 623-641.

Individuals with Disabilities Education Act Amendments of 1997, PL 105-17, 20 USC § 1400 et seq.

Lewit, E. M., Terman, D. L., & Behrman, R. E. (1997). Children and poverty: Analysis and recommendations. *Children and Poverty, 7,* 4-24.

McGrew, K. S., Bruininks, R. H., Thurlow, M. L., & Lewis, D. R. (1992). Empirical analysis of multidimensional measures of community adjustment for young adults with mental retardation. *American Journal on Mental Retardation, 96,* 475-487.

Schalock, R. L. (Ed.). (1996). *Quality of life Volume I: Conceptualization and measurement.* Washington, DC: American Association on Mental Retardation.

Stancliffe, R., & Abery, B. (1997). Longitudinal study of deinstitutionalization and the exercise of choice. *Mental Retardation, 35,* 159-169.

Stark, J. A., & Goldsbury, T. (1990). Quality of life from childhood to adulthood. In R. L. Schalock (Ed.), *Quality of life: Perspectives and issues* (71-83). Washington, DC: American Association on Mental Retardation.

Wagner, M. (1995). *Transition from high school to employment and postsecondary education: Interdisciplinary implications for youths with mental retardation.* Paper presented at the 119th annual meeting of the American Association on Mental Retardation, San Francisco, CA.

Wehmeyer, M. L., Agran, M., & Hughes, C. (2000). A national survey of teachers' promotion of self-determination and student-directed learning. *Journal of Special Education, 24,* 58-68.

Wehmeyer, M. L., & Bolding, N. (1999). Self-determination across living and working environments: A matched-samples study of adults with mental retardation. *Mental Retardation, 37,* 353-363.

Chapter 9
Supported Living

Paula Davis
Southern Illinois University

Key Questions
1. What is the continuum model of residential services?
2. What are the disadvantages of the continuum model?
3. What is supported living and how is it different from the continuum model?
4. What are the strategies for identifying the housing preferences of people with disabilities?
5. What types of supports may be necessary to assist someone to live in a preferred arrangement?
6. What are the key components of a systematic instructional program?
7. What are the alternative strategies to support an individual who is not independent in community living skills?
8. What types of personal support may assist people to live in their preferred arrangements?

It is hard to imagine a more important decision than where to live. Where one lives affects many other facets of life such as where one works, what one does in one's free time, which friends one visits, and what community resources one uses.

In the past, people with disabilities and their families had few choices available. A person either lived at home, in a state-operated institution, or in some other large group living arrangement. Beginning in the late 1960s and early 1970s, as a result of the normalization philosophy and the corresponding deinstitutionalization movement, the number of persons with mental retardation living in public residential facilities decreased and the number of people living in smaller community-based settings increased (Beirne-Smith, Patton, & Ittenbach, 1994). These community residential programs were established using a continuum approach to service delivery. In the late 1980s, there was recognition, however, that this approach had not been successful in assisting people access their chosen lifestyles (Taylor, 1987). As a result, current best practice follows an individualized, person-centered approach, often referred to as supported living.

This chapter provides an overview of residential services for people with disabilities. First, it describes and compares the continuum and the supported living approaches. Second, it examines strategies for identifying the residential preferences of people with disabilities. Finally, it discusses three broad types of supports for assisting people in living in their chosen arrangements.

Continuum and Supported Living Approaches to Community Living

Key Question #1: What is the continuum model of residential services?

Continuum Approach

In the continuum approach to residential services, residential options reflect the least restrictive environment (LRE), also known as the least restrictive alternative (LRA). Residential options are arranged in order on the continuum from those that provide a great deal of supervision and training to those that provide none. People live in the residential program that most closely reflects the skills they possess and the supervision and services they need. For example, a person who has few independent living skills and who needs continuous supervision probably would be in an arrangement on the more restrictive end of the continuum.

In contrast, a person who can demonstrate most or all of the skills needed to live independently and who requires little or no supervision would likely be in a residential setting on the less restrictive end of the continuum. In the continuum approach to residential services, as a person demonstrates skill mastery and less need for supervision, the person moves to a less restrictive arrangement on the continuum. The person continues to move in this fashion until she or he attains independence or ceases to make behavioral gains.

Residential Options in the Continuum

There are a number of residential options that could be placed on the residential continuum. Several of the most common ones are described in order from those that are considered to be most restrictive to those that are considered to be least restrictive.

Large Group Facilities

State-operated and privately-owned institutions are examples of facilities that provide services to a large group of people with disabilities in one setting (Beirne-Smith et al., 1994). These facilities are on the more restrictive end of the continuum because they do not meet the standards of a normalized living arrangement, are not very homelike, and often offer only limited opportunities for community integration. They vary in size from those that are quite large, serving several hundred people, to considerably smaller arrangements.

Group Homes

A group home is the form of community living most often used by people with developmental disabilities (Beirne-Smith et al., 1994). Some of the homes are small (e.g., three people), but they may have as many as fifteen residents. Because group homes are smaller than large group facilities, they are presumed to be more homelike and to provide a more normal daily routine. Their smaller size also may allow them to blend more easily into the surrounding community than a larger sized residential facility does. Additionally, the smaller number of residents allows for more personalized interactions between staff and residents.

Foster Homes

A foster home is one in which a person with disabilities lives with a family in the family's home (Heward & Orlansky, 1992). The person with the disability interacts with family members in a home rather than with paid staff members, goes on regular family outings into the community, and receives attention from the same small number of people on a twenty-four-hour a day basis rather than according to a work schedule. For these reasons, the foster home arrangement falls on the less restrictive end of the continuum.

Semi-Independent Living

Although semi-independent living can take various forms, it generally refers to a situation in which people with disabilities live in a home or an apartment, either alone or with one or two roommates, and receive support to allow them to maintain their lifestyles in the community. Three common variations of semi-independent living have been described (Heward & Orlansky, 1992):

- In the apartment cluster arrangement, people with disabilities live in a small number of apartments in a complex that primarily serves people without disabilities. Staff who supervise and support the residents with disabilities live in another apartment in the complex.
- In another variation of semi-independent living, persons with and without disabilities live together. The duties of the person without the disability depend on the needs of the person with the disability. The roommate without disabilities may be a paid staff member or an unpaid individual who lives rent-free or with a reduced rent.
- A third variation of semi-independent living is one in which the person with disabilities lives in a home or apartment alone or with one or two others with disabilities. The people who live in the home usually have the skills necessary to take care of their basic daily living needs, but may need daily, weekly, or occasional assistance for difficult tasks (e.g., grocery shopping) or those that occur infrequently (e.g., making a doctor's appointment, planning a monthly budget).

Independent Living

On the opposite end of the continuum from institutions is independent living. In the continuum approach to providing services, independent living is seen as the ultimate goal, which is achieved when formal services and supports are no longer necessary.

Key Question #2: What are the disadvantages of the continuum model?

Despite the apparent simplicity and logic of the continuum approach, problems with relying on it have become apparent (Taylor, 1987). First, the very existence of an option legitimizes that option and suggests that it is an appropriate and acceptable place for some people to live. Usually, those people are the ones with the most severe disabilities.

According to Taylor (1987), a second problem that arises with the continuum is that the location of the service (segregated versus integrated) is not separated from the amount of service and support needed by the person. While it would be possible to provide any level of support in an integrated setting, the structure of the traditional continuum is such that the most intensive services and supports are linked with a segregated setting (e.g., institution) and are less likely to be provided in integrated settings. This intertwining of location and amount of service precludes community placements for those who need intensive services and supports.

The continuum approach to residential services is based on the readiness model, the third flaw of the continuum approach (Taylor, 1987). The readiness model prevents someone from moving to a less restrictive residence until he or she demonstrates prerequisite skills. Therefore, someone who cannot master a particular skill with instruction and modifications is relegated, perhaps forever, to the more restrictive end of the continuum. Again, this usually will be people with the most significant physical and/or cognitive disabilities.

Another problem with the continuum approach to residential services is that it may be dehumanizing (Taylor, 1987). By constantly preparing people to move to the next level on the continuum, service providers may never focus on ensuring that people with disabilities have a high quality of life in the present. More attention may be paid to preparing people for their future happiness rather than to ensuring they are enjoying their current lifestyle. Furthermore, the emphasis on movement along the continuum actually may detract from a person's overall satisfaction with life because moving from one residential placement to another may be disruptive to the development of friendships and feelings of security and belonging that are essential to happiness.

The continuum model of residential services provided positive alternatives to permanent placement in large facilities at least for those with mild disabilities. As problems with the continuum approach became apparent, however, a new way of promoting community living for people with disabilities emerged. This new approach emphasizes the preferences and needs of individuals with disabilities and their families and provides options for those with significant disabilities as well as those with mild disabilities.

Key Question #3: What is supported living and how is it different from the continuum model?
Supported Living Approach

Just as supported employment was developed as an alternative in response to problems with the flow-through or continuum model of employment services for people with disabilities, supported living has emerged as an alternative to the continuum approach to residential services (Boles, Horner, & Bellamy, 1988). In supported living, people with disabilities receive the type and degree of support needed to live in the residential arrangement of their choice. The supports are individually determined, may vary with time and personal preference, and are provided as long as necessary without time restrictions. Unlike the continuum model, people are not required to "earn" the right to move to a less restrictive placement as they develop skills. Instead they are placed in the situation of their choice and supported in living in that arrangement. Promoting and honoring personal choice and providing a variety of individually determined supports indefinitely are two essential features of supported living.

Choice

In the continuum approach to residential services, people are given little opportunity to choose where to live. Their skill level determines which options are available to them and they live in an option that corresponds to their skills. In the supported living model, the person with the disability decides where and with whom to live. Skill level is not used to determine a person's readiness for a selected option, but rather it is used to determine the supports a person may need. With its emphasis on consumer choice, the supported living model corresponds with the philosophy of the independent living movement which advocates consumer control and empowerment (Chappell, 1995). Choice also has been identified as one indicator of quality of life (Guess, Benson, & Siegel-Causey, 1985; Keith, 1990). Attempts at improving the quality of life for persons with disabilities should include increased opportunities for them to express their preferences and to make decisions based on those preferences.

Key Question #4: What are the strategies for identifying the housing preferences of people with disabilities?

There are a variety of ways to find out where someone would like to live. The simplest and most direct way is simply to ask the person. This can be accomplished verbally or through the use of pictures. It has been demonstrated that people who are mildly mentally retarded can reliably indicate preferences regarding residential placements when they are presented various options in picture format (Faw, Davis, & Peck, 1996).

Even using pictures, people with significant cognitive disabilities may not be able to communicate their preferences or may not fully understand their options. Therefore, support personnel may need to spend time with individuals to identify their likes and dislikes. By watching what people do in their free time, with whom they spend their time, and how they react to different situations, it may be possible to identify what features to look for in a home.

A third way to identify what a person likes is to provide the person with opportunities to try out the options before making decisions because it may be hard for a person to select a residential option without having experienced it. For example, a person may be given the chance to spend several days in a group home or to stay overnight with a friend who lives in a supervised apartment. Observing a person's behavior in that environment and later discussing the experience with him or her (if possible) may provide clues to the person's reaction to the option.

Finally, significant others in the life of the person with the disability may have important insights into the person's preferences. Discussions with family members or friends, for example, may reveal that the person likes having his or her own room, enjoys assisting in meal preparation but cannot cook independently, and would be unhappy if he or she could not have a pet. By asking the person with the disability, observing what he or she does, providing opportunities to try out various options, and by working closely with significant others in the person's life, it is more likely that the residential option selected by and for the person will be one that reflects the person's desires and will help the person obtain a lifestyle that is congruent with his or her preferences.

One way to ensure that preferences of individuals with mild disabilities are considered when residential plans are made has been illustrated (Faw et al., 1996; Foxx, Faw, Taylor, Davis, & Fulia, 1993). In these studies, individuals with dual diagnoses of mild retardation and psychiatric disabilities were presented with pictures that represented options available in community living arrangements and asked which they preferred. For example, the person was shown a picture of a room with one bed and told that he or she would have a room alone. Simultaneously, the person also was presented with a picture showing a room with two beds and told he or she would share a room. With both pictures present, the individual was asked to point to the picture which represented his or her choice and to describe it. Thirty possible preferences were evaluated in this fashion. The assessment was conducted on three separate occasions and the mean test-retest reliability was 86%.

To determine the most important preferences, each of the thirty preferences were compared to one other of the thirty preferences. For example, a person who indicated preference for a private room and for shopping for oneself would be shown the corresponding photographs and asked which was more important. This pairing was done for all items three times ensuring that the same items were never compared to each other more than once. Items chosen repeatedly were considered strong preferences.

After the preference identification was completed, each person received a small photograph album containing the pictures of their ten strongest preferences. They were then taught to use those photographs to determine if their preferences were available in different living arrangements in the community. The instructional procedures were those described in Chapter 4 (e.g., task analysis, verbal instruction, modeling, reinforcement). At the completion of their training, all were able to take tours of homes, ask question regarding the availability of their preferences, report that information back to their social worker (Faw et al, 1996; Foxx et al., 1993) and make decisions about which homes they toured were good places for them to live based on the availability of their preferences (Faw et al., 1996).

Persons with more significant disabilities may need more assistance and support to identify preferences as described earlier. Of the strategies suggested, the one often used in person-centered planning is to ask significant others to identify preferences. Care should be taken when using this approach. Reid, Everson, and Green (1999) compared the person-centered planning approach to preference identification to the use of a preference assessment that examined the person's responses to the presentation of items and activities. Four individuals with profound multiple disabilities participated in the study. In the person-centered approach, persons who knew the individuals well identified preferences. The reported preferences were then presented to the persons with disabilities. Approaches to the items as well as avoidance behaviors were recorded. The results of this study revealed that asking people who know people with disabilities may identify some preferences accurately but also may incorrectly identify as preferences some things that are not liked by the individual. For this reason, it is recommended that the results of person-centered planning be supplemented with systematic preference assessments following the recommendations listed above.

A review of the Reid et al. (1999) and Faw et al. (1996) studies reveals two important considerations in using preferences to assist individuals with disabilities in accessing their chosen lifestyles. First, the manner in which preferences are identified depends on the skill level of the person with the disability. In the Faw et al. (1996) study, participants were able to identify their own preferences through the use of pictures and to verbalize their choices by describing what the picture represented. In contrast, in the Reid et al. (1999) study, participants had multiple and profound disabilities and were severely limited in their ability to communicate. To identify their preferences reliably, it was necessary to observe their behavior when presented with various items identified by others as potential preferences. This suggests that while reports by other people are useful, they need to be validated. These studies reveal that it may be necessary to use a variety of techniques to identify the preferences of individuals, especially those with more severe impairments.

A second important consideration has to do with the type of preferences being identified. The participants in the Faw et al. (1996) study identified preferences related to major lifestyle decisions (handling one's own money, curfew, sharing a room) and used their preferences to evaluate residential options. In contrast, the preferences identified in the Reid et al. study (1999) are those that may impact in significant ways on a person's daily routine in the current living arrangement. For individuals with the most significant disabilities such as those in the Reid study, preferences regarding larger issues such as where to live or work may not be easily assessed or honored (Bambara, Cole, & Koger, 1998; Brown, Gothelf, Guess, & Lehr, 1998). For persons with the most significant disabilities, decisions regarding where to live may require the use of a combination of procedures. This will more likely ensure that they live in a place most compatible with their preferences; that they have access to preferred activities, items, and events on a regular basis; and that they have the supports needed to be successful in their chosen homes.

Key Question #5: What types of supports may be necessary to assist someone to live in a preferred arrangement?

Once the living arrangement preferred by the individual is determined, the supports the person would need to live in that arrangement are identified. Supports are highly individualized and are determined through activities such as those described in Chapters 1 and 2. Davis and Cuvo (1997) identified three broad types of supports that might be provided to assist people with disabilities to live as independently as possible in the community. These include systematic instruction, environmental and task modifications, and personal supports.

Key Question #6: What are the key components of a systematic instructional program?

Whereas instruction is the primary method of increasing personal independence in the continuum model, it is only one of the supports (albeit an important one) provided to individuals in the supported living model. Systematic instruction focuses on

1. conducting an ecological assessment to identify the skills a person would need to live in a particular living arrangement or participate in a specific community environment (e.g., restaurant, movie theater),
2. assessing the person to determine which of those skills he or she has and which would need to be taught, and
3. teaching the person how to perform the tasks in order to overcome the skill deficits.

Effective instructional programs use applied behavior analytic techniques, which include selecting a chaining procedure, providing instructional prompts, reinforcing appropriate responses, and gradually and systematically reducing the prompts and reinforcers so that the person is responding in the natural environment without the instructional program (Cuvo & Davis, 1983). Effective programs also plan for the long-term maintenance of the newly acquired skill and the generalization of the skill to all relevant situations. Systematic assessment and instructional procedures are illustrated here in the context of a case study.

Window to the World
Bill

Bill is an eighteen-year-old male with moderate mental retardation. He is in his final year of high school. Through a school-based vocational program, he is working at a local trucking company twenty hours per week. His primary duties are washing trucks and vacuuming their interiors. After several weeks of intensive job coaching, he has limited support needs at his job. Bill plans to work for the company full-time when he finishes school.

Upon graduation, Bill hopes to move into a supervised apartment with one of his high school friends. His parents are supportive of that plan. To help Bill achieve that goal, his transition team (which includes Bill and his parents) developed a plan that listed the various supports Bill would need to be successful. One that was identified was community living skill instruction to permit Bill to function as independently as possible. Although supports will be available in his apartment, Bill would like to do as much as possible for himself.

Prior to beginning instruction, Bill's teacher, Mrs. Howell, conducted an ecological assessment to determine the skills necessary to function in the apartment and those necessary to access the places in the community Bill was likely to use frequently (e.g., fast food restaurant, grocery store, bank, movie theater). After the skills were identified, Bill's teachers and parents identified which of those skills Bill already could perform. Those skills that his teachers and parents thought that he could not perform yet or those that they were unsure about were considered for instruction. Based on Bill's preferences, teacher and parent recommendations, and other considerations, several of the skills that Bill needed to learn were selected for instruction.

Because Bill would like to cook for himself and doing so would increase his independence, cooking was identified as one instructional goal. This skill was further specified as making a grilled cheese sandwich, one of Bill's favorites. Mrs. Howell wrote a behavioral objective that specified the conditions under which Bill would make the sandwich and the criterion for goal completion. Then she began the instructional program using the following procedure:

1. Mrs. Howell developed a task analysis of making a grilled cheese sandwich.

2. Mrs. Howell identified the sites where she would do her assessment and instruction. She decided to assess Bill in the home economics classroom, which was equipped like a home kitchen. If instruction proved necessary, she would continue to work with Bill in the classroom and she would ask Bill's parents to observe and, if necessary, assist Bill in making a sandwich at home once or twice a week.

3. Using the task analysis, on three different occasions Mrs. Howell assessed Bill's ability to make a sandwich to determine if he needed instruction. The data revealed that Bill could perform only about 30% of the steps without assistance.

4. Bill's instruction was provided using the following format:

- **Chaining procedure:**
  Total task training was used. Bill completed each step of the task of making a grilled cheese sandwich on each training trial and received instruction as necessary.

- **Prompts:**
  Verbal instruction, modeling, and physical guidance were used to prompt Bill if he did not perform a step or when he made an error.

- **Prompt Fading:**
  The prompts were provided in the order of least to most, always starting with giving Bill the opportunity to perform a step with no help. Using this system, as Bill became more skilled, fewer and less intensive prompts were delivered until he was making the sandwich independently.

- **Reinforcement:**
  During initial training trials Bill was reinforced immediately with verbal praise for each correct step he performed even if prompts were needed. After completing the entire chain, he ate the sandwich along with a small bag of chips, thereby introducing the natural reinforcer involved in task completion. As Bill became more skilled, the verbal praise statements were provided less frequently until they were no longer provided at all. Throughout the training program, Bill continued to eat the sandwich and chips at the completion of the task.

- **Maintenance:**
  After Bill performed the task independently at home on two consecutive occasions and in the classroom on three consecutive occasions, he had met the behavioral objective and acquired the skill. To ensure that he maintained the skill, Bill's parents continued to monitor his sandwich making at home every week or two. They occasionally commented on his cooking skills and sometimes ate one of the sandwiches he cooked. Opportunities to continue to cook and to get reinforced (the sandwich itself as well as parent praise) helped maintain the skill. If his parents noticed a decline in his skills, they were to call Mrs. Howell for remedial training.

- **Generalization:**
  In this case, generalization was achieved by having Bill cook in two locations (school, home). Unfortunately, Bill's teacher cannot say for sure that Bill's cooking skill will generalize to his new apartment when he moves out upon graduation. It will be necessary for someone to observe Bill when he makes his first grilled cheese sandwich in his new apartment and to provide training for any steps that might be unique to cooking in his new kitchen. It is also important to note that learning to cook a grilled cheese sandwich does not mean Bill can cook other food items. To increase his cooking skills, additional training would be necessary.

- **Social Validation:**
  By having Bill, his teachers, and parents involved in the selection of the skill identified for instruction, the importance of the skill was verified. It was also validated by the results of the ecological inventory that revealed that cooking is a skill that Bill would use when living in the supported apartment. Having Bill's parents monitor his performance at home validated the results. Because his parents agreed with the teacher that Bill had mastered the skill, the outcome was validated. Perhaps most importantly, the outcome was validated because Bill continued to cook and eat a sandwich after the instructional program had ended. That would suggest that the skill selected was of value to Bill and that he learned the skill sufficiently well to maintain it after the formal instructional program was terminated.

Key Question #7: What are the alternative strategies to support an individual who is not independent in community living skills?

Even with appropriate instruction, it may be difficult or impossible for a person with disabilities to perform some community living skills. The difficulty may arise as a result of the academic, physical, or memory requirements of the task. For example, cooking may require reading and number skills. Budgeting money may require arithmetic skills. A person with severe mental retardation may not possess those skills. In contrast, tying one's shoes requires fine motor skill that a person with cerebral palsy may not have. Preparing a meal may require that the person remember to complete the cooking steps in the appropriate sequence. A person with traumatic brain injury may have difficulty with sequencing steps in the correct order. For these and similar situations, alternative strategies may be appropriate to support the individual (Davis & Cuvo, 1997).

Alternative Approaches

For some tasks, alternative approaches have been developed that are used by the general public. Examples include calculators to help with budgeting, shoes with Velcro™ so tying is not necessary, and a variety of frozen food items that reduce the cooking skills needed. Another example is a telephone with inserts for pictures of friends, family, or other frequently called numbers for speed dialing. Touching the photograph results in a call being placed to the pictured individual with no need to recall or dial the number. These may be the preferable forms of modifications because they present a simpler way of performing the task, are readily available, and are non-stigmatizing.

Modification or Development of Task Materials

For some people, the alternatives used by the general public may not be sufficient to support independent performance. Specially developed modifications may be necessary to make the task easier for the person to accomplish. One of the most common examples used by people with disabilities who have difficulty reading is to replace words with pictures such as using recipes and shopping lists that have pictures instead of words. Similarly, pictures could be used to remind someone of the steps needed to complete housekeeping or grooming chores. As another example, the person who has learned to ride the community bus, but for whom there are some safety concerns in case of an emergency, could carry a specially designed identification card with phone numbers and contact persons. The careful development or modification of materials may allow someone who would otherwise need personal assistance to perform a task without help.

Task Modification

In addition to altering or developing new materials, the tasks themselves could be modified to accommodate individual differences. For example, a person who does not have traditional money handling skills could make purchases by paying one more dollar than is requested (i.e., the dollar more strategy). Someone who is having a difficult time measuring laundry soap could receive assistance from someone to measure the appropriate amount of soap into plastic sandwich bags when the box of detergent is purchased. At laundry time, the person would not need to measure but simply would open the sandwich bag and pour the soap into the washer.

Several issues should be considered when selecting any of the alternative approaches (Davis & Cuvo, 1997). First, when possible, select alternatives that are identical to those used by the general public. When that is not possible, use modifications that are as similar as possible to those used by others to reduce any stigma that may be associated with their use. Second, make a decision about the long-term use of the alternative. In some cases, the alternative can be removed gradually as the person acquires a skill; in other situations, it may be desirable or necessary to leave the alternative in place indefinitely. Finally, it is important to remember that simply providing someone with an alternative rarely is sufficient. The person most likely will need instruction to ensure that the alternative is used correctly.

Key Question #8: What types of personal support may assist people to live in their preferred arrangements?

Using a combination of systematic instruction and individually determined alternative strategies, persons with disabilities can increase their level of independence in the community. These supports, however, are only two of a multitude of those used in supported living. In contrast to the continuum approach, the supported living model recognizes that some people may never acquire skills, even with appropriate instruction and modification. It advocates that they still should be given the opportunity to live in a situation of their own choosing with individually determined personal supports.

Because each person has different needs, it is impossible to list all the specific personal supports that might be provided. Examples might include, but are not limited to:

1. transportation to and from appointments, work, and leisure activities
2. assistance obtaining and maintaining employment
3. help in performing any or all of the activities of daily living such as engaging in self-care tasks, cleaning one's home, doing laundry, and cooking
4. assistance with budgeting money and paying bills
5. support in engaging in social and leisure time activities, such as going out to eat with friends, going to the movies, or visiting a museum (Walker & Racino, 1993)

People with disabilities are a heterogeneous group including people with cognitive impairments (e.g., mental retardation), sensory/neurological impairments (e.g., epilepsy, blindness), physical impairments (e.g., cerebral palsy), and emotional/behavioral impairments (Kiernan & Schalock, 1995). Therefore, supports must be determined individually and may vary in intensity from assistance that is provided only occasionally to assistance that is intensive and provided continuously (e.g., around the clock). Friends, family members, and neighbors may provide supports informally or a paid staff member of a human service agency may provided them. For example, someone with a learning disability may need assistance for an hour monthly from a sibling to set up a budget and pay bills. In contrast, someone with more significant disabilities may need a paid, live-in caregiver who assists with daily grooming, cooking, and cleaning, and is responsible for the day-to-day health and safety of the individual. The type and intensity of supports may vary with time and should be based on individual needs and desires. The case study presented below illustrates the use of various personal supports and alternative approaches.

Window to the World
Judy

Judy Birch is a twenty-year-old woman who has severe mental retardation and cerebral palsy. She has an unsteady gait and has difficulty using her hands and fingers to engage in tasks that require fine motor control. Due to her cognitive limitations and her physical disability, Judy has extensive support needs in nearly every area of community living.

Judy has just moved into an apartment with two other women with disabilities. Additionally, a staff member lives in the apartment. Judy's parents are supportive and visit her at least once a week. She usually goes home once a month for an overnight visit.

During the day, Judy works at a department store. In the evenings and on weekends, she participates in the typical activities of the home. She receives various amounts of assistance to do these tasks from the staff member who lives in the home. For example, she goes to the grocery store with her roommates and staff member. She assists at meal time by putting the plates on the table and by drying dishes. Once a week she does her laundry. During her leisure time, she listens to compact discs and watches videotapes.

At the most recent meeting to review Judy's progress, the team (which included Judy and her parents) decided that one way to improve Judy's life would be to make it easier for her to listen to music or watch videos without having to ask for assistance. Earlier attempts to teach her how to perform these tasks using the systematic instructional procedures described above had not been completely successful. The team decided to consider an alternative strategy.

They developed a series of pictures showing Judy performing each of the steps of selecting a CD, opening the player, opening the CD case, inserting the CD into the player, closing the CD player, and pushing the play button. Additionally, all of the critical buttons on the CD player were color coded and those color coded buttons were highlighted in the photographs that were taken. With instruction that included prompts provided in order from most to least assistance and praise, Judy was soon able to play CDs without asking for assistance.

Because of the success of the pictorial task analysis, the treatment team decided to develop a similar system to assist Judy in doing her laundry. Although the pictures were successful in helping Judy perform some of the steps, she had ongoing difficulty with others, such as identifying which water temperature to use, how to sort her clothes, and how to measure the detergent. Because all of her clothes could be washed with warm water, the warm water setting on the washer at her home was marked with a red permanent marker. She receives personal support from the staff to sort her clothes and to premeasure the detergent into sandwich bags after purchasing the detergent. With these various supports, Judy is successfully washing her own clothes.

As Judy's story illustrates, with systematic instruction, task and materials modification, and personal support alone or in combination, people with significant disabilities can be active participants in their own lives. The focus is on providing people with meaningful experiences in their current situations, not just planning for future opportunities.

Conclusion

One of the most important decisions made in adulthood is where to live. Many times that decision is made for (rather than by) people with disabilities and is based on their skill deficits. In the continuum model, movement to a less restrictive community placement is considered only if a person demonstrates a predetermined set of skills. In contrast, the supported living model emphasizes that persons with disabilities should be involved in the decision about where to live and that they should receive the level of support necessary to attain their chosen lifestyles.

Judy and Bill illustrate the variety of supports that could be provided to assist people with a wide range of disabilities to access their chosen lifestyles. Both Bill and Judy probably would benefit from all three types of support described: systematic instruction, environmental and task modifications, and personal supports. By receiving systematic instruction, people with disabilities can become more skilled and independent in the performance of some activities. With the development of individualized environmental and task modifications and the provision of personal supports, they also can experience greater access to the variety of activities all people participate in on a daily basis even if they cannot perform those activities independently.

This approach to the provision of residential services should be considered by community providers who want to ensure that people with disabilities are provided with a home that reflects their individually determined needs and desires. The goal of supported living is to ensure:

1. that people are living in homes of their own choosing
2. that they are active participants in the life of the community
3. that they have access to activities, events, and people that are enjoyable to them
4. that they are productive
5. that they are happy with their lives

Best Practice Recommendations

1. Ensure that the preferences of individuals are identified and honored in both the selection of where to live as well as in choices that are made on a daily basis.
2. Assist people to be as independent as possible by providing systematic instruction.
3. For difficult tasks, develop alternative approaches or provide personal supports.
4. Remember that preferences and needed supports change with time.
5. Continually evaluate the person's quality of life. Have less concern for people's ability to perform independently and more concern that they are active participants in the aspects of life that permit them to be productive, integrated, and happy members of their community.

Future Research Issues

1. Identifying the preferences of people with the most significant disabilities is challenging. This is especially true for major life decisions such as where to live. Continuing research in this area is essential if we are to afford people with severe disabilities the opportunities to be active participants in choosing their own lifestyles.
2. Most research in the area of community living skills has been on the development of easily defined and analyzed skills such as cooking, apartment cleaning, and grocery shopping. Few studies have examined more complex skills. Two notable exceptions are studies that evaluated procedures to teach people how to evaluate residential options (Faw et al., 1996) and how to self-advocate (Sievert, Cuvo, & Davis, 1988). More systematic research is needed to determine the most effective instructional methods for teaching people how to be self-determined and how to carry out the choices they make.
3. Research in the area of staff training has focused on teaching staff how to provide systematic instruction. Additional research is needed to develop the best methods for ensuring that staff identify and honor the preferences of people with disabilities. Such programs could follow the model established by the independent living movement in which personal care attendants are hired, supervised, and terminated by the person with the disability for whom they work. In a similar fashion, residential support workers could be hired, supervised, and terminated by the person with disabilities (or appropriately selected advocate). If the support worker reports directly to the individual with the disability (or advocate), it seems more likely that the preferences of the person with the disability will be honored.
4. The existence of social relationships, including those with family and those with friends, is important to the quality of life of all people (Kennedy & Itkonen, 1996). Assisting people to develop the social skills necessary to acquire friends and then to maintain their relationships is challenging. Most research in this area has focused on the development of specific social skills (e.g., greeting, asking questions, accepting feedback). It has not been demonstrated, however, that increases in specific social skills

result in the development of relationships (Haring & Breen, 1992). The majority of the empirical work into the development of relationships has focused on school-aged individuals in school settings. One exception is a study by Johnson and Davis (1998) in which a program to foster supported relationships between adults with traumatic brain injuries and their nondisabled peers was developed and evaluated. The program, which required little staff intervention, was moderately successful. Additional research is needed to (a) evaluate programs that teach complex social skills, and (b) examine the factors that support the development and maintenance of relationships among those with and without disabilities.

Discussion Questions

1. Imagine that you are the leader of a team working to assist a young man to achieve his desired lifestyle. Currently he is living at home with his parents, but he would like to live in an apartment with a friend. In his community there are several agencies available to provide the supports he will need to be successful. His parents are not supportive of his plan. They want him to live with them indefinitely. What would you do to resolve this situation?
2. You have been hired to work in an agency that provides residential services that historically have been provided following the continuum model. Most people being served by the agency live in group homes. The agency director has asked you to make a presentation to the board of directors about supported living as an alternative to the continuum approach. What would you include in that presentation?
3. You have been asked to organize an inservice training program for the support workers at an agency providing residential services. The goal of the inservice is twofold: (a) to teach the support workers to identify preferences of the people with whom they are working and incorporate those preferences into each person's daily life, and (b) to increase the choice opportunities the workers make available to individuals on a daily basis. Develop an outline of such an inservice and gather or develop materials to be used in making the presentation.

Community-Based Activities

1. Conduct a survey of your community to determine the types of residential options available to people with disabilities.
2. Contact a community provider of residential services and supports. Ask to conduct an inventory of the skills needed to live in that environment (e.g., supervised apartment, group home). Find out which skills are required to live there and for which skills supports are available if an individual does not have the skills to perform independently.
3. Select a place in the community used frequently in daily living (e.g., bank, grocery store, movie theater). Conduct an ecological inventory of the skills necessary to function independently in that community environment.
4. Select one of the skills identified in two or three above. Develop an instructional program to teach that skill using the guidelines reviewed in

this chapter and described more fully in Chapters 3 and 4. Describe specific environmental or task modifications that could be developed if a person has difficulty learning the task.

References

Bambara, L. M., Cole, C. L., & Koger, F. (1998). Translating self-determination concepts into support for adults with severe disabilities. *Journal of the Association for Persons with Severe Handicaps, 23*, 27-37.

Beirne-Smith, M., Patton, J. R., & Ittenbach, R. (1994). *Mental Retardation* (4th ed.). New York: Merrill.

Boles, S., Horner, R. H., & Bellamy, G. T. (1988). Implementing transition: Programs for supported living. In B. L. Ludlow, A. P. Turnbull, & R. Luckasson (Eds.), *Transition to adult life for people with mental retardation: Principles and practices* (101-117). Baltimore: Brookes.

Brown, F., Gothelf, C. R., Guess, D., & Lehr, D. H. (1998). Self-determination for individuals with the most severe disabilities: Moving beyond chimera. *Journal of the Association for Persons with Severe Handicaps, 23*, 17-26.

Chappell, J. (1995). National Association of Independent Living. *Journal of Rehabilitation, 61*(3), 36-37.

Cuvo, A. J., & Davis, P. K. (1983). Behavior therapy and community living skills. In M. Hersen, R. M. Eisler, & P. M. Miller (Eds.), *Progress in behavior modification* (Vol. 14, 125-172). New York: Academic Press.

Davis, P. K., & Cuvo, A. J. (1997). Environmental approaches to mental retardation. In D. M. Baer & E. M. Pinkston (Eds.), *Environment and behavior* (231-242). Boulder: Westview Press.

Faw, G. D., Davis, P. K., & Peck, C. (1996). Increasing self-determination: Teaching people with mental retardation to evaluate residential options. *Journal of Applied Behavior Analysis, 29*, 173-188.

Foxx, R. M., Faw, G. D., Taylor, S., Davis, P. K., & Fulia, R. (1993). "Would I be able to...?" Teaching clients to assess the availability of their community living lifestyle preferences. *American Journal on Mental Retardation, 98*, 235-248.

Guess, D., Benson, H. A., & Siegel-Causey, E. (1985). Concepts and issues related to choice-making and autonomy among persons with severe disabilities. *Journal of the Association for Persons with Severe Handicaps, 10*, 79-86.

Haring, T. G., & Breen, C. (1992). A peer-mediated social network intervention to enhance the social integration of persons with moderate and severe disabilities. *Journal of Applied Behavior Analysis, 25*, 319-333.

Heward, W. L., & Orlansky, M. D. (1992). *Exceptional children* (4th ed.). New York: Merrill.

Johnson, K., & Davis, P. K. (1998). A supported relationships intervention to increase the social integration of persons with traumatic brain injuries. *Behavior Modification, 22*, 502-528.

Keith, K. D. (1990). Quality of life: Issues in community integration. In R. L. Schalock (Ed.), *Quality of life: Perspectives and issues* (93-100). Washington, DC: American Association on Mental Retardation.

Kennedy, C. H., & Itkonen, T. (1996). Social relationships, influential variables, and change across the life span. In L. K. Koegel, R. L. Koegel, & G. Dunlap (Eds.), *Positive behavior support: Including people with difficult behavior in the community* (287-304). Baltimore: Paul H. Brookes.

Kiernan, W. E., & Schalock, R. L. (1995). Developmental disabilities. In A. E. Dell Orto & R. P. Marinelli (Eds.), *Encyclopedia of disability and rehabilitation* (249-257). New York: Macmillan.

Reid, D. H., Everson, J. M., & Green, C. W. (1999). A systematic evaluation of preferences identified through person-centered planning for people with profound multiple disabilities. *Journal of Applied Behavior Analysis, 32*, 467-477.

Sievert, A. L., Cuvo, A. J., & Davis, P. K. (1988). Training self-advocacy skills to adults with mild handicaps. *Journal of Applied Behavior Analysis, 21*, 299-309.

Taylor, S. J. (1987). Continuum traps. In S. J. Taylor, D. Biklen, & J. Knoll (Eds.), *Community integration for people with severe disabilities* (25-35). New York: Teachers College Press.

Walker, P., & Racino, J. A. (1993). Being with people: Support and support strategies. In J. A. Racino, P. Walker, S. O'Connor, & S. J. Taylor (Eds.), *Housing, support, and community: Choices and strategies for adults with disabilities* (81-106). Baltimore: Paul H. Brookes.

Chapter 10
Postsecondary Education for Students with Disabilities

Dawn Hunter
Chapman University, School of Education
Lisa O'Brien
Santa Ana Unified School District

Key Questions

1. What postsecondary education options are available for students with disabilities?
2. What students with disabilities are accessing postsecondary education options? What characteristics do these students have that are similar and dissimilar to their peers without disabilities?
3. How can students with disabilities adequately prepare themselves for attending a college; university; or vocational, trade, or technical school?
4. What barriers exist in accessing postsecondary education options for students with disabilities?
5. What financial assistance is available to students with disabilities wanting to attend a college, university, or trade school?
6. What supports, accommodations, and services are available to students with disabilities pursuing a postsecondary education?

In addition to the world of work, young adults with disabilities have a variety of options available if they wish to pursue a postsecondary education such as attending a community college, a four-year college or university, or a vocational, trade, or technical school.

Key Question #1: What postsecondary education options are available for students with disabilities?

The same postsecondary educational experiences available to students without disabilities are, by law, available to a students with disabilities if the student meets the admission requirements. However, for a variety of reasons, these options have not always been readily available to students with disabilities and in many places continue to be challenging to access. The Rehabilitation Act of 1973 (Section 504) outlines numerous protections for students with disabilities seeking to attend postsecondary educational programs. It states:

No otherwise qualified person with a disability in the United States ... shall, solely by reason of ... disability, be denied the benefits of, be excluded from participation in, or be subjected to discrimination under any program or activity receiving federal financial assistance.

The Americans with Disabilities Act (ADA) also addresses access to stated-funded community colleges, vocational schools, colleges, and universities in Title II and private colleges and vocational schools in Title III. According to this mandate, students with disabilities cannot be discriminated against during the recruitment or admissions process, or in the way they are treated. However, discriminatory practices are still evident in many postsecondary programs.

Community Colleges

Many states have outstanding community college systems that are readily accessible to students with disabilities. There are many reasons students may wish to attend a community college as their first college experience. For example, community colleges tend to offer a variety of vocational, occupational, and academic programs that lead to professional certificates or associate's degrees. Thus, students have many choices available to them. If students are undecided about a career path they can use the community college experience to explore their options.

In addition to the academic strengths community colleges can provide, there are many practical reasons a student may select a community college. For example, for some students it may be important to live at home as they begin their collegiate experience. Thus, proximity alone may provide a level of comfort, as well as support, for students with disabilities and their families. Community colleges also can be less intimidating than four-year colleges due to their size, thus allowing students to "ease into" the college scene. In addition, community colleges often allow for greater flexibility in the scheduling of classes to better meet the needs of students who may be juggling course schedules with health needs, transportation issues, and related supports. It is interesting to note that community colleges frequently have better support services available to assist students with disabilities than four-year colleges and universities.

Community colleges also have limitations that students should be aware of in their decision-making process. While some community colleges have residential housing available, most do not. If a student lives off campus, transportation issues also may have to be addressed. Like other students attending community colleges, students with disabilities planning on transferring to a four-year school should be sure there are articulation or transfer agreements between the community college they attend and the college or university they will transfer to.

Community college admission standards vary from state to state. Some states require a high school diploma or GED; others require entrance exams for placement purposes only (i.e., remediation course work versus for-credit coursework); Still others have an "open admission" policy welcoming all members of the community, including people with disabilities who may have graduated with a certificate of completion from high school rather than a diploma. Therefore, prospective students should ask about the admission requirements of the particular community college they are interested in when exploring possible educational opportunities.

Four-Year College or University

Many students with disabilities will decide to go to a four-year college or university right out of high school or shortly after, thus bypassing the community college system. Students may attend a four-year college or university for a variety of reasons, including diverse degree program choices leading to bachelor's degrees. If a student is undecided about a major or field of study, a student may complete required general education coursework while exploring possible majors. However, if a student transfers from another institution or community college, this option may not be available.

Admission standards to a four-year college or university tend to be similar throughout the US. Many colleges require a high school diploma or GED, a minimum grade point average, minimum scores on standardized tests such as the SAT or ACT, references or letters of recommendation, completed application and application fee, and a personal statement. Therefore, it is important to find out in advance what the application requirements are prior to submitting the application.

Vocational Schools, Trade Programs, and Technical Schools

Unlike the past when many students with disabilities were "pigeon holed" into occupations that carried limited expectations (e.g., repetitive and routine types of jobs) and limited salaries, career opportunities exist today that are challenging, creative, and personally rewarding, in addition to paying well. Many of these careers require that a student obtain a license, certificate, or other type of credential that can be earned through a vocational school, trade school, or technical program of study. Consequently, some students with disabilities choose to bypass the community college system and four-year institutions of higher education to pursue an education that focuses on learning a specific trade or occupation. While some of these programs actually may be located on a community college campus and be part of the community college system, others may not.

Vocational, trade, or technical programs can prepare a student for a career in many occupations (e.g., information technology, hotel and motel management, cosmetology, dental assistant, paralegals, medical technician, electrician, plumber, early childhood worker, auto mechanic, sign language interpreter). Because of the concentrated nature of these programs, students may be able to complete the them in a relatively short time, allowing them to enter the work force in their chosen field in a shorter period of time than their peers pursuing college degrees.

While some of the programs are relatively inexpensive compared to colleges and universities, others are not. Like community colleges, these programs typically do not have housing available to students; therefore, students will be required to find housing in the community. Because of the great variation in vocational, trade, or technical schools, application requirements differ. Therefore, students should make inquiries directly to the school to acquire the necessary information regarding the application process and requirements.

Key Question #2: What students with disabilities are accessing postsecondary education options? What characteristics do these students have that are similar and dissimilar to their peers without disabilities?

There are some interesting trends when looking at college access for students with disabilities over the past twenty years. Henderson (1999) reports that in 1978, slightly less than 3% of freshman attending college reported they had a disability. By 1988, approximately 7% of freshman reported having a disability and by 1998, approximately 9.4% of all first time, full-time students entering as college freshman reported that they had a disability.

Further analysis (Henderson, 1999) indicates that while the percentage of some groups of students with disabilities attending college have remained fairly consistent through the years (e.g., students with speech disabilities or hearing impairments), the percentage of other groups of students with disabilities attending college has increased since 1989 (e.g., students with learning disabilities or health-related disabilities). The most dramatic increase is in the number of students with learning disabilities, which was reported as 41% of all students with disabilities in 1998 compared to just 15.3% in 1988. On the other hand, during this same time period students who reported being blind or partially sighted dropped significantly from nearly 31.7% in 1988 to 13.3% in 1998. Students with orthopedic disabilities dropped from 13.8% in 1988 to 9.1% in 1999.

Factors such as gender, age, and race/ethnicity of entering college freshman offer other interesting patterns. For example, there is a greater representation of male students, compared to female students, in the freshman population of students with disabilities (Horn & Berktold, 1999; Henderson, 1999). However, the race/ethnicity of students with disabilities attending college versus students not reporting a disability were very similar (Henderson, 1999).

Henderson (1999) also found that freshman students with disabilities had lower perceptions of themselves than did their peers without disabilities in the areas of the drive to achieve, cooperativeness, leadership ability, competitiveness, self understanding, intellectual self confidence, emotional health, popularity, overall academic ability, writing ability, mathematical ability, and physical health. In the areas of artistic ability and creative ability, students with disabilities reported higher perceptions of themselves than did their peers without disabilities.

Many of the factors that influenced students with disabilities to attend college were similar to the factors influencing their peers without disabilities (e.g., to get a better job, to make more money, to gain a general education, to prepare for graduate or professional school, to become a more cultured person, to fulfill parental expectations to attend college). However, three reasons appeared more important to students with disabilities compared to students without disabilities: to prove to others they could succeed, to improve reading and study skills, and the encouragement of a mentor or role model (Henderson, 1999).

Key Question #3: How can students with disabilities adequately prepare themselves for attending a college; university; or vocational, trade, or technical school?

Early Preparation for Postsecondary Education

A key to ensuring that a student is prepared for a college experience is beginning the preparation process early in the student's educational career. It should be assumed, from the time a child with disabilities is in kindergarten, that he or she will be attending a college or university upon completion of high school. If this posture is not taken early in the child's school career, it is quite possible that the child will be "tracked" into a nonacademic or less academically rigorous program of study. This is especially true for students who are exhibiting challenges with reading and math at a young age or have been assigned labels such as learning disability, developmental delay, autism, traumatic brain injury, or cerebral palsy. If children miss valuable foundational experiences early in their school career and don't have access to the core curriculum early on, their chances of leaving school with a high school diploma or GED are very slim. Without a high school diploma or GED the chances of being admitted to a four-year college or university are nonexistent. Consequently, students with disabilities and their parents will want to work closely with guidance counselors as they plan their course of study. These issues also should be monitored closely during the Individual Transition Program (ITP) planning process. However, if families wait until a child is fourteen, it already may be too late.

Determining if Postsecondary Education Is the Right Path to Take

Determining if a postsecondary education is right for a student with a disability can be a challenging and complex process. Many factors will need to be considered in making this decision. Students must be ready to demonstrate their willingness to take risks, realistically assess their strengths and areas of weakness and limitations, and select academic strategies and supports that will effectively compensate for their disabilities (Brinckerhoff, Shaw, & McGuire, 1993; Quinn, 2001).

In addition, students and their families will need to know if the student is ready to handle additional academic responsibilities (e.g., advocating for himself or herself in seeking necessary accommodations, juggling assignment completion dates, being exposed to possibly new academic subjects, completing assignments independently at a level that is expected for students enrolled in the course). New personal and household responsibilities (e.g., laundry, household or dorm responsibilities, cooking if required, managing money, managing health issues and medications, managing personal care needs) also will need to be addressed. Students also will have to be ready to confront new social responsibilities and freedoms of college living (e.g., finding an acceptable balance between studying and socializing, meeting new people, flexibility in living with others in dorm or roommate situations, establishing and implementing social boundaries).

In order to gather information to make an informed decision about what kind of postsecondary educational experience will be the best choice for the student, carefully consider the following types of questions:

- What are the long range career plans of the student?
- What would be the purpose of going to school and how much education

will be needed (e.g., enjoyment or enrichment, remediation, leading to a profession, enhancing current skills, earn a degree, certificate, or license)?
- What are the student's strengths and support needs?
- Will the job market support the student's career choice upon program completion?

Selecting a College, University, or Vocational/Trade/Technical Program

Once a student determines that attending a postsecondary educational institution is the right path for achieving his or her ambitions, the next step is determining what program to attend. This is no easy process, with more 3,000 colleges and universities in the US (HEATH, January 31, 2000). Therefore, students will want to utilize a variety of resources to assist them in this decision-making process.

A wealth of information is easily obtained through conducting internet searches. Most colleges and universities have extensive web sites that include a vast amount of information about their degree programs (e.g., admission, costs, course description), housing, university policies, scheduled events, faculty biographies, student demographics). Some provide video mini tours. Commercially produced publications also are available to assist students with disabilities with the decision-making process. Some of these resources specifically address students with learning disabilities (e.g., Cobb, 2001; Brinckerhoff, McGuire, & Shaw, 2001; Koehler & Kravets, 1998; Dolber, 1996; Kravets, 1999) or attention deficit disorders (e.g., Quinn, 2001).

In addition to the internet and commercially available print materials, a valuable resource is people who are currently working in the field the student is hoping to enter. Teachers, school counselors, and friends of the family are also a good source of information on this topic. In fact, Henderson (1999) found that students with disabilities were more likely to select a college based on special programs and advice from teachers or guidance counselors than their peers without disabilities.

The key is for the student to acquire the information necessary to make an informed decision that will meet the student's needs. Consequently, students will want to explore questions such as:
- What programs exist that offer the course of study the student desires?
- Is the location of the program (e.g., urban, rural, close to family, accessible by bus) relevant to the decision-making process?
- What kind of living arrangements are most desirable given the student's interests, needs, and strengths? Is housing available?
- What is the cost of the educational opportunity? Is it affordable with financial aid?
- What accommodations, if any, are needed in order to facilitate success? Are the required academic, physical, and emotional supports and accommodations available? Will there be a fee for supports provided by the program?
- What are the admissions requirements of the institution? Will the student be able to meet the admission requirements (e.g., GPA, entrance exams, letters of recommendation, interview, documentation required to verify disability status)?

Housing and independent living issues can be of critical importance to students with disabilities. Colleges and universities are required to make available to students with disabilities options similar to their nondisabled peers. Many students with disabilities will not require special housing accommodations. That is, they will be able to access standard student housing options (e.g., dorms, on-campus houses and apartments, off-campus houses and apartments). In addition, some students with disabilities will elect to live with their parents or other family members.

However, for some students with disabilities, housing may present unique challenges and limited options. Many college campuses have limited accessible housing arrangements; students requiring accommodations should contact the residence life or housing office on the campus very early on. For students using wheelchairs or walking devices, physical accessibility will be a primary concern (e.g., ground level entrances, no steps, desks positioned at the correct height, adequate physical space, accessible restrooms and showering/bathing facilities). Still other students may require living space for attendants or work dogs. For students with hearing impairments, deaf alerting devices (e.g., security and safety alarm systems, door bells, telephone signaling systems) and aids (e.g., telephone amplifiers, TDDs, television decoders) may be needed in their residence.

Key Question #4: What barriers exist in accessing postsecondary education options for students with disabilities?

There are numerous barriers that can present significant challenges to students with disabilities wanting to experience a postsecondary education program. HEATH (January, 2000) reports that the most common deterrents for students with disabilities wanting to attend college are: attitudinal barriers (e.g., fear, low aspirations), lack of information and counseling, lack of family support or even family opposition, and the need for financial assistance. These potential deterrents, along with several others, are briefly described below:

Attitudes of Students with Disabilities

Students with disabilities may, in fact, be their own worst enemy when it comes to considering postsecondary education. Because many students with disabilities experience lower self-esteem than their peers without disabilities, they may lack confidence that they can be successful in attending a college program and sabotage their efforts before they start the process. Other students may not yet have come to a place of understanding and acceptance of their disability and, therefore, are reluctant to ask for necessary help. Still other students with disabilities may want to independently advocate for themselves but simply lack the skills required to do so. Resolving these issues prior to seeking a postsecondary experience will only benefit the student. This may be difficult for many students, however, as it requires a great deal of maturity that some at this age have yet to develop.

Family Concerns

It is not uncommon for families of persons with disabilities to be concerned about their daughters and sons attending college. For some students this may be the first time they will be required to use the public transportation system, navigate a large college campus, be responsible for obtaining and self administering their medications, arrange for their attendants and support providers, and maintain their living environment. For other students this may be the first occasion they have spent an extended period of time away from supportive family members and environments and routines that have been modified to meet their needs.

In addition, many students with disabilities have relied heavily upon their families to advocate for the services, accommodations and supports they have required (Thomas, 2000). Consequently, family members may struggle with "letting go" of the responsibility of advocating for their son or daughter, and students may be reluctant to accept their new responsibility for self-determination. The impact of this transition can be dramatic if students with disabilities have not been taught, or have not had the opportunity to practice, self-advocacy skills throughout their youth.

Discriminative Posture of Colleges and Universities

Unfortunately, negative and discriminatory attitudes of faculty, staff, and administrators at institutions of higher education are still evident on many campuses and may pose challenges to students with disabilities wishing to attend colleges and universities (Malakapa, 1997; Farone, Hall, & Costello, 1998; Thomas, 2000). Numerous examples of blatant institutional structural discrimination have been brought to light in court cases or are evident in the research.

However, sometimes the discrimination is more subtle. Professors, staff, and administrators may be unwilling to make reasonable accommodations required by law, may be uninformed of the law, or may disregard the law. Support services may be piecemeal, inadequate, or nonexistent. Admission personnel and faculty members may not be encouraging and welcoming to students with disabilities and may believe that students with disabilities don't belong in college. Buildings, housing, labs, and equipment may not be accessible, thus presenting a challenge to students.

Ensuring success will require proactive efforts of faculty, administrators, support staff, and the students themselves (Thomas, 2000). If students with disabilities are going to be successful in college and compete equitably, it is essential that faculty believe they have the right to be in college and that they can be successful with reasonable academic adjustments, and be willing to make reasonable accommodations in their classrooms (Brinckerhoff, Shaw, & McGuire 1993; Vogel, Leyser, Wyland, & Brulle, 1999; Beilke & Yssel, 1998).

Key Question #5: What financial assistance is available to students with disabilities wanting to attend a college, university, or trade school?

Due to the cost of postsecondary education, most students require assistance to finance their postsecondary educational experience. Obtaining financial aid can be a time consuming and complex task. Most students need to utilize a variety of partnership arrangements to fund their education. Fortunately, numerous helpful resources have been created to assist students with disabilities and their families as they navigate the maze of developing a sound financial aid package. A document that many students and their families have found useful is entitled *Creating Options: A Resource on Financial Aid for Students with Disabilities* (HEATH, March, 2000). Typically four types of financial support are available to students seeking aid. These include loans, grants, scholarships, and work-study programs (US Department of Education, 2000-2001).

Key Question #6: What supports, accommodations, and services are available to students with disabilities pursuing a postsecondary education?

Unlike high school, colleges and universities are under no legal obligation to provide students with disabilities all of the supplemental aids and services that may be needed to be successful in college. However, academic and physical accessibility to qualified students with disabilities is required by Federal legislation. As previously noted, colleges and universities are required to provide, if requested, "reasonable accommodations" that allow students with disabilities to access the same educational opportunities and services that are available to nondisabled peers. (See Tables 1 and 2.)

Student Support on Campus

Students with disabilities requiring support services or reasonable accommodations will want to seek out the campus office that provides disability related support services. This office goes by a variety of names, depending upon the college or university campus (e.g., Office for Students with Disabilities, Disabled Students Program, Center for Academic Success).

While the office may have different names, its purposes are generally quite similar. It typically provides students with disabilities information about what accommodations and services are available on campus, where the services are available, and how accommodations and services can be accessed. Many students find that this office provides a wealth of helpful information and is a critical resource especially when first entering the college or university.

Colleges and universities are not obligated to provide or pay for all the supports a student with disabilities may need. Once a student identifies what accommodations, supports, and aids will be required to be successful, the student will often need to be resourceful in determining who will provide and pay for these supports and services. It is not uncommon for a variety of sources to pay for or provide such services. This may include, but is not limited to, the college, vocational rehabilitation, the student, or the student's family. In addition, scholarships or financial aid also may fund some of these supports and services.

Accommodations

Students with disabilities have the right to request a variety of accommodations in order for them to successfully access an educational program once admitted. Table 1 provides a listing of the types of accommodations made available to students with disabilities on college and university campuses. Not all colleges and universities provide all of the accommodations listed. Necessary accommodations are individually determined and negotiated between the student and the institution.

Services

Similar to the accommodations a student may need to be successful, additional services also may be needed from the college or university to facilitate a student's success in the program. The types of services currently being provided by some colleges or universities are listed in Table 2.

Table 1
Types of Accommodations for Students with Disabilities

Continued eligibility for financial aid despite disability-related reduced course enrollment

Extended time on exams

Alternate testing locations

Substitution of similar or related work for a nonfundamental program requirement

Time extensions on papers and projects

Special testing procedures

Advanced notice regarding booklists for students with visual impairments and some students with learning disabilities

Use of academic aides in the classroom such as note takers and sign language interpreters

Early advisement and assistance with registration

Classroom accessibility for students who use wheelchairs and those with mobility impairments (e.g., moving scheduled classrooms if the classroom is not accessible)

Need for special classroom furniture or special equipment in the classroom

Adaptive technology (telecaption adapters or decoders, alternative keyboards, switches, alerting devices)

Part-time enrollment

Part-time enrollment with reduced fees

Exception to minimum academic progress requirements

Substitution of coursework for graduation upon dean's approval

Preferential seating in classrooms

Faculty member to wear wireless microphone

Books on tape

Readers for students with visual impairments

Telecommunication devices (TDD), telephone amplification devices

Accommodate attendance policy

Grammar/spelling/writing accommodations

Use of calculators

Use of word processor for exams and writing

Give oral directions clearly and in writing

Tape record lectures

Lab/library assistants

Materials enlarged/VTEK

Writer

Write on tests

Extended time in class writing assignments

Assistive listening device

Braille transcription

CCTV magnifier

Taped exams

Table 2
Types of Services Available for Students with Disabilities

Assistance with reading

Access to adaptive equipment

Priority enrollment

Liaison with faculty, staff, and community agencies

Sign Language interpreters

Registration assistance

Facilitation of access to programs

Specialized educational materials

On-campus transportation

Assistance with architectural barriers

Assistance in obtaining books and supplies from university bookstore

Information regarding accessible seating at sporting events

Auxiliary aid equipment loans

Assistive technology

Support for individual needs that are unique to a student's disability

Scholarships

Academic, career, and personal counseling

Readers, scribes, tutors, learning assistants

Special orientation to campus facilities and programs

Disabled parking access

Assessment and evaluations

Disability verification

Adapted fitness and wellness program

Special admissions process

Support groups

Equipment loan

Referral to other agencies

Admissions assistance

Attendant referral

Specialized computer lab

Braille transcription

Testing and evaluation of learning disabilities

Disability management

Mobility Assistance

Again, this listing is a compilation of the types of services that colleges and universities throughout the country are providing to students with disabilities. Not all institutions of higher education are providing all of these types of services. In addition, not all of these services are provided free of charge to the student. Students will want to make sure they discuss the supports, accommodations, and services they will need with their financial aid worker at the college or university, as some of these expenses may increase the dollar amount the student is eligible to receive through his or her financial aid award.

Window to the World
Juanita

Juanita is a nineteen-year-old university student who enjoys kayaking, dancing, movies, and hiking with her peers. She has an outrageous sense of humor that keeps her family and peers laughing and is enthusiastic in all that she does. Juanita experiences numerous academic challenges due to having a severe auditory processing disability, making it difficult to process complex oral information and directions. She also is distracted easily in noisy or chaotic environments. Juanita is a very articulate and persuasive speaker and demonstrates outstanding creativity in her written assignments. Juanita aspires to work in the field of marketing research upon graduation. Her family lives thirty miles from of the university and keeps a close eye on her and her studies. At times Juanita resents their involvement, and other times she deeply appreciates it.

Juanita's learning disabilities were formally diagnosed when she was in third grade. She received special education services primarily in the general education classroom throughout her school career. Juanita's parents insisted that class assignments be modified only when absolutely necessary and that she have access to the core curriculum. Juanita's parents closely monitored her educational progress and never lost sight of the goal that she would attend college upon graduation from high school. Juanita maintained a B average during high school and scored in the eightieth percentile on her SAT exam.

Juanita's life is very similar to her peers that are attending the university, although there are several notable differences. Because of her diagnosed disabilities, Juanita has requested several reasonable accommodations from the university. Juanita has a private room in the dorm so that she is not distracted from her studies. She has priority registration, which has allowed her to schedule most of her classes in the morning, as she becomes more distracted when she is tired. This schedule also gives Juanita the opportunity to study in the afternoons when the dorm area is somewhat quieter. Juanita tape records all class lectures and has a peer assigned to take notes for her in each class. She is allowed extra time on exams and takes the exams in a quiet area that is proctored by the Office for Student Services. Juanita utilizes the services of the writing center on campus to assist her in proofreading her written assignments.

Juanita has shared with her peers that she has a learning disability and is fully accepted by her peers. In fact, because of Juanita's sense of humor, seriousness about her coursework, creativity, and enthusiasm, she is actively recruited by her peers when assigned group projects. Juanita would like to take advantage of the full range of social, educational, and recreational opportunities offered at the university and she also would like to work part-time. But with a busy class schedule and the time it takes to complete course assignments, she has little time available for a social life or to work. Juanita, however, is hopeful that she will be working part-time by the middle of her sophomore year.

Window to the World
Melinda

Melinda is a nineteen-year-old student who loves music, drama, dancing, movies, and socializing with her peers. She has a delightful sense of humor and is very socially engaging. Melinda experiences numerous academic challenges due to having Down syndrome. However, she has reading skills at approximately the first grade level, can print her name, and can copy words from a printed model. Melinda's speech is somewhat difficult to understand to those who are unfamiliar with her.

Melinda has attended public schools since she was a preschooler. Her parents fought hard to ensure that she received special education services in an inclusive environment throughout her school career. When Melinda turned eighteen, her parents thought the high school setting was no longer age appropriate for Melinda to receive educational services. Consequently they contacted the school district and made arrangements to have Melinda enrolled in a model transition partnership between the school district and a private four-year comprehensive university in the community.

Melinda's day on the university campus is quite different from one in high school. Depending upon the semester, she attends university classes two or three days a week with her nondisabled peers. She also works on the campus approximately ten hours a week. Melinda spends the remainder of her school day working on specific academic goals in her special education classroom (which is located next to the university), or learning independent living skills (e.g., using a bus, shopping, banking) in the community.

Melinda has fully participated in a variety of university classes including modern dance, conditioning and weight training, critical thinking, the global citizen, archery, swimming, and woman's self-defense with her nondisabled collegiate peers. In addition, she currently works in the university book store, and has worked at the child care center on campus, in the School of Education and in the catering department. Melinda also enjoys serving as a locker room assistant and "bat woman" for the woman's softball team.

Melinda's peers without disabilities have willingly included and accepted Melinda into their classes. Melinda is actively recruited when students are required to work in small group activities. Her peers and the faculty encourage her to fully participate in and contribute to class discussions. On numerous occasions Melinda's contributions have added a novel perspective and rich dimension to the class discussions. Her sense of humor has also charmed her peers and professors.

Best Practices Recommendations

More students with disabilities are accessing and completing postsecondary educational experiences than ever before, although access to these experiences has required both legislation and litigation. During this process we have learned a great deal about the ingredients it takes for success. However, the practices identified below should serve only as a starting place for students with disabilities, their families, and practitioners.

1. Begin the postsecondary education planning process early: Although IDEA mandates that transition planning begin at age fourteen, it is wise to begin the postsecondary planning process early in elementary school. An early step that families and teachers can take is to ensure that students with disabilities have access to the core general education curriculum. Without this foundational knowledge, a student's opportunity for postsecondary education is severely limited.

2. Support students with disabilities and their families during the transition process: The decision-making process is complex for students seeking postsecondary education. The stress that change and uncertainty can create may be difficult for both students with disabilities and their parents. Both may need a variety of supports as students seek postsecondary educational options. Professionals can provide a valuable service to students and their families by assisting them in identifying and obtaining the supports they need.

3. Create learning environments that foster confidence: Because many students with disabilities struggle with issues of low self-esteem, it is critical that influential adults look for ways to foster the development of self-confidence in these students. This will include setting high but reasonable expectations and providing opportunities for students to take risks. Confidence and a willingness to take risks are essential when a student attends college.

4. Know the laws that protect a student's civil rights: Probably the two most important pieces of legislation that students with disabilities should know are Section 504 of the Rehabilitation Act of 1973 and the Americans with Disabilities Act (ADA) of 1990. Both Section 504 and the ADA require that postsecondary educational institutions provide accommodations to students with disabilities, if they are accepted for admission. This legislation also protects the rights of students to ensure that they are not discriminated against because of their disability during the admission process. If students need accommodations, it is their responsibility to notify the institution of higher education that they have a disability and are seeking accommodations. The institution will require the student to furnish documentation supporting verification of his or her disability. Because documentation requirements vary from institution to institution (e.g., what is required, age of testing scores), students will want to be clear about what precisely is needed. Generally no accommodations are made until such documentation is provided. All information pertaining to a student's disability is protected as confidential. Thus, access to the information is limited to only select individuals, unless the student grants permission for others to review the information.

5. Ensure that mandated rights are enforced: While legislation and litigation have articulated the mandated rights of students with disabilities, both the letter of the law and the spirit of the law frequently are not implemented. Thomas (2000) identifies eleven practices that may be used by higher education professionals to ensure that the rights of students with disabilities are protected, and at the same time protect institutions of higher education from unnecessary expenditures and costly litigation. These practices are summarized below:

   - Establish and publish reasonable and sufficient guidelines.
   - Review financial aid practices and remove provisions that may result in discriminatory practices.
   - Review admission procedures to ensure they do not arbitrarily deny or delay student admission.
   - Keep abreast of new technologies and instructional methodologies.
   - Employ staff that has knowledge of disability law and assessment procedures.
   - Ensure that the Student Disability Services Office is adequately staffed and funded.
   - Provide for inservice training for administrators, staff, and faculty members regarding accommodations and access.
   - Periodically assess buildings and grounds to determine accessibility.
   - Examine and eliminate academic and disciplinary procedures that may be discriminatory.
   - Handle inquiries and requests for accommodations in a timely fashion.
   - Investigate allegations of noncompliance and discrimination promptly and efficiently (Thomas, 2000, 255-266).

6. Become familiar with available resources: High school counselors, special education personnel, and high school teachers need to be aware of the resources and postsecondary opportunities available for students. This is especially true for students with disabilities—Henderson (1999) found that students with disabilities were more likely to ask their teachers for advice about postsecondary educational options than their peers without disabilities are.

   One of the most valuable resources to students with disabilities interested in pursuing a postsecondary education is the HEATH Resource Center, which operates The National Clearinghouse on Postsecondary Education for Individuals with Disabilities. This clearinghouse, which receives support from the US Department of Education, serves as an information exchange on educational support services; policies and procedures; and adaptations and opportunities available at US campuses, vocational/technical schools, adult education programs, independent living centers, and other postsecondary training entities. HEATH publications can be viewed and obtained from its website: www.heath-resources-center.org. HEATH provides a wealth of information in regard to financial aid, scholarships, and helpful resources both on-line and via printed materials.

7. Identify college mentors for students with disabilities: Identify a mentor on the campus who also has a disability, preferably a similar disability. Students will know how to work the system and can show the incoming student "the ropes." In addition the mentor may have experienced challenges similar to what the new student is experiencing, and may be able to share practical, simple, and cost effective solutions and strategies.
8. Self-advocacy and self-determination: Teach students with disabilities the skills they need to become effective self-advocates and change agents. Encourage students to discover and develop an effective style they feel comfortable with, yet is consistent with their own unique personalities. This will require the students to successfully communicate their wants and needs, demonstrate problem solving skills, and make decisions. These skills will be critical when a student attends college.

Future Research Issues

Although great strides have been made in ensuring that students with disabilities have access to and complete postsecondary educational experiences, there is a paucity of research on the topic. In order to better serve students with disabilities in postsecondary experiences, the knowledge base needs to be expanded. Field based research is needed to address pertinent questions such as:

1. What practices are most effective in encouraging and preparing high school students for a postsecondary education? What role should high school students, their families, high school teachers, guidance counselors, mentors, and colleges and universities play in the preparation process?
2. What are the most effective strategies for providing college and university faculty members, administrators, and staff with the knowledge they need to overcome the attitudinal barriers and discriminatory practices that people have toward students with disabilities? How can professors be educated about student needs and reasonable accommodations so that they can effectively use these strategies?
3. Should professional standards be developed for college and university faculty members, administrators, and staff who work with students with disabilities? Should disability organizations play a role in developing and implementing such standards?
4. How can service delivery be improved at the postsecondary level for students with disabilities? What constitutes effective service delivery and how should it be documented?
5. Why are some students with disabilities more successful in accessing college and universities than students with other disability labels? Is access correlated with characteristics of the students or are other factors influencing who is being granted access?
6. Henderson (1999) found that freshman with disabilities reportedly placed a higher level of importance on life objectives involving social concerns (e.g., promote racial understanding, participate in community action, be involved in environmental clean up efforts) than their peers without disabilities. Why was this the case? What role, if any, can students with disabilities play in raising the level of consciousness of their nondisabled

peers about issues of social justice? How can they most effectively do this?

7. What are some techniques that would enable college and university faculty members, administrators, and staff who work with students with disabilities to become more proactive?

8. What skills does a student with disabilities need to be an effective self-advocate on a college campus? What is the best way to teach students these skills?

9. While this chapter focuses primarily on "qualified" students with disabilities accessing postsecondary educational options, many students with disabilities who are not "otherwise qualified" could benefit both socially and academically from being on a community college, college, or university campus. High school settings for students with disabilities between the ages of eighteen and twenty-one often are not age appropriate. How can young adults with more significant disabilities, who are not "qualified" for college or university admission, still benefit from academic and social experiences on collegiate campuses?

As we think of our college days, most of us remember not only the joys but also the hardships of our college experience. Simply stated, college is a challenging enough venture without having to endure the additional burden of an inhospitable learning environment, such as students with disabilities often experience. The challenge is to eliminate those physical, academic, social, and attitudinal barriers that continue to promulgate unnecessary challenges for students with disabilities. While most of us have little or no control over how resources are utilized on college campuses, we can play an enormous role in being vehicles for change. By working side by side with our peers and colleagues with disabilities, we can create a free and democratic society in which we insist upon fair and equal access to educational opportunity.

Discussion Questions

1. How would your life have been different if you had a disability that required support services during your college experience?

2. What can be done to ensure that a greater number of students with disabilities have the opportunity for postsecondary educational experiences?

3. Compare and contrast postsecondary experiences for students with disabilities and their peers without disabilities?

Community-Based Activities

1. Interview high school counselors and ask how they help prepare students with disabilities for college. Use information to outline a model college preparation program for students with disabilities.

2. Interview a college student with disabilities and ask the student about the challenges he or she has experienced and the supports he or she uses at school.

3. Interview a parent of a student with disabilities and discuss from his or her perspective the whole college process. What were some of the parent's

fears or concerns? Did things go as planned? What surprises did he or she encounter along the journey to college?

4. Visit a student support service program at a local community college and investigate what types of assistance are available for students with disabilities.

References

Americans with Disabilities Act of 1990, 42 USC § 12102 et seq. (1998); title II §12131 et seq. (1998); 28 CFR §' 35.101-35.191 (1998); title III § 12181 et seq. (1998); 28 CFR §' 36.101-36.608 (1998)

Beilke, J. R., & Yssel, N. (1998). Personalizing disability: Faculty-student relationships and the importance of story. *Journal for a Just and Caring Education, 4*(2), 212-223.

Brinckerhoff, L. C., McGuire, J., & Shaw, S. F. (2001). *Postsecondary education for students with learning disabilities: A handbook for practitioners.* Austin, TX: Pro-Ed.

Brinckerhoff, L. C., Shaw, S. F., & McGuire, J. M. (1993). *Promoting postsecondary education for students with learning disabilities: A handbook for practitioners.* Austin, TX: Pro-Ed.

Cobb, J. (2001). *Learning how to learn: Getting into and surviving college when you have a learning disability.* Washington, DC: Child Welfare League of America.

Dolber, R. (1996). *College and career success for students with learning disabilities.* Lincolnwood, IL: NTC Contemporary Publishing Company.

Farone, M. C., Hall, E. W., & Costello, J. J. (1998). Postsecondary disability issues: An inclusive identification strategy. *Journal of Postsecondary Education and Disability, 13*(1), 35-45.

HEATH, Division of Programs and Analysis HEATH Resource Center (January 31, 2000). *Success in college for adults with learning disabilities.* Washington, DC: HEATH Resource Center.

HEATH Resource Center (March, 2000). *Creating options: A resource on financial aid for students with disabilities.* Washington, DC: HEATH Resource Center.

Henderson, C. (1999). *College freshmen with disabilities: A biennial statistical profile.* Washington, DC: HEATH Resource Center.

Horn, L., & Berktold, J. (1999). *Students with disabilities in a postsecondary education: A profile of preparation, participation, and outcomes. Postsecondary education descriptive analysis reports. Statistical analysis report* (Report No. NCES B 1999-187). Washington, DC: National Center for Education Statistics. (ERIC Document Reproduction Service No. ED 431 268)

Koehler, M., & Kravets, M. (1998). *Counseling secondary students with learning disabilities: A ready-to-use guide to help students prepare for college and work.* West Nyack, NY: Center for Applied Research in Education.

Kravets, M. (1999). *The K & W guide to colleges for students with learning disabilities or attention deficit disorders: A resource guide for students, parents and professionals* (5th Ed.). New York: Random

Malakpa, S. W. G. (1997). Problems in the admission and retention of students with disabilities in higher education. *Journal of College Admissions, 156*, 12-19.

Quinn, P. O. (2001). *ADD and the college student: A guide for high school and college students with Attention Deficit Disorder.* New York: Magination Press.

Rehabilitation Act of 1973, as amended by the Rehabilitation Act Amendments of 1974, 29 USC § 794 (1998); 34 CFR §' 104.1-104.47 (1998).

Thomas, S. B. (2000). College students and disability law. *The Journal of Special Education, 33*, 248-257.

United States Department of Education (2000-2001). *Funding your education.* [Brochure]. Washington, DC: Author.

Vogel, S. A., Leyser, Y., Wyland, S., & Brulle, A. (1999). Students with learning disabilities in higher education: Faculty attitude and practices. *Learning Disabilities Research and Practice, 14*(3), 173-186.

Appendix

It is important to join professional organizations, read professional journals, and visit web sites. Here is a list of suggestions. Joining an organization will help you in your professional development and assist you in staying current in the field.

GENERAL, PUBLIC POLICY, and LEGAL

Journals
Disability and Society
Disability Studies Quarterly
Educational Evaluation and Policy
    Analysis
Educational Forum
Educational Horizons
Educational Policy
Evaluation and Program Planning
Evaluation Review
Journal of Disability Policy
    Studies
Journal of Social Issues
Social Policy

Resources
Council for Exceptional Children
1920 Association Dr.
Reston, VA 22091-1589
888-232-7733
www.cec.sped.org

National Association of Protection
    and Advocacy Systems
900 Second St., NE, Ste. 211
Washington, DC 20002
202-408-9520
www.protectionandadvocacy.com

National Council on Disability
1331 F St., NW, Ste. 1050
Washington, DC 20004
202-272-2022
www.ncd.gov

American Council on Rural
    Special Education
Kansas State University
2323 Anderson Ave., Ste. 226
Manhatten, KS 66502
www.k-state.edu/acres

ERIC Clearinghouse on Handicapped
    and Gifted Children
The Council for Exceptional
    Children
1920 Association Dr.
Reston, VA 22091
http://ericec.org

Association on Higher Education and
    Disability
PO Box 21192
Columbus, OH 43221
614-488-4972
www.ahead.org

Disability Rights Education and
    Defense Fund
2212 Sixth St.
Berkeley, CA 94710
800-466-4232
www.dredf.org

Resource Center on Substance
    Abuse Prevention and
    Disability
1331 F St., NW, Ste. 800
Washington, DC 20004
Phone: 202-783-2900

National Center for Youth with
    Disabilities
Box 721-UMHC
420 Delaware St., SE
Minneapolis, MN 55455
800-333-6293
www.peds.umn.edu/centers/ncyd

National School-to-Work Office
400 Virginia Ave., SW, Ste. 210
Washington, DC 20024
800-251-7236
www.stw.ed.gov

The School-to-Work
   Intermediary Project
c/o Jobs for the Future
88 Broad St., 8th Floor
Boston, MA 02110
617-728-4446
www.intermediarynetwork.org

National Organization on
   Disability
910 16th St., NW, Ste. 600
Washington, DC 20006
202-293-5960
www.nod.org

National Association of State
   Directors of Special Education
1800 Diagonal Rd., Ste. 320
King St. Station 1
Alexandria, VA 22314
www.nasde.org

Bazelon Center for Mental Health
   Law
1101 15th St., NW, Ste. 1212
Washington, DC 20005-5002
202-467-4232
www.bazelon.org

World Institute on Disability
510 16th St., Ste. 100
Oakland, CA 94612
510-763-4100
www.wid.org

LEARNING DISABILITIES

Journals
Exceptional Children
Exceptional Education Quar-
   terly
Exceptionality
Journal of Learning Disabilities
Journal of Precision Teaching
Journal of Reading, Writing, and
   Learning Disabilities
Journal of Special Education
Learning Disabilities Forum
Learning Disabilities Quarterly
Learning Disabilities Research
   and Practice
Reading and Writing Quarterly:
   Overcoming Learning
   Difficulties
Remedial and Special Education

Resources
Learning Disabilities Association
   of America
4156 Library Rd.
Pittsburgh, PA 15234
412-341-1515
www.ldaatl.org

International Dyslexia Association
8600 LaSalle Rd., Chester
   Bldg., Ste. 382
Baltimore, MD 21286-2044
410-296-0232
www.interdys.org

Children and Adults with
   Attention Deficit Disorders
8181 Professional Plaza, Ste. 201
Landover, MD 20785
800-233-4050
www.chadd.org

National Attention Deficit
   Disorder Association
PO Box 1303
Northbrook, IL 60065-1303
www.add.org

National Center for Learning
   Disabilities
318 Park Ave., South, Ste. 1401
New York, NY 10016
888-575-7373
www.ncld.org

VISUAL IMPAIRMENTS

Journals
Journal of Visual Impairment
and Blindness

Resources
American Council of the Blind
1155 15th St., NW, Ste. 720
Washington, D.C. 20005
800-424-8666
www.acb.org

National Federation of the Blind
1800 Johnson St.
Baltimore, MD 21230
410-659-9314
www.nfb.org

American Foundation for the
Blind
11 Penn Plaza, Ste. 300
New York, NY 10001
800-232-5463
www.afb.org

National Association for the
Visually Handicapped
22 West 21st St.
New York, NY 10010
212-889-3141
www.hauh.org

COMMUNICATION DISORDERS

Journals
American Journal of Speech
Language Pathology
Augmentative and Alternative
Communication
Communication Education
Human Communication
Research
Journal of Child Language
Journal of Childhood Communi-
cation Disorders
Journal of Communication
Journal of Communication
Disorders
Journal of Fluency Disorders
Journal of Speech and Hearing
Disorders
Journal of Speech and Hearing
Research
Language
Language and Communication
Language and Speech
Language, Speech and Hearing
Services in the Schools
Seminars in Child Language
Seminars in Speech and Lan-
guage
Speech Communication Teacher
Speech and Hearing Services in
the Schools
Topics in Language Disorders

Resources
American Speech, Language,
and Hearing Association
10801 Rockville Pk.
Rockville, MD 20852
888-821-ASHA
www.asha.org

Stuttering Foundation of
America
PO Box 11749
Memphis, TN 38111-0749
800-992-9392
www.stuttersfa.org

BEHAVIOR DISORDERS/EMOTIONAL DISTURBANCE

Journals
Behavior Modification
Behavior Therapy
Behavioral Disorders
Journal of Applied Behavior
  Analysis
Focus on Autistic Behavior
Journal of Autism and Develop-
  mental Disorders
Journal of Emotional and
  Behavioral Disorders

Resources
The Association for Behavior
  Analysis
Room 258 Wood Hall
Western Michigan University
Kalamazoo, MI 49008-5052
www.wmich.edu/aba

National Alliance for the
  Mentally Ill
2107 Wilson Blvd., Ste. 300
Arlington, VA 22201
800-950-6264
www.naimi.org

National Mental Health
  Association
1021 Prince St.
Alexandria, VA 22314-7722
www.nmha.org

Cambridge Center for
  Behavioral Studies
1170 Massachusetts Ave., #123
Cambridge, MA 02140
617-491-9020
www.behavior.org

DEAF CULTURE/HEARING IMPAIRMENTS

Journals
American Annals of the Deaf
Audiology
British Journal of Audiology
Journal of the American
  Deafness and Rehabilitation
  Association
Journal of the British Associa-
  tion of Teachers of the Deaf
Perspectives for Teachers of the
  Hearing Impaired
Sign Language Studies
Silent News
Teaching English to Deaf and
  Second Language Students

Resources
National Association of the Deaf
814 Thayer Ave.
Silver Spring, MD 20910
http://nad.policy.net

National Technical Institute for
  the Deaf
1 Lomb Memorial Dr.
Rochester, NY 14623
716-475-6700
www.rit/~418www/new/
  ntid.html

COMPUTERS AND TECHNOLOGY

Journals
Journal of Special Education
Technology
Technology and Disability

Resources
Center for Applied Special
Technology
39 Cross St.
Peabody, MA 01960
978-531-8555
www.cast.org

Alliance for Technology Access
2175 East Francisco Blvd., Ste. L
San Rafael, CA 94901
415-455-4575
www.ataccess.org

Trace Research and Development
Center
Waisman Center
University of Wisconsin at
Madison
5901 Research Park Blvd.
Madison, WI 53719-1252
608-262-6966
http://trace.wisc.edu

Center for Accessible Technology
2547 8th St., 12-A
Berkeley, CA 94710
510-841-3224
www.el.net/CAT

PHYSICAL DISABILITIES

Journals
American Journal of
Occupational Therapy
Canadian Journal of
Occupational Therapy
Physical and Occupational
Therapy in Pediatrics
Physical Therapy
Physical Therapy Practice
Adapted Physical Activity
Quarterly
Journal of Developmental and
Physical Disabilities
Mainstream: Magazine of the
Able-Disabled
The Ragged Edge

Resources
National Easter Seal Society
230 West Monroe St., Ste. 1800
Chicago, IL 60606
800-221-6827
www.seals.com

Research and Training Center on
Independent Living
University of Kansas
4089 Dole Bldg.
Lawrence, KS 66045
913-864-5063
www.lsi.ukans.edu/rtcil/rtcil.htm

National Multiple Sclerosis Society
733 Third Ave.
New York, NY 10017
800-344-4867
www.nmss.org

American Disabled for Attendant
Programs Today (ADAPT)
201 S. Cherokee
Denver, CO 80233
303-733-9324
www.adapt.org

AMERICANS WITH DISABILITIES ACT

Resources
Pacific Disability and Business
 Technical Assistance Center
2168 Shattuck Ave., Ste. 301
Berkeley, CA 94704
510-848-2980
www.pacdbtac.org

US Architectural and
 Transportation Barriers
 Compliance Board
1331 F. St., NW, Ste. 1000
Washington, DC 20004-1111
800-872-2253
www.access-board.gov

Office of the Americans with
 Disabilities Act
Civil Rights Division
US Department of Justice
PO Box 66118
Washington, DC 20035
800-514-0301
www.usdoj.gov/crt/ada/
 adahoml.htm

TRANSITION AND EMPLOYMENT

Journals
American Rehabilitation
Canadian Journal of Rehabilitation
Career Development for
 Exceptional Individuals
Career Development Quarterly
Cognitive Rehabilitation
Disability and Rehabilitation
International Journal of
 Rehabilitation Research
Journal for Vocational Educational
 Special Needs Education
Journal of Applied Rehabilitation
 Counseling
Journal of Back and
 Musculoskeletal Rehabilitation
Journal of Career Development
Journal of Employment Counseling
Journal of Head Trauma
 Rehabilitation
Journal of Occupational
 Rehabilitation
Journal of Rehabilitation
Journal of Rehabilitation
 Administration
Journal of Rehabilitation Research
 and Development
Journal of Vocational Behavior
Journal of Vocational Education
 Research
Journal of Vocational Rehabilitation
NeuroRehabilitation: An
 Interdisciplinary Journal

Psychosocial Rehabilitation Journal
Rehabilitation Counseling Bulletin
Rehabilitation Education
Rehabilitation Psychology
Rehabilitation World
Vocational Education Journal
Vocational Evaluation and Word
 Adjustment Bulletin
Work: A Journal of Prevention,
 Assessment and Rehabilitation
Worklife

Resources
The Association for Persons in
 Supported Employment
1627 Monument Ave., Room 301
Richmond, VA 23220
804-278-9187
www.apse.org

President's Committee on Employment of People with Disabilities
1331 F St., NW, Ste. 300
Washington, DC 20004-1107
202-376-6200
www.pcepd.gov
Abledata
National Rehabilitation Information
 Center
8401 Colesville Rd., Ste. 200
Silver Spring, MD 20910
Phone: 800-227-0216
www.abledata.com

National Clearinghouse on
   Postsecondary Education for
   Individuals with Disabilities
HEATH Resource Center
American Council on Education
One Dupont Cir., NW, Ste. 800
Washington, DC 20036
Phone: 800-544-3284
www.acenet.edu

National Clearinghouse of Rehabilitation Training Materials
Oklahoma State University
5202 N. Richmond Hill Dr.
Stillwater, OK 74078-4080
800-223-5219
www/nchrtm.okstate.edu

Job Accommodation Network
West Virginia University
PO Box 6080
Morgantown, WV 26506-6080
800-232-9675
http://janweb.icdi.wvu.edu

National Rehabilitation Information
   Center
1010 Wayne Ave., Ste. 800
Silver Spring, MD 20910-3319
800-346-2742
www.naric.com/naric

National Rehabilitation Association
633 S. Washington St.
Alexandria, VA 22314
703-836-0850
www.nationalrehab.org

Association for Career and Technical
   Education
1410 King St.
Alexandria, VA 22314
800-826-9972
www.avaonline.org

National Alliance of Business
1201 New York Ave., NW, Ste. 700
Washington, DC 20005-6143
202-289-2972
www.nab.org

DEVELOPMENTAL DISABILITIES/MENTAL RETARDATION

Journals
American Journal on Mental
   Retardation
Australian and New Zealand
   Journal of Developmental
   Disabilities
Disability, Handicap, and Society
Education and Training in Mental
   Retardation
Education and Treatment of
   Children
Applied Research in Intellectual
   Disabilities (formerly Mental
   Handicap Research)
Journal of Intellectual Disabilities
   Research
Journal of the Association for
   Persons with Severe Handicaps
Mental Retardation
Research in Developmental
   Disabilities

Resources
The Association for Persons with
   Severe Handicaps
29 West Susquehanna Ave., Ste. 210
Baltimore, MD 21204
www.tash.org

American Association on Mental
   Retardation
444 North Capitol St., NW, Ste. 846
Washington, DC 20001-1570
800-424-3688
wwww.aamr.org

National Association for Down
   Syndrome
PO Box 4542
Oak Brook, IL 60521
630-325-9112
www.nads.org

President's Committee on Mental
  Retardation
200 Independence Ave.
352 G. Hubert Humphrey Bldg.
Washington, DC 20201-0001
202-619-0634
www.acf.dhhs.gov/programs/pcmr

The Arc
500 East Border St., Ste. 300
Arlington, TX 76010
817-261-6003
www.thearc.org

National Down Syndrome Society
666 Broadway, 8th Floor
New York, NY 10012
800-221-4602
www.ndss.org

National Association of Developmental Disabilities Council
1234 Massachusetts Ave., NW, Ste.
  103
Washington, DC 20005
202-347-1234
www.igc.org/NADDC/index4.html

PARENTS/FAMILIES

Journals
Contemporary Family Therapy
Families in Society
Family Process
Journal of Child and Family
  Studies
Journal of Divorce and Remarriage
Journal of Family History
Journal of Family Practice
Journal of Family Psychology
Journal of Family Violence
Journal of Marriage and the Family
Parent
PTA Today
Studies in Family Planning
The Exceptional Parent
Working Mother

Resources
Parent Advocacy Coalition for
  Education Rights
4826 Chicago Ave. S.
Minneapolis, MN 55417-1098
612-827-2966
www.pacer.org

Sibling Information Network
University of Connecticut
249 Glenbrook Rd.
Storrs, CT 06269-2064
www.parentsoup.com/library/
  organizations/bdfa009.html

National Parent Network on
  Disability
1130 17th St., NW, Ste. 400
Washington, DC 20036
202-463-2299
www.npnd.org

Beach Center on Family and
  Disability
Bureau of Child Research
University of Kansas
3111 Haworth Hall
Lawrence, KS 66045
785-864-7600
www.lsi.ukans.edu/beach/
  beachhp.htm

POSTSECONDARY EDUCATION

Journals
College Teaching
Higher Education Policy
Innovative Higher Education
Journal for Higher Education and
    Policy and Management
Journal of Career and Technical
    Education
Journal of College and University
    Law
Journal of Higher Education

Journal of Postsecondary Education
    and Disability
Journal of Student Financial Aid
New Directions for Higher
    Education
Planning for Higher Education
Quality Higher Education
Research in Higher Education
Studies in Higher Education
Thought and Action

AUTISM

Journals
Autism Research Review
    International
Focus on Autistic Behavior
Journal of Autism and
    Developmental Disorders

Resources
Autism Society of America
7910 Woodmont Ave., Ste. 300
Bethesda, MD 20814-3015
800-328-8476
www.autism-society.org

MISCELLANEOUS

Epilepsy Foundation of America
4351 Garden City Dr.
Landover, MD 20785
800-332-1000
www.efa.org

Tourette Syndrome Association,
    Inc.
42-40 Bell Blvd.
Bayside, NY 11361
718-224-2999
http://tsa.mgh.harvard/edu

Anxiety Disorders Association of
    America
11900 Parklawn Dr., Ste. 100
Rockville, MD 20852
www.adaa.org

American Therapeutic
    Recreation Association
1414 Prince St., Ste. 204
Alexandria, VA 22314
703-683-9420
www.atramtr.org

National Mental Health
    Association
1021 Prince St.
Alexandria, VA 22314-2791
703-684-7722
www.nmha.org

National Alliance for the
    Mentally Ill
2107 Wilson Blvd., Ste. 300
Arlington, VA 22201-3042
800-950-6264
www.nami.org

B. F. Skinner Foundation
PO Box 84
Morgantown, WV 26507
304-293-2146
www.bfskinner.org

About the Contributors

Keith Storey, Ph.D., (Editor) received his degree from the University of Oregon. He is currently an associate professor of education at Chapman University in Concord, CA. He served six years as a classroom teacher working with people with a variety of disability labels. Dr. Storey is the recipient of the 1988 Alice H. Hayden Award from The Association for Persons with Severe Handicaps; the 1996 Hau-Cheng Wang Fellowship from Chapman University, which is presented for exceptional merit in scholarship; and the 2001 Robert Gaylord-Ross Memorial Scholar Award from the California Association for Persons with Severe Disabilities. He is a member of the Illinois State University College of Education Alumni Hall of Fame. He is currently forum editor for *Education and Treatment of Children* and assistant editor of the *Vocational Evaluation and Work Adjustment Journal*, and serves on the editorial boards of the *Journal of The Association for Persons with Severe Handicaps* and *Education and Training in Mental Retardation and Developmental Disabilities*. His proudest achievements are his children Evan and Anna.

Paul Bates, Ph.D., (Editor) received his degree in 1978 and took a position in the Department of Special Education at Southern Illinois University. For the past twenty-three years, he has been involved in personnel preparation of special educators at SIU and has conducted several innovative research and demonstration projects in the southern Illinois area involving supported employment, community-based training, person-centered transition planning, and the self-directed IEP. The results of Dr. Bates' work have been published in leading professional journals, books, and monographs. He has provided consultation to state and local programs in over thirty states. Dr. Bates' research interests focus on assisting students, their families, and professionals to work collaboratively through the transition planning process.

Dawn Hunter. Ph.D., (Editor) is an associate professor in the School of Education at Chapman University. Previously, she served the branch chief of the Severe Disabilities Branch, Office of Special Education Programs, US Department of Education. Dr. Hunter has published in the areas of inclusive schooling, transition, positive behavioral support, recreation, educational change, and collaborative partnerships. She coordinates the Chapman University/Tustin Unified School District Transition Partnership. Through this partnership, students with severe disabilities have access to the social, educational, vocational, and recreational opportunities offered at the university and university students have access to new educational and career options and the opportunity to become involved with issues of social justice confronting persons with disabilities.

Michael P. Brady, Ph.D., received his degree in special education from George Peabody College of Vanderbilt University in 1985. Dr. Brady has worked as a preschool and special education teacher, school administrator, and vocational educator. He currently is a professor and chair of the Department of Exceptional Student education at Florida Atlantic University in Boca Raton, FL, and also has served as a faculty member at the University of Houston and Florida International University. His professional affiliations include the Council for Exceptional Children (Divisions on Mental Retardation and Developmental Disabilities, Behavioral Disorders, and Teacher Education) and he is a lifetime member of The Association for Persons with Severe Handicaps.

Janis Chadsey, Ph.D., is a professor in the Department of Special Education at the University of Illinois at Urbana-Champaign. In addition, she is the director of the National Transition Alliance and has been affiliated with the Transition Research Institute for over fifteen years. Dr. Chadsey studies the social interactions and relationships experienced by youths and young adults as they make their transition from school to adulthood. She is on numerous editorial boards, has been the recipient of several federally funded grants, and has over sixty publications in journals and books. Several years ago, she received a University of Illinois Scholar Awards, which is given to university professors for noteworthy research.

Penny Church-Pupke, Ed.S., is a graduate student at the University of Florida Department of Special Education pursuing a doctoral degree. She has twenty years of experience working in the school system in Palm Beach County, FL, both as a classroom teacher and as a district level resource teacher. While there, she taught in classrooms and supervised programs for children with cognitive disabilities. Her current work includes co-teaching an undergraduate course in severe disabilities and supervising practicum students who are working toward special education certification.

Susan R. Copeland, Ph.D., is assistant professor of special education in the Department of Educational Specialties at the University of New Mexico. She received her Ph.D. in special education from Vanderbilt University. Her research interests include self-management strategies for individuals with severe and moderate disabilities, instructional supports for students with disabilities in general education settings, and transition from school to adult life. Dr. Copeland teaches courses at UNM in classroom management and advocacy and empowerment for individuals with severe disabilities.

Paula Davis, Ph.D., is a professor in the Rehabilitation Institute at Southern Illinois University. She is the coordinator of the undergraduate program in rehabilitation services. Her areas of interest include self-determination and choice for persons with disabilities. Previously, Dr. Davis was the co-director of an interdisciplinary program to prepare special educators and rehabilitation professionals to work with students with disabilities as they leave high school. She has presented and published on the topic of community living skills and supported living.

Stephanie E. Fowler, Ph.D., is a special education teacher in Nashville, TN. In 2001, she completed her doctoral program at Vanderbilt University, specializing in the area of goal setting for high school students with mental retardation. While at Vanderbilt, Dr. Fowler worked on several federally funded research projects, including the Metropolitan Nashville Peer Buddy Project and Project OUTCOME, which is designed to improve postschool outcomes for students from high poverty backgrounds.

Teresa A. Grossi, Ph.D., is the director for the Center on Community Living and Careers at the Indiana Institute on Disability and Community, the Indiana's University Center for Excellence at Indiana University. Dr. Grossi has extensive background in education and employment for individuals with disabilities. She has worked in North Carolina and Ohio as a community-based instructor, transition coordinator, and job coach and managed a vocational training program and a supported employment agency. Prior to working in Indiana, Dr. Grossi directed Ohio's systems change grant in supported employment and co-chaired the cross-training teaching for the Transition from School to Adult Life systems change grant. She conducts research, consultation, and training and technical assistance on supported employment and community supports for persons with severe disabilities.

Carolyn Hughes, Ph.D., is associate professor in the Department of Special Education at Vanderbilt University. In 1990, she received her Ph.D. in special education from the University of Illinois at Urbana-Champaign, specializing in the area of secondary transition. At Vanderbilt, Dr. Hughes conducts several federally funded research projects including a self-determination program, the Metropolitan Nashville Peer Buddy Program, and Project OUTCOME, which addresses postschool outcomes for students from high poverty backgrounds. Dr. Hughes serves on the editorial board of several professional journals and teaches courses at Vanderbilt in transition to adult life and classroom management.

Margaret (Meg) Hutchins, Ph.D., is an associate professor at Illinois State University, where she is primarily involved as an instructor of teacher candidates who are preparing to teach individuals with moderate, severe, or multiple disabilities. Dr. Hutchins' research interests and focus on promoting employment outcomes for individuals with disabilities began early in her career as a vocational specialist in a federally funded model demonstration program in the Albemarle County, VA, public schools and continued throughout her graduate studies. She has been the co-director and coordinator of several federally funded grants that targeted the design of vocational services in secondary schools in order to promote positive employment outcomes for youth and young adults with disabilities.

David M. Mank, Ph.D., is the director of the Indiana Institute on Disability and Community at Indiana University, Indiana's University Center for Excellence. He is also a full professor in the School of Education, Department of Curriculum and Instruction. Dr. Mank has an extensive background in the education and employment for persons with disabilities. His interest also includes a focus on the transition of persons with disabilities from school to adult life and community living. Dr. Mank is on the editorial boards of the *Journal of The Association for Persons with Severe Handicaps,* the *Journal of Vocational Rehabilitation,* and the *Journal of Disability Policy Studies.* He was president of the American Association of University Affiliated Programs board for 1999-2000 and is a member of the board of the American Association on Mental Retardation.

Craig Miner, Ph.D., is an assistant professor in the Department of Counseling and Special Education at California State University, Fresno. He has been involved in applied research, training, and implementation of person-centered planning activities. Dr. Miner has experience in education and adult service programs for individuals with severe, profound, and multiple disabilities. He has presented widely at state, regional, and international conferences on issues related to severe disabilities. In addition to person centered planning, Dr. Miner has research interests in self-determination, transition, family partnerships, and applied behavior analysis.

Lisa O'Brien, M.A., M.A.E., is a special education teacher working with students with severe disabilities in the Santa Ana Unified School District in California. In 1991 she earned her master's degree in Spanish at California State University, Long Beach. In 2000 she received her M.A.E. in special education at Chapman University in Orange, CA. She is currently a doctoral student at Claremont Graduate School in Claremont, CA.

Adelle Renzaglia, Ph.D., is a professor in the Department of Special Education at the University of Illinois at Urbana-Champaign. She coordinated the program to prepare teachers of children and youth with moderate and severe disabilities for twelve years and became department head in 1996. She continues to participate in the teacher preparation program as an advisor and course instructor. Dr. Renzaglia has directed (or co-directed) research and demonstration projects funded by the Department of Special Education from the Office of Special Education and Rehabilitation Services, US Department of Education. She also serves as a consultant to school districts, state departments of education, and other university preparation programs in this field. She has authored a number of professional publications in the areas of vocational training, transition, community-based and individualized curriculum and instruction, and personnel preparation.

Howard Rosenberg, Ed.D., received his degree in special education (mental retardation and vocational rehabilitation) from Teachers College, Columba University, in 1975. He has worked professionally as a special education teacher and school psychologist, and as director of job development and career counseling for adults with disabilities. Dr. Rosenberg is currently an associate professor of special education at Florida International University in Miami, FL, where he has been a faculty member since 1976. His professional affiliations include the Council for Exceptional Children (Division on Mental Retardation and Developmental Disabilities, and the Division on Career Development and Transition), the American Association on Mental Retardation, and the National Rehabilitation Association.

Larry Schaaf, M.S., is a member of the staff at the Center on Community Living and Careers at the Indiana Institute on Disability and Community. He received an MS in adult education from Indiana University-Purdue University in Indianapolis in 2002. His experiences as a business owner, a parent coordinator on Indiana's transition change grant, and a parent of a young adult with a disability gives multiple dimensions in his duties of providing training and technical assistance in the areas of transition, employment, and community-based services for parents, schools, and adult agencies.

Debra Shelden, M.S., C.R.C., is currently a research associate at the Transition Research Institute at the University of Illinois at Urbana-Champaign. She has ten years of experience conducting training and providing technical assistance related to transition, supported employment, and natural supports. She is currently the project director for the Social Security Transition Project, a model demonstration project addressing public benefits issues in transition planning. Prior to her work at the Transition research Institute, she provided support to individuals with disabilities in both residential and employment settings.

Marcia Steigerwald, B.S., works at the Center on Community Living and Careers at the Indiana Institute on Disability and Community as regional transition field coordinator providing technical assistance and training in the areas of transition, employment, and community-based services. Her background includes working as a special education teacher and as a vocational rehabilitation counselor.

Index